INDEX

SOLVED PAPERS(PAPER II)

AUTHOR HAS QUALIFIED PATENT AGENT EXAMINATION.

PATENT AGENT EXAMINATION, 2023

(Under Section 126 of the Patents Act, 1970)

PAPER II

TIME: 02.30 p.m. to 05.30 p.m. (Three Hrs) Total Marks: 100

Instructions

1. This paper consists of 3 parts - Part A (20 marks). Part B (30 marks) & Part C (50 Marks).

2. All questions in Part A and B are compulsory.

3. Part C comprises Part CI of 20 marks and C2 of 30 marks. Part CI consists of 2 questions and the

Candidate is required to answer anyone of them, Part C2 consists of 2 questions and the candidate is required to answer anyone of them.

4. Candidates should read the questions very carefully before answering.

5. In case a candidate answers more questions than required, the first attempted question shall be evaluated. .

6. No clarification will be provided during the course of the examination.

7. There is no negative marking.

8. All references to "Act" and "Rules" may be read as The Patents Act, 1970 and The Patent Rules. 2003 respectively, as amended until now and their related applications.

9. Candidate is expected to quote relevant sections and rules as well as prescribed fees and forms in theanswer.

PART A

4 Questions * 5 Marks= 20 Marks

1. State the factors that need to be considered for deciding the date of filing of the request for examination,after filing an application for patent?

Ans. Factors that need to be considered for deciding the date of filing of the request for examination, after filing an application for patent:

1. Time Limit for filing Examination Request: The first important factor to consider is the time limit for filing an examination request. In India, a request for examination must be filed within 48 months of the filing date or the priority date, whichever is earlier.

2. Automatic vs. Early Publication: In India, there is automatic publication of the patent application after 18 months from the date of filing. If an early publication is requested, it may expedite the examination process.

For Form 9, fee is 2500 and 12500(electronic mode)

3. Form 18 or 18A: In India, the request for examination may be filed in Form 18 or Form 18A. Form 18A can be used to request expedited examination, which could be useful if there is a commercial urgency and eligibility. The choice of form would depend on the circumstances of each case.

For Form 18: Fee under 11B and rule 24(1) 4000 and 20000(electronic mode)

For Form 18: Fee under rule 24C, 4000 and 40000(electronic mode)

In summary, the timing of the request for examination will depend on several factors, including publication, request for early examination and corporate or personal eligibility.

2. Raju is a creative person who is engaged in the business of printing wherein he mixed paints with somefluorescent chemicals in a particular ratio so that the amalgamated painting material while using appearsvisible

2

during night even without any kind of light source. He has applied for patent for theamalgamated painting material and also sought copyright protection for the painting he made using thismaterial. In both the applications he did not disclose the composition of the amalgamated paintingmaterial. What will be the effect of such a nondisclosure on the protection of his IP rights?

Ans. The non-disclosure of the composition of the amalgamated painting material in patent application may have adverse effects on the protection of Raju's Patent rights. This is because the disclosure of the invention is an essential requirement for obtaining a patent protection.

Firstly, with regard to the patent application, Section 10(4)(a) of the Indian Patents Act 1970 requires the applicant to disclose the invention fully, clearly, and completely such that a person skilled in the art can understand and replicate the invention. The inclusion of the compositional details of the amalgamated painting material may be crucial in establishing the novelty and inventive step required for patentability. Failure to comply with the disclosure requirements may result in the patent application being rejected or invalidated for lack of novelty or inventive step.

Secondly, Section 3(e) of the Indian Patents Act, which prohibits the grant of patents to mere admixture or aggregation of known substances, may also be a hurdle to patentability if the disclosure does not reveal any additional advantages or technical effect beyond the known substances' properties.

In summary, failure to disclose the composition of the amalgamated painting material may jeopardize the protection of Raju's Patent rights. Therefore, it is essential to comply with the disclosure requirements and provide comprehensive and clear details of the invention in patent application. Further, to qualify for copyright protection, Raju may have to demonstrate that the painting made using the material represents a unique, original artistic expression that qualifies for copyright protection.

3. Karan, an Indian citizen, owns a shipping company in Visakhapatnam. He got a call from his friend. John, a US citizen who also owns a shipping company registered in USA, informing that John's Ship- "Discovery" developed some technical snag while passing through Indian coast and needed urgentrepairs. He requested Karan to get it repaired at his dock in Visakhapatnam.On inspection of the ship Karan realized that technical snag can be repaired using technology thatis patented by SHIPREP, an Indian company. The SHIPREP's patented technology can repair suchdamages in few hours as compared to conventional process of repair which takes weeks. Karan usedthat technology to repair "Discovery" at the Indian coast without the permission from SHIPREP. Afterfew months one of the ships owned by Karan also developed the same problem and Karan got it repairedusing the same patented technology of SHIPREP without permission. SHIPREP came to know aboutsuch uses of their patented technology by Karan and approaches you for your expert guidance, what isyour advice to SHIPREP.

Ans. Based on the information provided, it appears that Karan used SHIPREP's patented technology on Indian vessel without obtaining permission or a license from SHIPREP. This constitutes patent infringement. SHIPREP may take legal action against Karan for patent infringement.

However, use of patent on foreign vessel does not constitute infringement.

Section 49: Patent rights not infringed when used on foreign vessels, etc., temporarily or accidentally in India;

(1) Where a vessel or aircraft registered in a foreign country or a land vehicle owned by a person ordinarily resident in such country comes into India (including the territorial waters thereof) temporarily or accidentally only, the rights conferred by a patent for an invention shall not be deemed to be infringed by the use of the invention--

(a) in the body of the vessel or in the machinery, tackle, apparatus or other accessories thereof, so far as the invention is used on board the vessel and for its actual needs only; or

(b) in the construction or working of the aircraft or land vehicle or of the accessories thereof, as the case may be.

(2) This section shall not extend to vessels, aircraft or land vehicles owned by persons ordinarily resident in a foreign country the laws of which do not confer corresponding rights with respect to the use of inventions in vessels, aircraft or land vehicles owned by persons ordinarily resident in India while in the ports or within the territorial waters of that foreign country or otherwise within the jurisdiction of its courts.

4. Explain about the Start-ups Intellectual Property Protection (SIPP) scheme and the roles of the IPfacilitator and compare the benefits offered under the scheme in the years 2020 and 2023.

Ans. The Start-ups Intellectual Property Protection (SIPP) scheme is an initiative of the Government of India, implemented by the Department for Promotion of Industry and Internal Trade (DPIIT), aimed at enabling start-ups to protect their intellectual property rights such as patents, trademarks, copyrights, and designs.

Under this scheme, start-ups can avail facilitator service of free drafting, filing and prosecuting patents applications in India.However, statutory fees have to be borne by the start ups. The role of the IPfacilitator is to assist the start-ups in filing and prosecuting their patent, design and trademark applications. IPfacilitators are selected by DPIIT from among professionals such as Patent Agents or Advocates engaged in IP rights work.

The benefits offered under the SIPP scheme in the year 2020 and 2023 are likely to be similar, but with some improvements. In 2023, the scheme might cover innovators and educational institutions along with start-ups with easier access to Intellectual Property services.

PART B]

3 Questions * 10 Marks= 30 Marks

5. What would be the reasons for advising your client to file a request for early publication? What are theadvantages of waiting till 18 months for

publication? Discuss citing the appropriate provisions under the Patent Act 1970 (as amended).

When a patent application is filed, it is not immediately published. The Patent Act 1970 (as amended) provides for the publication of patent applications after 18 months from the date of filing or priority date, whichever is earlier. Section 11A(7) of Indian Patent Act provides that on and from the date of publication of the application for patent and until the date of grant of a patent in respect of such application, the applicant shall have the like privileges and rights as if a patent for the invention had been granted on the date of publication of the application:

However, there may be situations where the applicant may wish to get their patent application published earlier than 18 months.

In such cases, the applicant can make a request for early publication.

On the other hand, waiting for the 18-month period to end for publication of the patent application has its own advantages. One of the major benefits of waiting for 18 months is that it allows the applicant to keep their invention confidential for a period of time. This may be important in some industries where maintaining confidentiality is critical to the success of the invention. Upon publication, the details of the invention become publicly available, which may be advantageous in some scenarios, but not necessarily in all cases.

6. PS Polymers Ltd designed an attractive paper cup with corrugated design and got the design registeredin India. An inventor Raghu made a patent application for a corrugated paper cup which includes a cupbody, a cup bottom and a cup sleeve having horizontally and vertically corrugated stripes on whichthere are many grooves which provides a grip to the user of the said cup. Designer team of PS polymersLtd. finds this application in the patent office journal and while checking the drawings of patentapplication, the designer team found that the claimed cup in the patent application is substantiallysimilar to the corrugated design registered in the name of PS polymers Ltd.During search on the above said application by PS Polymers Ltd, they also found one patent documentIN123456 where corrugated shape

of different pattern was patented which appears to be for the samepurpose. Further they also found out that Raghu had not explained the process of making the cup in thedescription. PS polymers Ltd. approaches you to file representation against the grant of patent to Raghu.Prepare a representation under the provisions of the Act and Rules.

Ans:

To the Hon'ble Controller of Patents,

Indian Patent Office

[Address of Patent Office]

Subject: Representation against the grant of patent for the invention titled "Corrugated Paper Cup"

Sir,

We, PS Polymers Ltd. (hereinafter "the Applicant"), hereby file this representation against the grant of patent application No. _____ filed by Mr. Raghu for a corrugated paper cup. We request the patent office to reject the claims made in the said application in accordance with Section 25(1)(e) of the Patents Act, 1970.

We respectfully submit that the claimed corrugated paper cup in Mr. Raghu's patent application is substantially similar to the corrugated design that was registered in the name of PS Polymers Ltd. This corrugated design was incorporated into an attractive paper cup that was designed by our team and registered in India. The design registration provides us exclusive right to use and commercialize the said design, and Mr. Raghu's patent application would be in conflict with our rights.

Furthermore, we have found that the corrugated design of different pattern was patented under Indian patent document IN123456. We believe this prior art and our design registration exemplify that the claimed invention is neither novel nor inventive in nature, and therefore not entitled to patent protection.

Additionally, we note that the patent application submitted by Mr. Raghu fails to provide a detailed explanation of the process for making the claimed cup. The absence of such technical details violates the requirements under Section 10(4)(e) of the Patents Act, which specifies that a patent specification shall fully and particularly describe the invention and its operation.

In light of these reasons, we respectfully urge the Hon'ble Controller of Patents to reject the claims made by Mr. Raghu in his patent application.

Thank you for your attention to this matter.

Sincerely,

[Name and signature of the authorized representative of PS Polymers Ltd.]

Enclosed:

a. Copy of the registered design certificate of the corrugated paper cup owned by PS Polymers Ltd.

b. Copy of Raghu's patent application and drawings showcasing the similarity with our registered design.

c. Copy of the prior patent document IN123456 demonstrating a corrugated shape for the same purpose

7. Ramashankar a farmer whose farm is subject to periods of drought, has developed a new process ofmanufacturing solar power operated pumps that improves the water obtained from the pump by 75%.

There is no other technology in the market that gives the same results in terms of water flow. Further,Gopika, who is daughter of Ramashankar, an engineering student, has developed a system comprising of a logic Controller with electronic modules to keep track of water yield from any type of pumps usedin a farm. This system could display the exact output of water from each pump. Ramashankar and hisdaughter together own an agro start-up company named RAGO Solutions. They wish to protect theirinvention(s) in India. Gopika attended "NIPAM?", the IP awareness program of the Indian Patent Officewhere she came to know about expedited examination. Advise them how to protect the inventions inIndia at the earliest. ;

Ans: Since RAGO Solutions wishes to protect its inventions as soon as possible, they can consider requesting expedited examination of their patent applications under the amended patent rules. It is designed to expedite the examination of patent applications filed by startups and small entities in India. By making use of this program, RAGO Solutions can expedite the processing of its patent applications, potentially reducing the time required for grant of patents.

PARTC

Parts C1 & C2 consist of 2 questions each and the candidate is required to answer any 1 of them ineach part. In case a Candidate answers both the questions in any part, the first attempted questionwill be considered for evaluation.

Part C1

After reading the specification:

i. Provide an appropriate title,

ii. Draft an abstract (maximum of 150 words) and .

iii. Draft at least 2 independent claims and subsequent dependent claims.

8a. Fire-resistant wires typically comprise a conductor wrapped with inorganic material in conjunction withone or more polymer layers. In case of a fire the inorganic material provides electrical insulation around bthe conductor once the usual layers of organic polymer insulation have been melted or burnt away. Ofvarious known inorganic fire-resistant wrappings, mica tapes are generally preferred. This is due to thismineral's excellent thermal and dielectric properties which provide good fire resistance and high insulationvalues. Fire resistance is often achieved by use of several layers of inorganic materials such as glass whichmakes the cables large and heavy whereas light weight and small size are achieved by thin layers ofpolymeric insulation. Large, heavy cables are not well suited for aerospace industry where small diameter,lightweight and high performance are important requirements for wire harnesses. In accordance with thepreferred embodiments of this invention, an electrical cable is provided with a primary insulation ofmicaceous material, a secondary insulation of a fluoropolymer and a third layer of a fluoropolymer. Thecable itself may comprise one or more electrical conductors formed of any suitable metal, preferably copperor aluminum. In a preferred embodiment, the cable comprises one or more twisted electrical conductors orstrands. The primary layer is composed of a micaceous material. Preferably, this layer is in the form of amica paper tape and is wrapped about the bare cable by conventional cable taping equipment or by directfeed into extrusion heads. The mica tape may, for example, have a thickness of about 12.7 pm (0.5 mils) toabout 1.27 mm (50 mils), more preferably about 25.4 pm (1 mil) to about 101.6 pm (4 mils). The mica tapeis spirally wrapped with an overlap and an opposite lay direction to the strand layer.

The fluoropolymer secondary insulation may be applied to the covered conductor by any suitablemanner including tape wrapping. Especially preferred fluoropolymers include tetrafluoroethylenehomopolymers (PTFE) and copolymers with hexafluoropropene, propylene or perfluorovinylpropyl ether,chlorotrifluoroethylene homopolymers. The tape width and thickness will be selected by those skilled inthe art according to the conductor size and the degree of overlap required. Tapes can be approximately 5mm - 25 mm, more preferably 10-20 mm, wide and between about 10 to 1000 um, more preferably about25 to about 100 pm, thick.

The tertiary insulation layer may be applied to the covered conductor by any suitable mannerincluding extrusion coating, powder coating and the like. The extrusion of the fluoropolymer onto thesecondary insulation is preferred since high rates of production can be obtained. Preferred fluoropolymersare copolymers of ethylene and tetrafluoroethylene (ETFE).

The fluoropolymer layer may also include conventional additives, such as stabilizers, fillers,crosslinking agents, pigments and the like. The thickness of the fluoropolymer layer may be in the range ofabout 127 um (5 mils) to 2.54 mm (100 mils) or more, preferably about 254 pm (10 mils) to 508 pm (20mils). The fire-resistant wire is prepared by wrapping a bare conductor with mica tape followed by a layerof polytetrafluoroethylene (PTFE), sintering the PTFE layer and extruding and crosslinking a layer ofpoly(ethylene-co-tetrafluoroethylene) (ETFE) over the PTFE layer. Further the product is preferablycrosslinked by electron beam irradiation to further enhance the properties of the insulation. Following figureshows schematic end view the structure of a fire wire according to the present invention having a metallicwire conductor 1, two layers 2, 3 of mica tape, PTFE tape layer 4, ETFE layer 5.

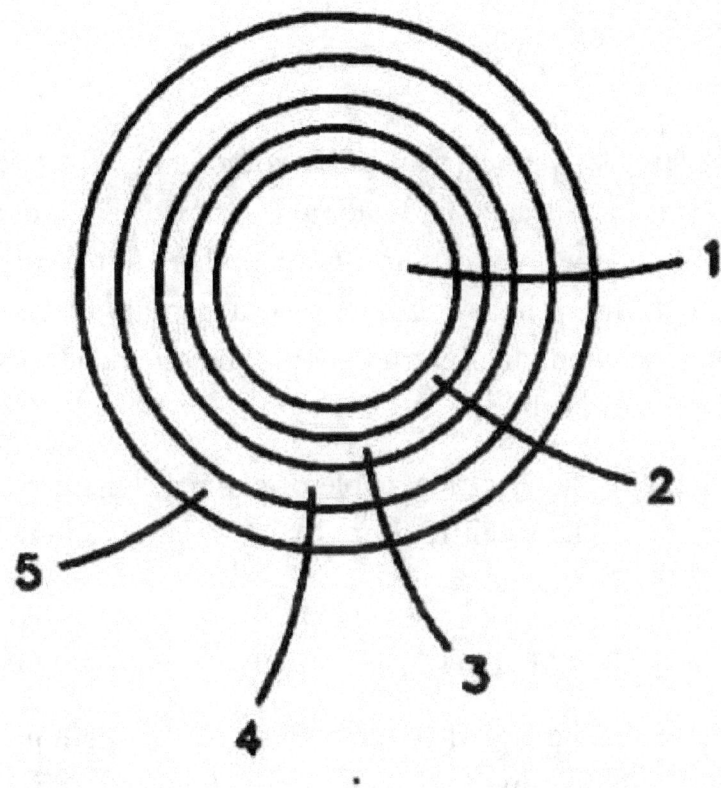

Ans. You may refer to Patent No. KR1020110125917A

Title: Fire-Resistant Electrical Cable with Micaceous Material and Fluoropolymer Insulations

Abstract: This invention relates to an electrical cable that is lightweight, small in size, and equipped with high-performance fire-resistant insulating materials. The proposed electrical cable comprises a conductor wrapped in multiple layers of fire-resistant materials. The primary layer is composed of micaceous material, while the secondary and tertiary insulation layers are made of fluoropolymer material. The use of micaceous material provides electrical insulation around the conductor in the event of fire, ensuring fire-resistance. The layer of fluoropolymer material is applied onto the primary layer in any suitable manner, including tape wrapping or extrusion coating. The fluoropolymer layer can also include additives such as stabilizers, fillers, crosslinking agents, or pigments. The proposed electrical cable demonstrates excellent performance characteristics, is preferred for use in aerospace industries, and is cost-effective.

Claims

I claim

Independent Claim 1: An electrical cable comprising a metallic wire conductor, a primary layer of micaceous material wrapped around the metallic wire conductor, a secondary layer of tetrafluoroethylene homopolymer or copolymer wrapped around the primary layer, and a tertiary layer of ethylene and tetrafluoroethylene copolymer extruded onto the secondary layer, thus forming a fire-resistant electrical cable.

Dependent Claim 2: The electrical cable of claim 1, wherein the thickness of the micaceous material is between 12.7 pm (0.5 mils) to1.27 mm (50 mils).

Dependent Claim 3: The electrical cable of claim 1, wherein the thickness of the tetrafluoroethylene homopolymer or copolymer is between 10 to 1000 um.

Dependent Claim 4: The electrical cable of claim 1, wherein the thickness of the ethylene and tetrafluoroethylene copolymer is between 127 um (5 mils) to 2.54 mm (100 mils).

Independent Claim 2: An electrical cable comprising at least one twisted electrical conductor formed of any metal, a primary layer of micaceous material spirally wrapped around the twisted electrical conductor, a secondary layer of a fluoropolymer tape wrapped around the primary layer, and a tertiary layer of a copolymer of ethylene and tetrafluoroethylene extruded onto the secondary layer of the fluoropolymer tape, thus forming a fire-resistant electrical cable.

Dependent Claim 5: The electrical cable of claim 2, wherein the thickness of the micaceous material is between 25.4 pm (1 mil) to 101.6 pm (4 mils).

Dependent Claim 6: The electrical cable of claim 2, wherein the width of the fluoropolymer tape is between 5 mm - 25 mm.

Dependent Claim 7: The electrical cable of claim 2, wherein the thickness of the fluoropolymer tape is between 25 to 100 pm.

8b. The invention consists of a device for crushing or mincing garlic or similar items. The device has anopen topped receptacle formed with sides and a perforated bottom. A plunger fits within but is removable from the receptacle to allow garlic to be placed within it. A forcing means is provided to enable the plungerto be forced towards the bottom of the receptacle thereby crushing the garlic. Rotating means enables theplunger to be rotated to assist in breaking up the garlic. The preferred embodiment has two pivotallyattached elongated members, one supporting. the receptacle and the other a forcing member to which theplunger is rotatably attached.One problem with existing garlic crushers when used for crushing garlic is that they generally worksimply by compressing the cloves of garlic between two surfaces. This does, to a degree, crush the garliccloves but is not particularly effective in causing the cloves to disintegrate and allowing the juice to beextracted unless large forces are applied. The present invention broadly consists in a garlic crusher and/ormincer comprising: a receptacle having an open top, sides, and a bottom which is perforated; a plungerwhich fits within but which is removable from the receptacle; forcing means which, in use, forces theplunger towards the bottom of the receptacle; and rotating means which, independently of the forcingmeans, enables the rotation of the plunger within the receptacle.

FIG. 1 shows a side view of the garlic crusher and/or mincer in the closed position, FIG. 2 shows a planview from above of the garlic crusher and/or mincer in its closed position, FIG. 3 shows a plan view from above of part of the garlic crusher and/or mincer in an open position, FIG. 4 shows a side view of the plunger, and FIG. 5 shows a detail of part of the bottom of the plunger.

The garlic crusher and/or mincer of the present invention is designed particularly to have its components formed by molding of suitable plastics materials or casting of suitable metals. The preferred garlic crusher and/or mincer comprises basically three main components, these being a first elongated member 1, a second elongated member 2 and a plunger 3. The first and second elongated members are preferably molded or cast as unitary pieces although this is not an essential aspect of the invention. The first elongated member supports a receptacle 4 having an open top, sides 5 and a bottom 6 which is perforated, preferably by a plurality of holes 7. The receptacle preferably has the shape of a truncated cone so that its sides 5 taper inwardly towards the bottom. The first elongated member provides a pivot means 8 to one side of the receptacle and a handle 9 to an opposite side of the receptacle. The underside of this handle may be provided with finger grips.

The second elongated member supports a forcing member 10 of a generally circular disc shape but preferably reinforced, for example, by ribs 11 across its top surface. The second elongated member provides a pivot means 12 to one side of the forcing member and a handle 13 to an opposite side of the forcing member. The first and second members are pivotally connected together at their respective pivot means by a pivot pin 14. This enables the first and second members to be pivotally moved relative to each other from an open position, or rather a variety of open positions where the open top to the receptacle is exposed, to a closed position. One open position is shown in FIG. 3 where the first and second members have been opened to lie at 180° relative to each other. In the closed position the forcing member 10 and the handle 13 of thesecond member 2 are superimposed over the receptacle 4 and the handle 9 of the first member 1respectively, the forcing member then being located over the open top of the receptacle. The plunger 3which is shown separated from the rest of the garlic crusher in FIG. 4 is rotatably attached to the forcing member 10 such that when the first and second members are in an open position the plunger is clear of the receptacle. This allows cloves of garlic or other things to be placed in the receptacle for crushing and/or mincing. As the first and second elongated members are brought together the plunger enters the receptacle and as the handles 10 and 13 are squeezed further together the plunger crushes the garlic in the receptacle.

The first and second elongated members are preferably designed so that when they are brought together to their closed position their handles are not brought completely together, a gap being left between them toprevent the skin of the hand of a user from being pinched between the handles. The plunger as shown hasa body, the lower portion 15 of which is shaped to correspond generally with the shape of the bottom portionof the receptacle, the dimensions of the lower portion 15 being slightly reduced from this however. Thebottom surface 16 of the plunger is preferably corrugated or grooved, and preferably corrugated or groovedin two directions at right angles so that a plurality of points 17 is provided as shown in FIG. 5. Thisconfiguration assists in the crushing and the disintegration of the thing being crushed, especially when theplunger is rotated within the receptacle while pressure is being applied to the plunger by the handles 10 and13 being squeezed together. From the upper portion of the body of the plunger a shaft 18 projects and passesthrough a hole 19 in the forcing member. A third handle 20 is attached to the shaft on the side of the forcingmember opposite the plunger. This handle 20 enables the plunger to be rotated independently of the forcingmeans. In use, when pressure is being applied, rotation of the plunger causes a shearing action between thebottom of the plunger and the bottom of the receptacle. The top and bottom surfaces of the thing beingcrushed tend to be gripped by the corrugations on the bottom of the plunger and by the sides of the holeson the bottom of the receptacle respectively. This assists the shearing action. The holes of course also allowthe juice, if any, from the thing beingcrushed to pass through. If the handle20 is made to be detachable from the plunger, the plunger can be separatedfrom the forcing member for more'effective cleaning.

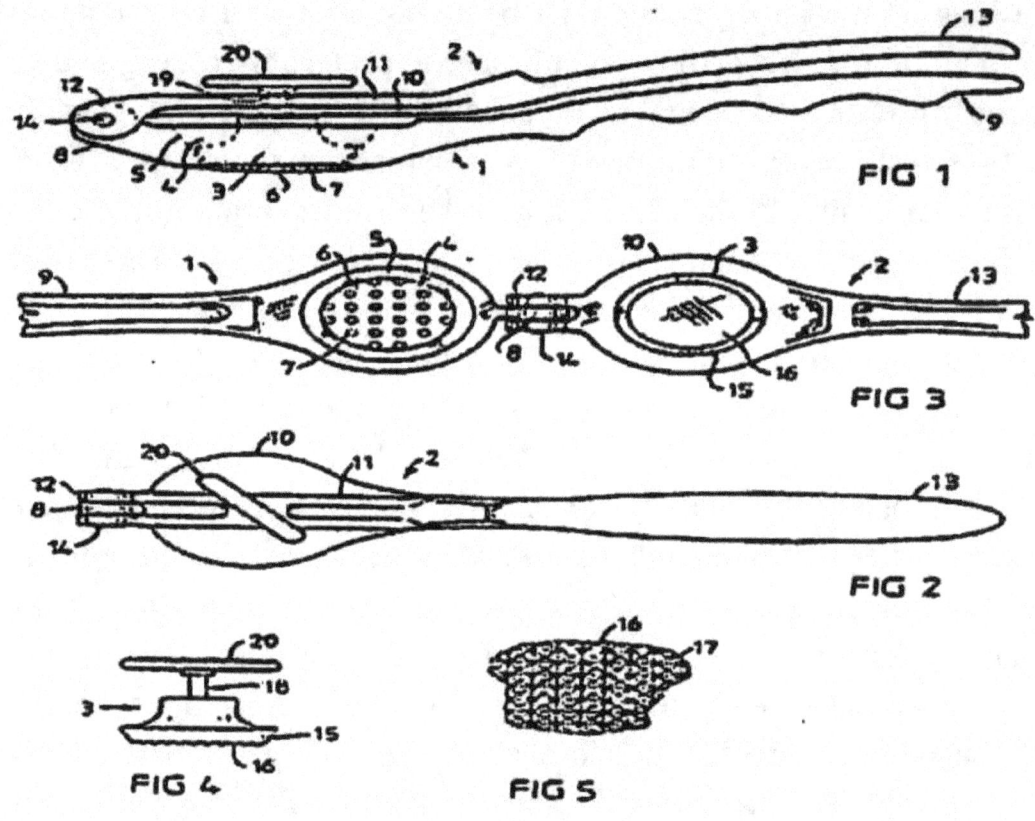

FIG 1

FIG 3

FIG 2

FIG 4

FIG 5

Ans. You may refer to United States Patent 4582265

Title: Garlic Crusher and Mincer with Rotating Plunger

Abstract: The present invention relates to a device for crushing or mincing garlic or similar items. The device comprises an open-topped receptacle with sides and a perforated bottom, a removable plunger that fits within the receptacle, a forcing means to push the plunger towards the bottom of the receptacle, and rotating means to rotate the plunger within the receptacle. In the preferred embodiment, the device consists of two elongated members. The first elongated member supports the receptacle while the second elongated member supports a forcing member and a circular reinforced disc-shaped plunger, which is rotatably attached to the forcing member with a separate handle for rotational movement. The unique design of the device provides efficient crushing and disintegration of the garlic cloves without applying large forces. The device is easily cleaned and constructed with molding of suitable plastics materials or casting of suitable metals.

17

Claims

I claim

Independent Claim 1: A garlic crusher and/or mincer comprising a receptacle having an open top, sides, and a perforated bottom, a removable plunger, forcing means which forces the plunger towards the bottom of the receptacle, and rotating means which enables the rotation of the plunger within the receptacle.

Dependent Claim 2: The garlic crusher and/or mincer of claim 1, wherein the perforated bottom of the receptacle has a plurality of holes.

Dependent Claim 3: The garlic crusher and/or mincer of claim 1, wherein the plunger has a grooved or corrugated base to assist in crushing and disintegration.

Dependent Claim 4: The garlic crusher and/or mincer of claim 1, wherein the rotating means includes a handle attached to the plunger to provide independent rotational movement of the plunger.

Independent Claim 2: A garlic crusher and/or mincer comprising a first elongated member supporting a truncated cone-shaped receptacle having an open top, sides, and a perforated bottom, a second elongated member pivotally attached to the first elongated member, supporting a circular reinforced disc-shaped forcing member with a circular detachable handle, a circular reinforced disc-shaped plunger rotatably attached to the forcing member with a separate handle, forcing means to move the plunger towards the bottom of the receptacle, and rotating means for independent movement of the plunger within the receptacle.

Dependent Claim 5: The garlic crusher and/or mincer of claim 2, wherein the detachable handle is detachable from the plunger for effective cleaning.

Dependent Claim 6: The garlic crusher and/or mincer of claim 2, wherein the perforated bottom of the receptacle has a plurality of holes.

Dependent Claim 7: The garlic crusher and/or mincer of claim 2, wherein the plunger has a grooved or corrugated base to assist in crushing and disintegration.

Part C2

A client meets you and provides technical information regarding his invention. Draft a complete specification with at least two claims and a title for anyone of the following descriptions, for filing in the Indian Patent office. While preparing the complete specification, no need to draw the figures. However, you may refer to the figures in the specification as fig. 1, fig. 2 etc.

1X 30M = 30 Marks

9a. The motorcycles nowadays still use internal combustion engines as a primary source of power, electric motorcycles will prevail in the foreseeable future due to technological advancement. Hence, it is imperative to apply wind power generation in electric motorcycles such that a wind power generating module canfunction as an auxiliary recharging device for use with an electric motorcycle and achieve the goal ofenhancing the range and the energy-saving capacity of the motorcycle. The inventors of the presentinvention endeavors to improve the prior art and thus proposes a wind power generating module for usewith an electric scooter. The proposed wind power generating module introduces external air thereintowhile the electric scooter is moving so as for fan blades to be driven to rotate by a current of the air andcomprises a duct for enhancing the rotational efficiency of the fan blades, thereby increasing the powergeneration capacity of a power generator.

A wind power generating module for use with an electric scooter is disclosed. The wind power generatingmodule is installed on an electric scooter and includes: at least one fan blade being driven to rotate byexternal air introduced into the wind power generating module while the electric scooter is moving; a disctype generator with a rotor configured to rotate in conjunction with the fan blades and generate electricpower, a duct circumferentially disposed at an outermost portion of the fan blades and having an opening,the opening receiving the fan blades, wherein the opening has a front opening portion functioning as aninlet for the external air and a rear opening portion functioning as an outlet for the external air, the frontopening portion being smaller than the rear opening portion; a front protective cover and a rear protectivecover disposed at the inlet and the outlet, respectively.

It is an objective of the present invention to provide a wind power generating module whichcomprises multiple blades each having a wing-shaped cross-section and an enlarged duct and therebygreatly enhances the output of electric power, and, as a result, the wind power generating module canfunction as an auxiliary recharging device for use with an electric scooter and achieve the goal of enhancingthe range and the energy-saving capacity of the electric scooter. Another objective of the present inventionis to provide a wind power generating module which is portable and thus can be installed at any appropriateposition of a motorcycle, such as above the motorcycle head and thus functioning as a semi wind shield, at a motorcycle handle, outside the motorcycle front board, or inside the motorcycle front board, therebydispensing the need for changing motorcycle structure and shape.The objective of the present invention is to provide a wind power generating module with a wheelhub, and the wheel hub is coupled to a disc type generator to thereby achieve modularization and cut costs.

In order to achieve the above and other objectives, the present invention provides a wind power generatingmodule for use with an electric scooter, wherein the wind power generating module is disposed in an electricscooter, comprising: at least one fan blade being driven to rotate by external air introduced into the windpower generating module while the electric scooter is moving; a disc type generator with a rotor configuredto rotate in conjunction with the fan blades and generate electric power; a duct circumferentially disposedat an outermost portion of the fan blades and having an opening, the opening receiving the fan blades,wherein the opening has a front opening portion functioning as an inlet for the external air and a rear"opening portion functioning as an outlet for the external air, the front opening portion being smaller thanthe rear opening portion; a front protective cover and a rear protective cover disposed at the inlet and theoutlet, respectively.

FIG. 1A is a front view of a wind power generating module for use with an electric scooter according to the present invention; FIG. 1B is a rear view of the wind power generating module for use with an electric scooter according to the present invention; FIG. 2 is a perspective view of the wind power generating module for use with an electric scooter according to the present invention; FIG. 3A is a schematic view of the wind power generating module installed on an electric motorcycle according to the present invention;

FIG. 3B is a schematic view of the wind power generating module installed on an electric bicycle according to the present invention;

FIG. 3C is a schematic view of the wind power generating module installed above the head of the electric motorcycle according to the present invention. Referring to figures, a wind power generating module 10 for use with an electric scooter according to the present invention is a portable wind power generating module and thus can be installed at any appropriate position of an electric scooter. The following description of the wind power generating module 10 is exemplified by an electric motorcycle.

The wind power generating module is installed above the electric motorcycle head and thus functioning as a semi wind shield, at the electric motorcycle handle, outside the electric motorcycle front board, or inside the electric motorcycle front board. External air is introduced into the wind power generating module while the electric motorcycle is moving. The current of the external air drives the fan blades 101 to rotate. The rotation of the fan blades drives the rotor of a disc type generator 103 to rotate. Hence, the disc type generator 103 is capable of generating electric power. According to the present invention, the wind power generating module 10 comprises at least one fan blade 101, the disc type generator 103, a duct 105, a front protective cover 107a, and a rear protective cover 107b, which are described hereunder.

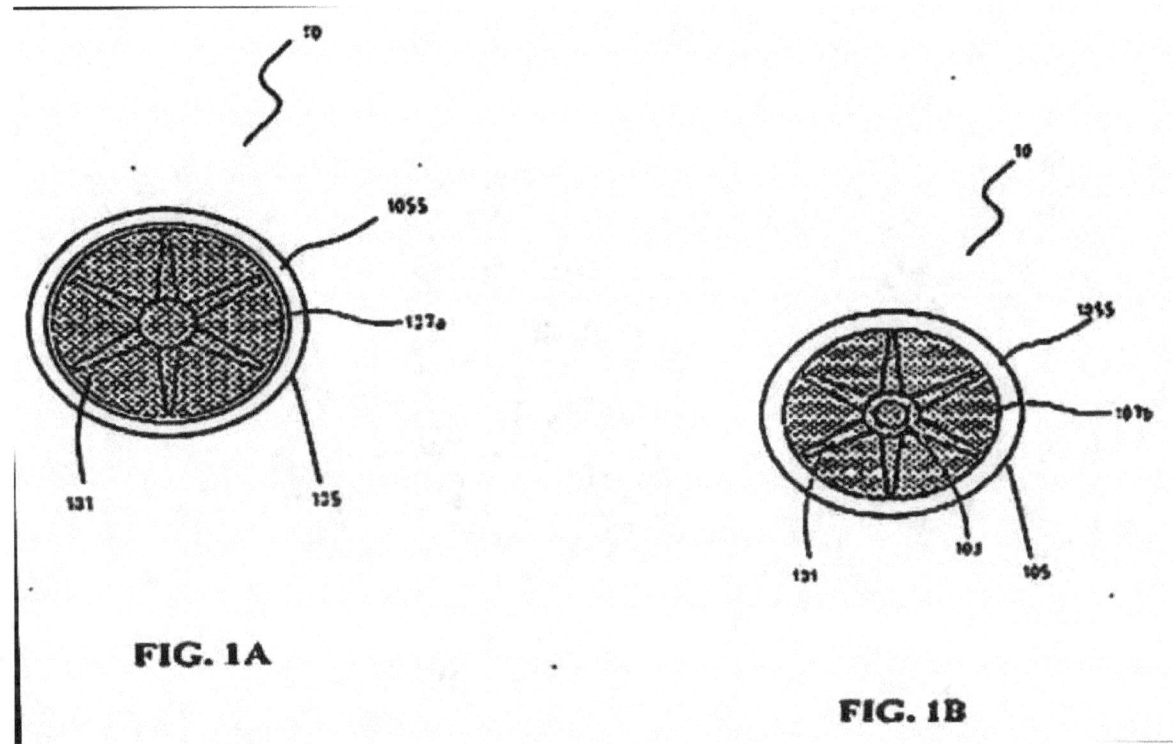

FIG. 1A

FIG. 1B

The fan blades 101 rotate when driven by the flowing external air current. The fan blades consistof a plurality of the fan blades. The fan blades each have a wing-shaped cross-section. The disc typegenerator 103 and a wheel hub 101a of the fan blades 101 are coupled together. Once the fan blades startto rotate, the rotation of the fan blades will drive the rotor of the disc type generator to rotate, therebycausing the disc type generator to generate electric power. In practice, the disc type generator can also be aconventional disc type generator. In addition, the disc type generator can be replaced by any other type ofpower generators. The duct 105 is circumferentially disposed at an outermost portion of the fan blades 101,and has an opening 105a. The opening 1052 receives the fan blades 101. The duct is spaced apart from theoutermost portion of the fan blades by a gap. The fan blades can rotate within the opening a freely.

22

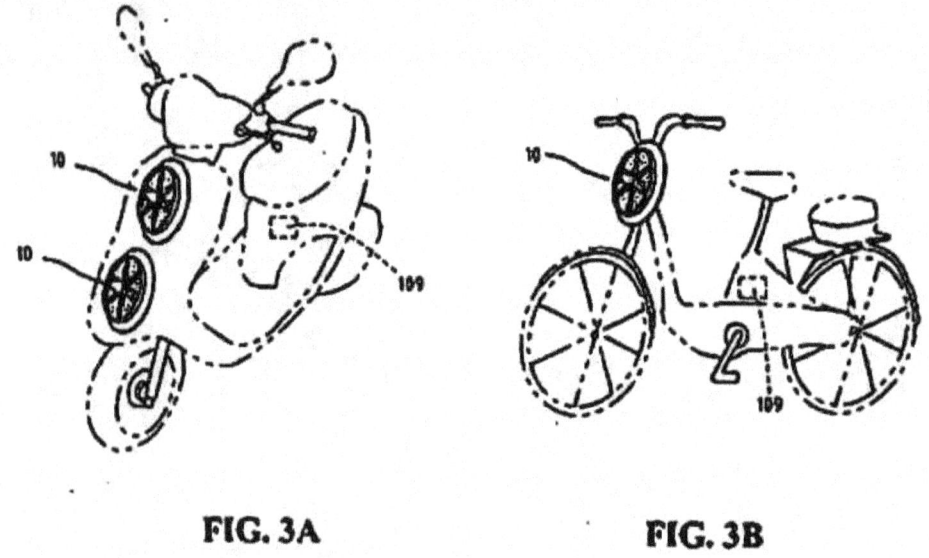

FIG. 3A   **FIG. 3B**

Ans.You may refer to **US20120038158A1**

Title: Wind Power Generating Module for Use with Electric Scooter

Abstract: The present invention relates to a wind power generating module for use with an electric scooter. The wind power generating module introduces external air into the module while the electric scooter is in motion, driving fan blades to rotate and generating electric power through a disc-type generator attached to the fan blades. The module includes an enlarged duct with multiple fan blades each having a wing-shaped cross-section to enhance efficiency, resulting in improved output of electric power, thus serving as an auxiliary recharging device and improving the range and energy-saving capacity of the electric scooter. The module is portable and can be installed at any appropriate position on the electric scooter without changing its structure or shape. The invention provides a wind power generating module with a wheel hub, allowing for modularization and cutting costs.

FIELD OF INVENTION The present invention relates to a wind power generating module for use with an electric scooter. The module introduces external air into the device while the electric scooter is in motion, driving fan blades to rotate and generating electric power through a disc-type generator attached to the fan blades.

BACKGROUND OF THE INVENTION Electric scooters are becoming increasingly popular due to their low carbon emissions and eco-friendliness. However, they face a limitation in their range and energy-saving capacity. Given that electric motorcycles primarily use internal combustion engines as a primary source of power presently, it is imperative to apply wind power generation to electric motorcycles so that a wind power generating module can function as an auxiliary recharging device for the electric scooter and achieve the goal of enhancing its range and energy-saving capacity. The invention provides a wind power generating module that utilizes wind energy to generate electricity for the electric scooter, thus addressing the aforementioned limitations.

SUMMARY OF THE INVENTION The present invention provides a wind power generating module for functions as an auxiliary recharging device for use with an electric scooter, enhancing its range and energy-saving capacity. The module introduces external air thereinto while the electric scooter is moving, driving fan blades to rotate and generating electric power through a disc-type generator attached to the fan blades. A duct is circumferentially disposed at the outermost portion of the fan blades, with an enlarged opening on the front side functioning as an inlet for receiving external air and a rear side with a smaller opening functioning as an outlet for blowing out the air. A front and rear protective cover is disposed at the inlet and outlet, respectively. To achieve efficient power generation, the present invention employs a plurality of fan blades, each with a wing-shaped cross-section and an enlarged duct, enhancing the output of electric power. The wind power generating module is portable, capable of installation at any suitable position of the electric scooter, such as above the head functioning as a semi wind shield, at the motorcycle handle, outside motorcycle front board, or inside the motorcycle front board, thus eliminating the need to change the motorcycle structure and shape. The module can be made more cost-effective by attaching a wheel hub to the fan blades to achieve modularization.

BRIEF DESCRIPTION OF THE DRAWINGS

FIG. 1A: Front view of a wind power generating module for use with an electric scooter according to the present invention. FIG. 1B: Rear view of a wind power generating module for use with an electric scooter according to the present invention. FIG. 2: Perspective view of a wind power generating module for use with an electric scooter according to the present invention. FIG. 3A: Schematic view of a wind power generating module installed on an electric motorcycle according to the present invention. FIG. 3B: Schematic view of a wind power generating module installed on an electric bicycle according to the present invention. FIG. 3C: Schematic view of a wind power generating module installed above the head of an electric motorcycle according to the present invention.

DETAILED DESCRIPTION OF THE INVENTION The present invention provides a wind power generating module for use with an electric scooter to address the limitations regarding the electric scooter's range and energy-saving capacity. The invention generates electric power by utilizing wind energy, which can serve as an auxiliary recharging device for the electric scooter, enhancing its range and energy-saving capacity. Referring to FIGS. 1A, 1B, and 2, the wind power generating module 10 of the present invention comprises at least one fan blade 101, a disc type generator 103, a duct 105 circumferentially disposed at the outermost portion of the fan blades, and a front protective cover 107a and a rear protective cover 107b disposed at the inlet and outlet, respectively. The fan blades 101 rotate when external air is introduced into the module while the electric scooter is moving, driving the fan blades to rotate. The fan blades are coupled with the rotor of the disc type generator 103 enabling the rotation of the fan blades to rotate the disc type generator. Hence, the disc type generator can generate electric power effectively. The fan blades consist of multiple blades, and each blade has a wing-shaped cross-section. The fan blades incorporate the wheel hub 101a, which connects the rotor of the disc type generator and the fan blades, facilitating modularization to cut costs effectively. The duct 105 is circumferentially disposed at the outermost portion of the fan blades, and has an opening 105a that receives the fan blades. The outermost portion of the fan blades is spaced apart from the duct by a gap, which enables the fan blade to rotate freely. The duct 105 has an enlarged front opening portion serving as an inlet for receiving external air. Correspondingly, the rear of the duct has a smaller opening portion functioning as an outlet to blow out the air. The front and rear protective covers 107a, 107b are disposed at the inlet and outlet, respectively. The protective covers enable streamlined airflow entry and exit. FIG.3A, FIG.3B, and FIG.3C depict exemplary modules installed on an electric scooter, electric bicycle, and above the head of an electric scooter respectively. The wind power generating module 10 shows as a portable device installed at any appropriate position of the electric scooter. The front protective cover 107a and the rear protective cover 107b effectively protect the fan blades 101 of the module. The enlarged duct 105 and fan blades with the wing-shaped cross-section have enhanced the electric power output. The present invention provides a wind power generating module that produces electric power by utilizing wind energy, thereby serving as an auxiliary source of power for the electric scooter and improving its range and energy-saving capacity. The module can be installed at any suitable position of the electric scooter without changing the structure or shape of the electric scooter. The wind power generating module provides a wheel hub for modularization, facilitating cost cutting.

Claims

I claim

Independent Claim 1: A wind power generating module for use with an electric scooter, comprising at least one fan blade, a disc type generator with a rotor attached to the fan blades, a duct circumferentially disposed at the outermost portion of the fan blades with an opening receiving the fan blades, and a front and rear protective cover at the inlet and outlet, respectively, wherein external air is introduced into the module while the electric scooter is moving to drive the fan blades and generate electric power.

Dependent Claim 2: The wind power generating module of claim 1, wherein the fan blades have a wing-shaped cross-section and therfore rendering improved efficiency.

Dependent Claim 3: The wind power generating module of claim 1, wherein the module is portable and can be installed at any appropriate position on the electric scooter without changing the scooter's structure or shape.

Dependent Claim 4: The wind power generating module of claim 1, further comprising a wheel hub attached to the fan blades to allow for modularization and reduced costs. Independent Claim 2: An electric scooter comprising a wind power generating module, wherein the wind power generating module comprises at least one fan blade, a disc type generator with a rotor attached to the fan blades, a duct circumferentially disposed at the outermost portion of the fan blades with an opening receiving the fan blades, and a front and rear protective cover at the inlet and outlet, respectively, wherein the wind power generating module introduces external air into the module while the electric scooter is moving to drive the fan blades and generate electric power.

Dependent Claim 5: The electric scooter of claim 2, wherein the fan blades have a wing-shaped cross-section to improve efficiency.

Dependent Claim 6: The electric scooter of claim 2, wherein the wind power generating module is portable and can be installed at any appropriate position on the electric scooter without altering its structure or shape.

Dependent Claim 7: The electric scooter of claim 2, wherein the wind power generating module further comprises a wheel hub attached to the fan blades to allow for modularization and reduced costs.

9b. The present invention is broadly concerned with temperature regulated cookware and servingwareitems, such as pots, pans, buffet serving pans, serving dishes, platters, and the like. More particularly, theinvention is concerned with sealed cookware and servingware objects, such as pressure cookers, that aretemperature and pressure regulated using control technology such as Radio Frequency Identification(RFID) technology and temperature sensors associated with the objects. The use of thermometers or othertemperature sensors to monitor and control the cooking process is well known. Such thermometers areundesirable for use with cookware/serving ware objects that have a lid as the use of a probe-typethermometer requires removal of the lid each time a temperature reading is taken. Generally, pressurecooker is placed on a stove or other similar heat source and heated until the desired pressure as indicatedon

pressure regulator is achieved. Once the desired pressure is obtained, the heat is reduced to maintain aconstant temperature and pressure within cooker. Maintaining a constant temperature and pressure withinpressure cooker is often difficult to do manually, taking a considerable amount of trial and error in adjustingthe stove temperature. Therefore, it would be beneficial to provide a means of easily regulating/maintaininga constant temperature and pressure within the pressure cooker.

The above-described objects are achieved using a temperature regulated object including a heatable body,a temperature sensor, an RFID tag (or another suitable transmitter/receiver), and a lid. The temperaturesensor can be embedded in the base of the pressure cooker and connected to an RFID tag or the temperaturesensor can extend through a tunnel in the wall of the heatable body of the object, which includes a sealingcap to cover the tunnel and prevent air and/or liquid from escaping the interior of the object, and isconnected to the RFID tag by a pair of wires. The RFID tag acts as a transmitter (and sometimes as receiver)to communicate with a reader/writer located in a cook-top for heating the object, providing temperatureinformation and other information regarding the object (such as heating characteristics) to the cook-top.

The temperature information and the heating information are used by the cook-top to control thetemperature and pressure within the object.

FIG. 1 is an elevation view of a prior art pressure cooker, in which temperature within pressurecooker is regulated by measuring and controlling the pressure within cooker. The pressure cooker includestypical components found in many pressure cookers, including pressure regulator, which is connected tothe inner chamber of pressure cooker by vent pipe, over-pressure plug, sealing ring, air vent/cover lock,lock pin, cover handle, and cocking rack. In a preferred embodiment the heatable object is a sealed objectsuch as a pressure cooker in which the temperature sensor extends through the wall of the cooker, the headof the temperature sensor is inserted through the tunnel in the body of the cooker from the outer surface soas to be generally flush with the inner surface of the wall of the body. A sealing cap is then positioned andcrimped over (or otherwise connected to or in close contact with) the head of the sensor. In an alternativeembodiment, the sealing cap is an integral part of the temperature sensor, and the sensor is inserted throughthe tunnel in the body of the cooker from the inner surface toward the exterior surface. The tunnel and thesealing cap may also include a potting material to surround the sensor. The tunnel through the wall of theobject of the instant invention is located at a position towards the top half to top third of the object, abovethe food/liquid line for the object. In a preferred embodiment the body and lid are manufactured in a mannerknown in the art for pots and pan, and in particular pressure cookers, and the tunnel is then drilled throughthe wall of the body. Nevertheless, it will be appreciated that the body can be manufactured to include thetunnel, such as by casting or any other suitable process. The RFID tag is located within a cavity formed inthe handle of the object of the instant invention to position the tag outside of the heat-generation zone forthe object. This reduces the temperature to which the tag is subjected, maximizing the life of the tag. Thehandle holds the RFID tag parallel to the cook-top surface for maximum signal strength during operation.

A section elevation view of an RFID controlled pressure cooker of the instant invention in which atemperature sensor extends through the wall of the cooker is shown in figure 2 and further an explodedpartial section view, taken along circle A-A of FIG. 2, showing the pressure cooker, temperature sensor andRFID tag in detail is shown in figure 3. As shown in figure 2, pressure cooker 110 includes heatable body120, handle 180 in which RFID tag 130 is located, and temperature sensor 150 located within a tunnel that. passes through the wall of body 120. Temperature sensor 150 is connected to RFID tag 130 by conductors140, and includes sealing cap positioned over the head of sensor 150. As is shown in Figures 2 and 3,sealing cap 160 includes a diameter that is greater than the diameter of the tunnel that passes through the wall of body 120.

The RFID tag.assembly includes RFID tag 130, a tag overmolding, temperature sensor, andconductor wires 140 connecting RFID tag 130 to temperature sensor 150. The tag overmolding is a shellthat surrounds the RFID tag and which is filled with an epoxy-based material to waterproof and generallyprotect RFID tag. The shell also functions as a stiffener for conductor wires that are connected to terminalpads on RFID tag. Conductor wires include two conductor wires (such as nickel metal copper, or othersimilar conducting material) that are embedded within a mineral insulation of a mineral insulated cable.Temperature sensor is attached to the exposed opposing ends of conductor wires from RFID tag. Sealingcap is positioned over sensor with a potting material (such as a silicone or ceramic material) in capsurrounding temperature sensor. Sealing cap is then laser welded to a stainless steel sheath of the mineralinsulated cable to provide a sealed connection between temperature sensor and wires. Sealing cap may bewelded over sensor prior to positioning of sensor through the wall of cooker body. In such case, wires arepushed through the tunnel in the wall of body from the interior (cooking area) of cooker towards the exteriorprior to being connected to the terminal pads of RFID tag. Alternatively, temperature sensor may be pushedthrough the tunnel in the wall of body from the exterior towards the interior, and then cap is positionedaround sensor from the interior of cooker and laser welded.

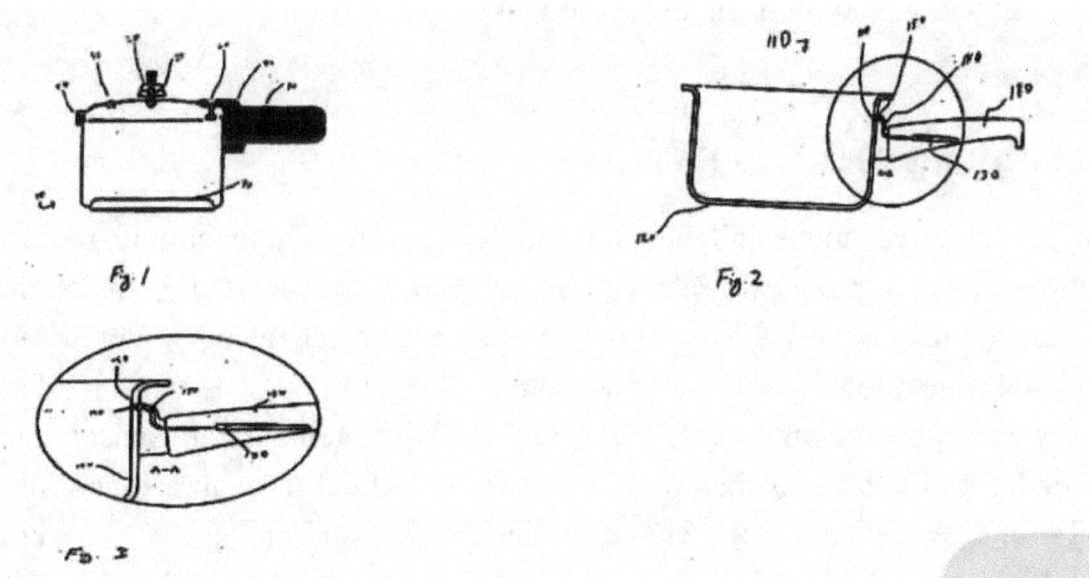

Fig. 1

Fig. 2

Fig. 3

Ans: Kindly refer to US7157675B2

TITLE- Radio frequency identification controlled heatable objects

FIELD OF THE INVENTION

The present invention relates to temperature regulated cookware and servingware items, such as pots, pans, serving dishes, platters, and the like. More particularly, the invention pertains to sealed cookware and servingware objects, such as pressure cookers, that are temperature and pressure regulated using control technology such as Radio Frequency Identification (RFID) technology and temperature sensors associated with the objects.

BACKGROUND OF THE INVENTION

Temperature regulation and control are essential in the cooking and serving of food using cookware/serving ware objects such as pressure cookers. The use of traditional thermometers is unsuitable for cookware/serving ware objects that have lids, as the use of a probe-type thermometer requires removal of the lid to take a temperature reading. There is a need for a means of maintaining constant temperature and pressure within the cookware/serving ware object, such as a pressure cooker, without manual adjustments.

SUMMARY OF THE INVENTION

The present invention significantly enhances the art of temperature regulated cookware and servingware objects by providing a means for maintaining constant temperature and pressure within the object using a temperature regulated object including a heatable body, a temperature sensor, an RFID tag (or other suitable transmitter/receiver), and a lid. The temperature sensor can be embedded in the base of the pressure cooker or extend through a tunnel in the wall of the heatable body of the object, which includes a sealing cap to cover the tunnel and prevent air and/or liquid from escaping the interior of the object. The RFID tag can communicate with a reader/writer located on a cook-top for heating the object, providing temperature information and other information regarding the object to the cook-top. The cook-top then controls temperature and pressure within the object according to the transmitted information.

FIG. 1 depicts a prior art pressure cooker that regulates temperature within the pressure cooker by monitoring and controlling the pressure within the cooker, while FIG. 2 shows an elevation view of an RFID controlled pressure cooker of the present invention including a heatable body, handle, RFID tag, sealing cap, and temperature sensor connected by conductors. A section elevation view of the RFID controlled pressure cooker showing the temperature sensor extending through the wall of the cooker is shown in FIG. 3.

DETAILED DESCRIPTION OF THE INVENTION

The present invention provides a temperature regulated object including a heatable body, a temperature sensor, an RFID tag, and a lid for maintaining constant temperature and pressure within the object, such as a pressure cooker. The temperature sensor can be embedded in the base or extend through the wall of the heatable body of the object, which includes a sealing cap to cover the tunnel and prevent air and/or liquid from escaping the interior of the object. The RFID tag communicates with a reader/writer located on a cook-top for heating the object and transmitting temperature and heating information to the cook-top.

The heatable body can be manufactured in a manner known in the art for pots, pans, and specifically pressure cookers, and the tunnel can be drilled through the wall of the body or manufactured with the body. The tunnel passes through the wall of the object, being located at a position just above the food/liquid line. The sealing cap can be laser welded to a stainless steel sheath of the mineral insulated cable providing a sealed connection between temperature sensor and wires and preventing air or liquid from escaping the pressure cooker.

The RFID tag assembly includes RFID tag, tag overmolding, temperature sensor, and conductor wires connecting RFID tag and temperature sensor. The tag overmolding is a shell that surrounds the RFID tag and is filled with waterproof epoxy-based material to protect the RFID tag. The conductor wires can be made of conducting materials such as nickel metal copper, or the like, and can be embedded within a mineral insulation of a mineral insulated cable. The temperature sensor is attached to the opposing ends of conductor wires from the RFID tag. The sealing cap is positioned over the sensor, and is laser welded to the stainless steel sheath of the mineral insulated cable to provide a sealed connection between temperature sensor and wires.

The handle includes an RFID tag cavity, where the RFID tag is located, and holds the RFID tag parallel to the cook-top surface for maximum signal strength during operation. The tunnel through the wall of the object and the sealing cap are positioned toward the top half to top third of the object, above the food/liquid line for the object.

Claims

I claim

Independent Claim 1: A temperature regulated object comprising a heatable body, a temperature sensor, an RFID tag (or another suitable transmitter/receiver), and a lid, wherein the temperature sensor is embedded in the base of the object or extends through a tunnel in the wall of the heatable body of the object, and the RFID tag communicates with a reader/writer located on a cook-top for heating the object, providing temperature information and other information regarding the object to the cook-top, which then maintains constant temperature and pressure within the object.

Dependent Claim 2: The temperature regulated object of claim 1, wherein the tunnel in the wall of the heatable body of the object is located at a position near the top half to top third of the object, above the food/liquid line for the object.

Dependent Claim 3: The temperature regulated object of claim 1, wherein the sealing cap covering the tunnel in the wall of the heatable body of the object is laser welded to a stainless steel sheath of a mineral insulated cable providing a sealed connection between the temperature sensor and the wires.

Dependent Claim 4: The temperature regulated object of claim 1, wherein the handle of the object includes an RFID tag cavity, where the RFID tag is located, which holds the RFID tag parallel to the cook-top surface for maximum signal strength during operation.

Dependent Claim 5: The temperature regulated object of claim 1, wherein the temperature sensor includes a sealing cap that is laser welded to a stainless steel sheath of a mineral insulated cable, which is surrounded by a potting material, such as silicone or ceramic material, to further seal the connection between the temperature sensor and the wires.

Dependent Claim 6: The temperature regulated object of claim 1, wherein the temperature sensor is connected to the RFID tag by two conductor wires embedded within a mineral insulation of a mineral insulated cable.

PATENT AGENT EXAMINATION, 2022

[Under Section 126 of the Patents Act, 1970

PAPER II

TIME: 02.30 p.m. to 05.30 p.m. (Three Hrs.) Total Marks: 100

Instructions:

1. This paper consists of 3 parts - Part A (20 marks), Part B (30 marks) & Part C (50 Marks).

2. All questions in Part A and B are compulsory.

3. Part C comprises Part Cl of 20 marks and C2 of 30 marks. Part Cl consists of 2 questions and thecandidate is required to answer any one of them, Part C2 consists of 2 questions and the candidate is requiredto answer any one of them.

4. Candidates should read the questions very carefully before answering.

5. In case a candidate answers more questions than required, the first attempted question shall be evaluated.

6. No clarification will be provided during the course of the examination.

7. There is no negative marking.

8. All references to "Act" and "Rules" may be read as The Patents Act, 1970 and The Patent Rules, 2003respectively, as amended until now and their related applications.

9. Candidate is expected to quote relevant sections and rules as well as prescribed fees and forms in the answer.

PART A

4 questions * 5 marks= 20 marks

Q.1.Explain the importance of prior art search before filing of patent application and drafting ofspecification.

Ans. Prior art search is a crucial step in the patent process that involves conducting a search to determine whether an invention has been previously disclosed or described in the same or similar form. The search involves analyzing various sources such as patents, publications, and databases to identify relevant prior art. Prior art search is essential before filing a patent application and drafting the specification for several reasons, including:

1. Avoiding Patent Rejection: Patent offices require a thorough prior art search before granting a patent. A prior art search helps identify existing patents and publications that may pose a threat to the novelty of an invention. By conducting a prior art search, inventors can identify any existing patents or publications that may conflict with their invention and modify their claims or specification accordingly.

2. Improving Patentability: A prior art search can help improve patentability by identifying alternative technical solutions to a problem that are not disclosed in published materials. By reviewing prior art, inventors may even find new ideas or approaches to their invention that may make the invention more unique and patentable.

3. Reducing Patent Costs: A prior art search helps avoid the costs associated with preparing and filing a patent application that will eventually be rejected by the patent office. By conducting a prior art search, inventors can ensure that their invention is patent-worthy and reduce the costs of filing subsequent patent applications.

4. Supporting Patent Application Drafting: A prior art search can provide valuable insights that can help draft a patent specification. By reviewing the relevant prior art, inventors can better understand the scope of the invention and draft claims that are specific, accurate, and not overreaching.

In conclusion, prior art search is critical to the success of the patent process. It helps inventors identify alternative technical solutions, avoid infringement, and improve the patentability of their invention. It also helps reduce patent costs and supports the drafting of patent specifications and claims.

Q2. **Suma is a home maker in rural Karnataka. She has a patent for a fish feed formulation. She hasbeen selling the patented product through e-commerce platforms and has got very encouragingfeedback from market. Suma has now realized that the addition of 10 % by weight of coconut oil intothe formulation extends disintegration time for fish feed pellets in water. Suma knows that addition ofcoconut oil into the fish feed formulations to extent disintegration is well known in the art. Nevertheless, she approaches you seeking means to protect this improved/modified formulation. How would you advice her?**

Ans:

Dear Suma,

I am writing to advise you regarding the protection of your modified fish feed formulation, which involves the addition of 10% by weight of coconut oil to extend the disintegration time of the fish feed pellets in water.

As per the information provided in your case, the addition of coconut oil to fish feed formulations for extended disintegration is well known in the art. Therefore, it is likely that the modified formulation may not satisfy the novelty and inventive step requirements under The Patent Act, 1970.

However, it is worth noting that Section 54 of The Patent Act, 1970 provides for the protection of improvements. Under this section, if an improvement is made to an already known invention, and such improvement is novel and non-obvious, it may be eligible for patent protection. In such cases, the patent protection will be limited to the improvement only, and not the original invention.

Therefore, Suma, you can consider filing a separate patent application for your improved formulation, highlighting the novelty and non-obviousness of the addition of coconut oil to extend the disintegration time of the fish feed pellets in water. You may also need to provide data and evidence to support the improvement and its effectiveness.

It is also advisable to conduct a prior art search to confirm the novelty and non-obviousness of the improvement before filing a patent application. The search will help identify any existing patents or publications that may affect the patentability of your improvement.

Please feel free to contact me for any further guidance or assistance.

Sincerely,

[Your Name]

[Your Designation]

[Your Contact Information]

Q3. Mr. Gopi, an applicant from Madya Pradesh, filed a Patent application in his individual capacityalong with the request for Examination. Patent office has issued First examination report (FER)wherein some documents were cited to prove that invention lacks Novelty and Inventive step. Gopinow realized that many features of the invention were not disclosed in the specification at the time ofthe original filing. Gopi asked you to incorporate the missing features in the original specification.

(a)Explain to Gopi the procedure to make voluntary amendments under the Patents Act.

(b) Briefly discuss whether Gopi can make use of such provisions for voluntary amendments inabove scenario.

Ans.(a) Dear Mr. Gopi,

I am writing to advise you regarding the procedure for making voluntary amendments to your patent application under The Patents Act, 1970.

As per the information provided in your case, you have received a First Examination Report (FER) from the Patent Office, which cited some documents to prove that your invention lacks novelty and inventive step. Additionally, you have realized that some features of your invention were not disclosed in the original specification at the time of filing. You now wish to incorporate these missing features in the original specification.

The procedure for making amendments to your patent application is governed by Section 57 and Section 59 of The Patents Act, 1970, as well as Rule 81 of The Patents Rules, 2003. To make amendments to your patent application, you need to follow the steps below:

(a) File a request for amendment in the prescribed format, along with a copy of the proposed amended specifications.

(b) Pay the requisite fee for the proposed amendment.

© It is important to note that the amendments made by Gopi should be supported by the original disclosure of the invention in the specification. In other words, the amendments should not introduce new matter that was not originally disclosed in the specification.

(d) If the Patent Office approves the proposed amendment, it will be incorporated into the patent application.

(e) such amendments should not result in expanding the scope of the invention disclosed in the original specification.

Therefore, Mr. Gopi, in your case, since you have already received the FER and the objections raised indicate a lack of novelty and inventive step, it may be possible to make amendments to the specifications to overcome those objections. I hope this advice is useful to you. Please feel free to reach out to me for any further guidance or assistance.

Sincerely,

[Your Name]

[Your Designation]

[Your Contact Information]

(b) Section 57 of Indian Patent Act: Amendment of application and specification before Controller;

(1)Subject to the provisions of section 59, the Controller may, upon application made under this section in the prescribed manner by an applicant for a patent or by a patentee, allow the application for the patent or the complete specification [or any document relating thereto] to be amended subject to such conditions, if any, as the Controller thinks fit:

Provided that the Controller shall not pass any order allowing or refusing an application to amend an application for a patent or a specification [or any document relating thereto] under this section while any suit before a court for the infringement of the patent or any proceeding before the High Court for the revocation of the patent is pending, whether the suit or proceeding commenced before or after the filing of the application to amend.

(2) Every application for leave to amend an application for a patent [or a complete specification or any document relating thereto] under this section shall state the nature of the proposed amendment, and shall give full particulars of the reasons for which the application is made.

[(3) Any application for leave to amend an application for a patent or a complete specification or a document related thereto under this section made after the grant of patent and the nature of the proposed amendment may be published.]

(4) Where an application is [published] under sub-section (3), any person interested may, within the prescribed period after the [publication] thereof, give notice to the Controller of opposition thereto; and where such a notice is given within the period aforesaid, the Controller shall notify the person by whom the application under this section is made and shall give to that person and to the opponent an opportunity to be heard before he decides the case.

(5) An amendment under this section of a complete specification may be, or include, an amendment of the priority date of a claim.

[(6) The provisions of this section shall be without prejudice to the right of an applicant for a patent to amend his specification or any other document related thereto to comply with the directions of the Controller issued before the grant of a patent.]

Rule 81: Amendment of application, specification or any document relating thereto.—(1) An application under section 57 for the amendment of an application for a patent or a complete specification or any document related thereto shall be made in Form 13.

(2) If the application for amendment under sub-rule (1) relates to an application for a patent which has not been granted, the Controller shall determine whether and subject to what conditions, if any, the amendment shall be allowed.

(3) (a) If the application for amendment under sub-rule (1) is made after grant of patent and the nature of the proposed amendment is substantive, the application shall be published.

(b) Any person interested in opposing the application for amendment shall give a notice of opposition in Form 14 within three months from the date of publication of the application.

(c)The procedure specified in rules 57 to 63 relating to the filing of written statement, reply statement, leaving evidence, hearing and costs shall, so far as may be, apply to the hearing of the opposition under section 57 as they apply to the hearing of an opposition proceeding.

Form 13

Fee for e filing

Natural persons before grant=800; after grant 1600,

Others before grant =4000; after grant 8000.

Section 59 of Indian Patent Act: Supplementary provisions as to amendment of application or specification.

[(1) No amendment of an application for a patent or a complete specification or any document relating thereto shall be made except by way of disclaimer, correction or explanation, and no amendment thereof shall be allowed, except for the purpose of incorporation of actual fact, and no amendment of a complete specification shall be allowed, the effect of which would be that the specification as amended would claim or describe matter not in substance disclosed or shown in the specification before the amendment, or that any claim of the specification as amended would not fall wholly within the scope of a claim of the specification before the amendment.]

[(2) Where after the date of grant of patent any amendment of the specification or any other documents related thereto is allowed by the Controller or by *** the High Court, as the case may be,--

(a) the amendment shall for all purposes be deemed to form part of the specification along with other documents related thereto;

(b) the fact that the specification or any other documents related thereto has been amended shall be published as expeditiously as possible; and

(c) the right of the applicant or patentee to make amendment shall not be called in question except on the ground of fraud].

(3) In construing the specification as amended, reference may be made to the specification as originally accepted.

Rule 81 of Indian Patent Rules: (1) An application under section 57 for the amendment of an application for a patent or a complete specification or any document related thereto shall be made in Form 13.

Fee for Form 13,before grant , INR 800 and 4000(Electronic mode)

Fee for Form 13,post grant , INR 1600 and 8000(Electronic mode)

In the given scenario, Gopi cannot make use of the provisions for voluntary amendments under the Patents Act as he has to opt for mandatory amendment.

Q4. An application was filed with a provisional specification (PS) by a MSME in Ladakh.Subsequently, the MSME made further developments to the invention disclosed in the PS contributedby Bikram, a citizen of Nepal,

who joined the MSME after the provisional had been filed. The MSMEseeks your advice-

(a) whether improvements can be included in the complete specification?

(b) if Bikram can be mentioned as Inventor while filing complete specification (CS)?

(a) Yes, the improvements made by Bikram after the filing of the provisional specification can be included in the complete specification. As per the Indian Patent Act, an applicant can file a complete specification at any time before the expiry of 12 months from the date of filing of the provisional specification. The complete specification can include a detailed disclosure of the invention, including any improvements or modifications made after the filing of the provisional specification.Regarding including improvements in the complete specification, Section 10 of The Patents Act, 1970, provides that the complete specification must fully and particularly describe the invention and its operation or use and disclose the best method of performing the invention known to the applicant.

Therefore, in your case, the improvements made by Bikram may be included in the Complete Specification through suitable amendments, provided that the amendments do not substantially alter the nature of the invention or change the scope of the claim.

(b) According to Indian Patent Law, an inventor is a person who contributes to any material extent to the invention. Regarding mentioning Bikram as an inventor, Section 6 of The Patents Act, 1970, defines an inventor as a person who contributes to the conception of the invention. Therefore, if Bikram contributed to the conception of the improved invention, he may be mentioned as an inventor in the Complete Specification filing.

PART B

3 questions * 10 marks= 30 marks

Q5. (a) Ujjwal, an enterprenuer and owner of startup "UJWsolar", has developed a cheap solar based battery. He wishes to have patent for said invention at the earliest. Ujjwal came to know aboutexpedited examination. Explain the same as per the provisions of the Patents Acts and Rules.

Ans : Expedited examination is a special provision provided under the Patents Act, 1970, and the Patents Rules, 2003, which enables an applicant to expedite the examination of their patent application.

According to Rule 24C of the Patents Act, an applicant can request expedited examination of their patent application in India by filing Form 18A along with the prescribed fee. The applicant must also submit a statement that the invention is of strategic importance from a national perspective or that the applicant is a startup.

Once the request for expedited examination is granted, the patent application will be examined by the Indian Patent Office within a period of one month from the date of the request. This is significantly faster than the usual time taken for examination, which can sometimes take years.

Section 11B of Patent Act: Request for examination;

[11B. Request for examination.--[(1) No application for a patent shall be examined unless the applicant or any other interested person makes a request in the prescribed manner for such examination within the prescribed period.]

* * * * *

[(3) In case of an application in respect of a claim for a patent filed under sub-section (2) of section 5 before the 1st day of January, 2005 a request for its examination shall be made in the prescribed manner and within the prescribed period by the applicant or any other interested person.]

(4) In case the applicant or any other interested person does not make a request for examination of the application for a patent within the period as specified under sub-section (1)*** or sub-section (3), the application shall be treated as withdrawn by the applicant:

[Provided that--

(i) the applicant may, at any time after filing the application but before the grant of a patent, withdraw the application by making a request in the prescribed manner; and

(ii) in a case where secrecy direction has been issued under section 35, the request for examination may be made within the prescribed period from the date of revocation of the secrecy direction.]

Rule 24B of Patent Rules: Examination of application.—(1) (i) A request for examination under section 11B shall be made in Form 18 within forty-eight months from the date of priority of the application or from the date of filing of the application, whichever is earlier;

(ii)The period within which the request for examination under sub-section (3) of section 11B to be made shall be forty-eight months from the date of priority if applicable, or forty-eight months from the date of filing of the application;

(iii)The request for examination under sub-section (4) of section 11B shall be made within forty-eight months from the date of priority or from the date of filing of the application, or within six months from the date of revocation of the secrecy direction, whichever is later;

(iv) The request for examination of application as filed according to the 'Explanation' under sub-section (3) of section 16 shall be made within forty-eight months from the date of filing of the application or from the date of priority of the first mentioned application or within six months from the date of filing of the further application, whichever is later;

(v)The period for making request for examination under section 11B, of the applications filed before the 1st day of January, 2005 shall be the period specified under the section 11B before the commencement of the Patents (Amendment) Act, 2005 or the period specified under these rules, whichever expires later.

(2) (i) Where the request for examination has been filed under sub-rule (1) and application has been published under section 11A, the Controller shall refer the application, specification and other documents related thereto to the examiner and such reference shall be made in the order in which the request is filed:

In conclusion, Ujjwal, as a startup owner, can apply for expedited examination of his patent application by submitting Form 18A along with the prescribed fee. Upon granting of expedited examination, the patent application will be examined within a period of one month from the date of the request.

(b) In another patent application Ujjwal has already filed a request for examination. The application has been awaiting examination for a long time. If he wants that application to be taken for examination immediately what steps are required?

Ans: To request expedited examination of the pending patent application, Ujjwal needs to file a request for expedited examination under Rule 24(c) and submit Form 18A. The request must include valid reasons for expedited examination, such as commercialization, infringement, or funding requirements, and must meet the requirements of Section 11B. Additionally, Ujjwal may need to pay an extra fee for requesting expedited examination. Once the request is granted, the patent application will be examined immediately, and the patent office will issue a first examination report within one month of the grant of the request.

Form 18

Online Fee: Natural Persons or small entity: 4000, Others 20000;(electronic mode)

Online Conversion fee from Rule 24B to 24C: Natural Persons: 4000, Others 40000; (electronic mode)

Q6. Your schoolmate Gopika is now a final year student at an engineering college at Chennai. She has invented dust repellant coating composition for solar panels. Her engineering college has agreed to pursue a patent application for the said invention. How will you explain to her the most important aspects of prosecuting a patent application in India upto grant, with the relevant forms, fees and time limits?

Ans: The following are the aspects of prosecuting a patent application in India up to grant with the relevant forms, fees, and time limits.

STEP 1. FILING OF PATENT APPLICATION: The first step to obtaining a patent is to file a patent application with the Indian Patent Office. The application can be filed either through the e-filing facility or by physically submitting the patent application at any of the patent offices. Patent Documents can be filed either through online or at the patent office in respective jurisdiction: Kolkata, Delhi, Mumbai, and Chennai.

1. Covering indicating the list of documents;

2. Application for Grant of Patent in Form 1 in duplicate [section 7, 54 & 135 and Rule 20(1)];fee is INR1600 and 8000(electronic mode)

3. Provisional/Complete specification in Form 2(No fee, if already paid) in duplicate [Section 10; Rule 13]; comprising

• Description

• Claims

• Drawing (if any)

• Abstract

4. Statement and Undertaking in Form 3 in duplicate [Section 8; Rule 12];(No fee)

5. Power of Attorney in Form 26 (in case a patent agent is assigned) (in original) (ii));(No Fee)

6. Declaration of Inventorship in Form 5 in duplicate (only where applicant and inventor[s] are different; (No Fee)

7. Form 28 (in case the applicant is a small entity) (Rule 2 (fa) & 7); (No Fee)

8. Certified true copy of the Priority document (in case priority is claimed); and

9. Requisite Statutory fees (cheque / DD)

STEP 2: PUBLICATION

[Rule 24] A patent application will be published automatically in the official journal after expiry of 18 months from date of filing or date of priority of the application containing title, abstract, application no. and name of applicant[s] and inventor[s].

Request for early publication: [Rule 22A] To expedite the process of grant of patent a request for publication under Section 11(A)(2) can be made in Form 9 any time after filing of the application. Upon such request the application will be published in one month from the date of such request.

STEP 3: OPPOSITION (IF ANY)

1. Pre grant Opposition

[Section 25(1)] Upon publication but before the grant of patent, any person, based on different grounds may file a pre grant opposition, in writing, represent by way of opposition to the Controller against the grant of patent. However the opposition will be taken by the patent office only after the filing of Request for Examination.

STEP 4: REQUEST FOR EXAMINATION

Examination request: After filing the patent application, the next step is to request for examination by submitting Form 18 along with the prescribed fees.

In Form 18 [sec 11B; rules 20(4)(ii) and 24B(1)(i)] (in duplicate when filed in physical copy) within period of 48 months from date of filing or priority, whichever is earlier.

Examination proceedings: The Indian Patent Office usually assigns a patent examiner to examine the patent application. The examiner checks whether the invention meets the patentability criteria of novelty, inventive step, and industrial applicability. The applicant may receive an examination report, and again a response can be filed.

STEP 5: FIRST EXAMINATION REPORT

[Section 12; 24B(3)] After proper examination of patent application on the criteria of novelty, inventiveness and industrial application, the Patent Examiner will issue a First Examination Report (FER) and will send along with the application and specification to the applicant or authorized agent

STEP 6: AMENDMENT OF OBJECTIONS BY THE APPLICANT

The issued FER give an opportunity to the applicant to file a response and overcome the objections raised by the Examiner.

Time limit: [Rule 24B(4)(iii)] Within 12 months from the date on which the First Examination Report has been issued to the applicant.

STEP 7: GRANT OF PATENT

The Controller will grant the application upon satisfactory response by the applicant to overcome all of the objections raised in the FER.

On the grant of a patent, the application will be accorded a number, called serial number in the series of numbers accorded to patents under the Indian Patents Act, 1970(39 of 1970).

The relevant forms with their fees are as follows:

- Form 1: Application for Patent- Rs 1,600 to Rs 8,000 (depending on the category of the applicant).

- Form 18: Request for Examination- Rs 4,000 to Rs 60,000 (depending on the category of the applicant).

- Response to Examination Report (On request)-

- Form 9: Application for Publication of Patent- Rs 2500 to Rs 13,750 (depending on the category of the applicant).

The time limits for prosecuting a patent application in India include:

- Filing of the request for examination within 48 months from the date of filing or the date of priority, whichever is earlier.

- Submitting the response to the examination report within six months from the receipt of the report.

In conclusion, it is important to note that prosecuting a patent application in India can be a time-consuming and complex process. It is wise to seek the assistance of a patent agent who can help with the process and ensure a successful outcome.

Q7. CropPro is a pesticide manufacturing company based in South Korea. CropPro developed apesticide composition comprising ingredients A and B to mitigate earworm infestation in tomatoplants. CropPro identified that when A and B are used in a ratio of 25-30% and 75-70% respectively,the pesticide composition nat only mitigated worms but also improved the flowering rate. Patentapplication was filed with a single claim-

"1. A pesticide composition comprising A and B."

Patent office has cited a prior publication in the first statement of objections (FER) which discloses apesticide composition comprising 5- 55 wt% A and 95-45 wt. % B for mitigating earworm infestationin tomato fields.

(a) How will you respond to this FER?

(b) If the complete specification did not have any examples evidencing increase in flowering rate,how can CropPro provide further evidence?

In response to this FER, CropPro can file a written response arguing that the prior publication does not anticipate their claimed composition because their composition comprises very specific amounts of A and B in a ratio of 25-30% and 75-70%, respectively. CropPro can also argue that the prior publication does not disclose the unexpected improvement in the flowering rate associated with their composition. They can provide technical arguments to highlight the differences between the claimed composition and the prior publication and why their invention should be patentable.

(b) If the complete specification did not have any examples evidencing an increase in flowering rate, CropPro can provide further evidence by filing an affidavit or declaration under the Patents Act. The affidavit or declaration should provide experimental data demonstrating the improved flowering rate using their claimed composition. Additionally, if possible, CropPro can provide technical literature or research articles supporting the improved flowering rate, which can help strengthen their position during prosecution. CropPro can also consider amending the claim language to specifically cover the improved flowering rate to demonstrate novelty and inventive step under Section 57.

PART C

Part C1 consists of 2 questions and the candidate is required to answer any 1 of them. Part C2also consists of 2 questions and the candidate is required to answer any 1 of them. In case acandidate answers more questions than required, the first attempted question will be evaluated.

Part C1

After reading the specification:

i. Provide an appropriate title,

ii. Draft an abstract (maximum of 150 words) and

iii. Draft 2 claims

1 X20 M = 20 marks

Q8. Diclofenac (2-(2-[2,6-dichlorophenylamino]phenyl)acetic acid) is one of the most widely usednon-steroidal anti-inflammatory drugs due to its marked pharmacological activity. Thiocolchicoside,also known as 3-demethyl-thiocolchicine glucoside, is a glucoside extracted from the seeds ofColchicum autumnale, which possesses a muscle-relaxant, anti-inflammatory, analgesic andanaesthetic action. The prior art 1 demonstrates that diclofenac is a substance which is relativelyunstable in solution, and that the liquid formulations of said substance therefore require the presenceof a stabilising agent. The patent prior art 2discloses stable aqueous solutions of diclofenac containinga mixture of propylene glycol and polyethylene glycol. The chemical stability of said solutions isobtained by adding a reducing agent which can be a sulphite, such as sodium bisulphite, cysteineand/or cysteine hydrochloride, acetylcysteine and/or acetylcysteine hydrochloride, or a thiosulphate.

Their chemical stability is further improved by the presence of lidocaine in addition to the reducingagent. When preparing a liquid composition containing diclofenac and thiocolchicoside, the inventorsof the present application have found that it is necessary to overcome a number of technologicaldifficulties, the most important requirement being to prevent the degradation of one or both of theactive ingredients when formulated in a single unit dose solution. The antioxidant most widely used tostabilize diclofenac in liquid solutions is sodium bisulphite. There are numerous formulations on themarket containing this antioxidant. Other antioxidants used are cysteine, acetylcysteine and reducedglutathione. Thiocolchicoside also presents stability problems in solution. The chemical and physicalcompatibility of thiocolchicoside with other injectable medicaments frequently combined with it,including anti-inflammatories, is described in prior art 3. The authors of the present invention havefound that the addition of thiocolchicoside to a formulation containing diclofenac makes the use of theabove-mentioned antioxidants problematic, if not impossible, as their presence in the solution causessignificant degradation of thiocolchicoside and diclofenac under ambient and supra-ambient storageconditions (40°C). As the number of antioxidants suitable for parenteral/injectable use is limited, theimpossibility of using said stabilizing agents makes it very complex to obtain formulations which arepotentially stable under the conditions required by the health authorities when the product isregistered. Tert-butyl-4-hydroxyanisole, also known as butylated hydroxyanisole or BHA, is anantioxidant widely used in the food and pharmaceutical industry. It is used in fats and oils, foodscontaining fats, essential oils, and food packaging materials. BHA is a mixture of two isomers: 2-tert-butyl-4-hydroxyanisole (2-BHA) and 3-tert-butyl-4-hydroxyanisole (3-BHA). The present inventionsolves the technical problem of the instability of liquid formulations containing a combination ofdiclofenac and thiocolchicoside. Accordingly the composition of the invention contains tert-butyl 4-hydroxyanisole (BHA) as antioxidant. Diclofenac is preferably present in the composition as sodiumsalt. The composition of the invention can optionally also contain excipients suitable forpharmaceutical use, such as mannitol and sorbitol, and can also contain a local anaesthetic, such aslidocaine. The composition according to the invention can also contain solubilising agents, chelatingagents, buffering agents or pH correctors, such as sodium or potassium hydroxide, sodiumbicarbonate, tromethamine, mono ethanolamine or other organic bases. In one embodiment of theinvention the composition takes the form of an aqueous solution consisting of a mixture of water andpropylene glycol. In a preferred embodiment of the invention the composition takes the form of anaqueous solution containing propylene glycol and diclofenac sodium salt. Diclofenac sodium salt ispreferably present in the composition in quantities ranging from 25 to 75 mg per unit doseadministered. Thiocolchicoside can be present in the composition in quantities ranging from 1 to 10mg per unit dose administered. BHA can be present in the composition in quantities ranging from 0.1to 1.2 mg per unit dose administered. The excipients mannitol or sorbitol can be present in thecomposition in quantities ranging from 6 to 32 mg per unit dose administered. Propylene glycol canbe present in the composition in quantities ranging from 800 to 2000 mg per dosage unit. In apreferred embodiment of the invention the composition contains diclofenac sodium salt at theconcentration of 18.75 mg/mL. corresponding to a dosage unit amount of 75 mg, and thiocolchicosideat the concentration of 1 mg/mL, corresponding to a dosage unit amount of 4 mg. A further aspect ofthe invention relates to the use of the composition according to the invention for the treatment ofrheumatic or traumatic pain and inflammation of the joints, muscles, tendons and ligaments. Thecomposition according to the invention can be administered in dosage unit amounts of 75 mg ofdiclofenac sodium and 4 mg of thiocolchicoside once or twice a day.

Ans. This problem is based on Patent no. WO2014064030A1.

Title-Stable injectable composition containing diclofenac and thiocolchicoside

Abstract

The invention relates to a stable injectable aqueous solution containing diclofenac and thiocolchicoside, or pharmaceutically acceptable salts thereof, and the use thereof in the treatment of painful and inflammatory rheumatic or traumatic conditions of the joints, muscles, tendons and ligaments.

Claims

I claim:

1. Pharmaceutical composition in the form of an injectable aqueous solution comprising diclofenac and thiocolchicoside or a pharmaceutically acceptable salt thereof as the active ingredients and tert-butylhydroxyanisole as stabilizer.

2. Composition according to claim 1, comprising diclofenac sodium salt.

3. Composition according to claims 1-2, wherein said aqueous solution consists of a mixture of water and propylene glycol.

4. Composition according to claims 1-3, further comprising an additional ingredient selected from local anaesthetic, solubilising agent, chelating agent, buffering agent and pH corrector.

5. Composition according to claims 1-4 comprising diclofenac sodium salt in amounts ranging from 25 to 75 mg per dosage unit.

6. Composition according to claim 5, wherein said amount is 75 mg.

7. Composition according to claims 1-6 comprising thiocolchicoside in amounts ranging from 1 to 10 mg per dosage unit.

8. Composition according to claim 7, wherein said amount is 4 mg.

9. Composition according to claims 1-8 comprising tert-butylhydroxyanisole in amounts ranging from 0.1 to 1.2 mg per dosage unit.

10. Composition according to claim 9, wherein said amount is 0.2 mg.

1 1. Composition according to claim 1 , consisting of the following ingredients and amounts per dosage unit:

Ingredient mg

Diclofenac sodium salt 75

Thiocolchicoside 4

Mannitol 6

tert-butylhydroxyanisole 0.2

Propylene glycol 1600

Sodium hydroxide q.s. for pH 8.0-8.5

Purified water q.s. for 4 mL

12. Composition according to any one of the preceding claims, for use in the treatment of joint, muscle, tendon or ligament pain and inflammation of rheumatic or traumatic origin.

OR

Q9. A regular electronic mosquito racket generally comprises a frame body, a grip, and a shaft. Theframe body holds a charged mesh on the inside. The grip houses a battery, which is electricallyconnected to the charged mesh, and an on/off switch, which controls electrical connection betweenthe battery and the charged mesh. The shaft is a hard rod member connected between the frame body'and the grip. When the user presses on the on/off switch, an electric current goes through the chargedmesh to kill insects that touch the charged mesh. However, because the shaft of the aforesaidelectronic mosquito racket is a hard rod member, the speed of the swiping motion of the electronicmosquito racket is not fast enough, and the operation angle will be limited, so the insects may escapebefore touching the charged mesh. Further, when the user swiping the electronic mosquito racket tokill insects staying on a wall, shocks produced when the frame body touches the wall will betransmitted to the user's hand. At this time, the shaft may be damaged. or the user's hand may feeluncomfortable. Therefore, this prior art design is not satisfactory in function.

As depicted in the attached images, the electronic mosquito racket in accordance with the presentinvention comprises a frame body, a gripand a shaft. The frame body comprises two openframes arranged in a stack, and an internal charged mesh set within the open frames. The grip is ahollow

member for enabling the user to grasp with the hand. The grip houses a power control unit,which comprises a battery set (not shown) and an on/off switch (not shown) for control electricalconnection between the battery set and the internal charged mesh of the frame body. The shaft is aflexible member made out of plastics, rubber, carbon fibers, or any other suitable materials.

According to the present preferred embodiment, the shaft is molded from plastics, having one endfixedly connected to the frame body and the other end fixedly connected to one end of the grip.Further, the shaft houses an electric circuit that is electrically connected between the internal chargedmesh and the battery set in the grip. Further, the shaft has a plurality of grooves extending around theperiphery and spaced along the length of the shaft to enhance the flexibility of the shaft.

The mosquito bat when using the electronic mosquito racket to kill insects, hold the grip with thehand and press on the switch to power the internal charged mesh by electric current, and move theelectronic mosquito racket to hit bugs, flies. mosquitoes, and harmful insects. Because the shaft is aflexible rod member, operate the electronic mosquito racket with a swiping motion causes the shaft tovibrate, enhancing the swiping speed. Further, the grooves around the periphery of the shaft enhancethe flexibility of the shaft. When an insect is staying on a wall, the user must move the electronicmosquito racket toward the wall. When the open frames of the frame body touch the wall, theshaft will be curved to absorb shocks, preventing damage to the shaft or potential injury of the hand.

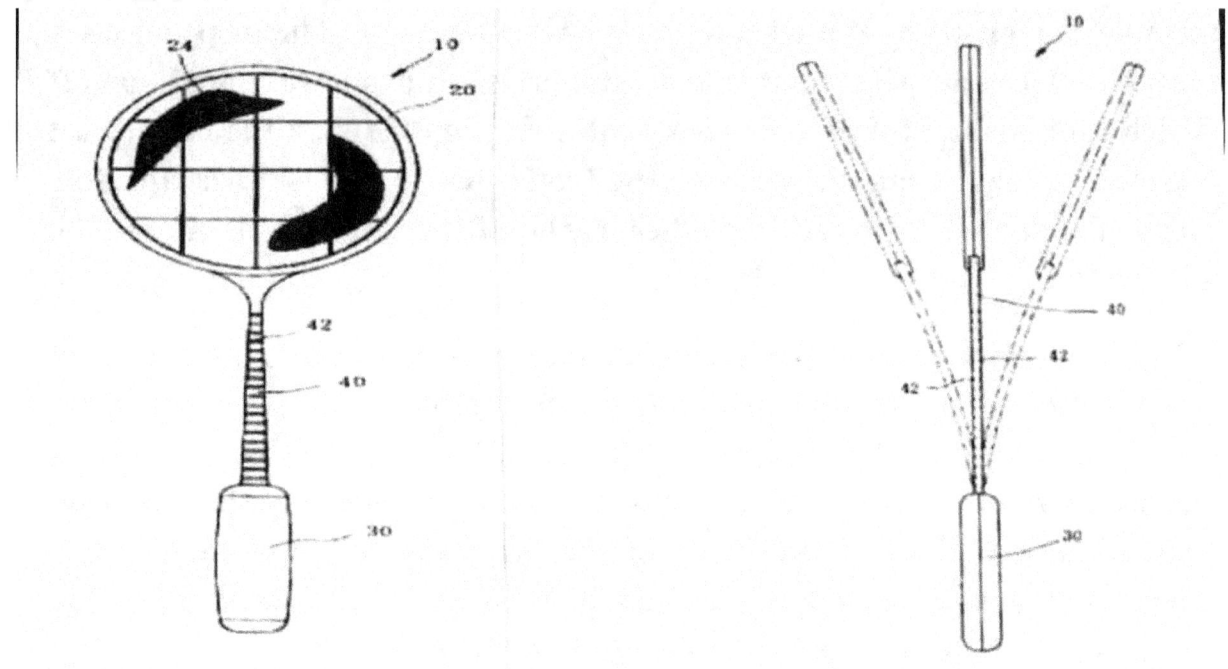

Ans: This problem is based on US Patent Application no. 20070271839

Abstract

An electronic mosquito racket includes a frame body holding a charged mesh, a grip accommodating a power control unit that is electrically connected to the charged mesh, and a shaft made out of a flexible material and connected between the frame body and the grip to enhance the swiping speed of the electronic mosquito racket and to provide a shock absorbing effect.

Claims (5)

I Claim:

1. An electronic mosquito racket comprising

a frame body, said frame body holding a charged mesh;

a grip, said grip accommodating a power control unit that is electrically connected to said charged mesh; and

a shaft connected between said frame body and said grip, said shaft being made out of a flexible material.

2. The electronic mosquito racket as claimed in claim 1, wherein said flexible material is a plastic material.

3. The electronic mosquito racket as claimed in claim 1, wherein said flexible material is rubber.

4. The electronic mosquito racket as claimed in claim 1, wherein said flexible material is carbon fibers.

5. The electronic mosquito racket as claimed in claim 1, wherein said shaft has a plurality of grooves extending around the periphery and spaced along the length thereof.

Part C2

A client meets you and provides technical information regarding his invention. Draft a completespecification with at least two claims and a title for anyone of the following descriptions, forfiling in the Indian Patent Office.

While preparing the complete specification, do not redraw the figures. However, you may referto the figures in the specification as Fig. 1, Fig. 2 and Fig. 3 etc.

1 X 30 M = 30 marks

Q10. PET bottle containers for selling beverages such as fruit juice, tea, and water are made ofpolyethylene terephthalate (PET) blow-molded bottles and caps made of polyethylene (PE) orpolypropylene (PP) by injection molding. The PET bottle body is light, strong and transparent, and isexcellent as a beverage container. The bottle body is filled with a beverage from the mouth at theupper end, and a lid is screwed into the threaded mouth of the bottle body to seal the beverage andkeep it aseptic. The PET bottle container containing the beverage is opened by removing the lid fromthe threaded mouth of the bottle body, opening the bottle body with the person who drinks thethreaded mouth of the bottle body, tilting the bottle body, and drinking the bottle body beverage todrink. When the drink 1s empty. the bottle body and lid are separated and discarded.

The discardedbottle body is crushed, washed, and reused as a raw material. When the beverage is left undrinked, theplastic bottle container for the beverage is screwed into the threaded opening of the bottle body andstored. Then. open and drink the remaining beverage.

In prior art, it has been considered to adhere an antibacterial titanium oxide photocatalyst powder tothe mouth of the bottle body in order to make the remaining beverage unhygienic when drinking. PETbottle containers are not hygienic after opening because the bottle body and lid do not haveantimicrobial properties. PET bottle containers without antibacterial properties require time-consuming cleaning after drinking. They are not collected after drinking, washed, and reused as PETbottle containers. Unlike glass bottles of milk, sake or beer, it is not a returnable bottle that can bewashed and used many times. Even at home, it scems that washing a PET bottle container afterdrinking and reusing it as a beverage container is rarely performed.

In addition, in the PET bottle container, when drinking the remaining beverage, if the elapsed timeafter opening is long, various bacteria may be propagated. It is unsanitary. In the PET bottle containerdisclosed in prior art, a photocatalyst used as an antibacterial agent does not exhibit an antibacterialeffect unless light having predetermined characteristics is applied. Since the mouth of the bottle bodyis covered with an opaque cap-shaped lid, the photocatalyst attached to the mouth of the bottle body ishardly exposed to light and hardly exerts an antibacterial action. The powder of the titanium oxidephotocatalyst attached to the mouth of the bottle body is casy to fall off.

The PET bottle body loses its superiority as a beverage container if it loses its properties such as beinglight, strong and transparent because of its antibacterial properties.

Antibacterial molded articles of polyethylene or polypropylene kneaded with silver zeolite powder asan antibacterial agent are known. However, there is no known antibacterial molded product ofpolyethylene terephthalate into which silver zeolite powder as an antibacterial agent has beenkneaded. Then, a granular masterbatch of polyethylene terephthalate mixed with silver zeolite powderas an antibacterial agent was prepared, and a bottle body of a blow molded article was prepared usingthe granular masterbatch as a raw material. Then, it was found that an antibacterial bottle body havingcharacteristics such as lightness, strongness, and transparency was obtained.

A PET bottle container comprising a bottle body of a molded article of polyethylene terephthalate anda lid of a synthetic resin molded article in a cap shape screwed into a threaded opening of the bottlebody. The bottle body is a molded product of polyethylene terephthalate kneaded with silver zeolite asan antibacterial agent and has antibacterial properties on the inner and outer surfaces, The lid is amolded article of a synthetic resin into which silver zeolite as an antibacterial agent has been kneaded,and is characterized in that the inner surface and the outer surface have antibacterial properties. Themain body of the bottle is a blow molded product made of a granular masterbatch of polyethyleneterephthalate mixed with silver zeolite powder as an antibacterial agent. The lid is an injection-moldedproduct made of a granular masterbatch of polyethylene or polypropylene mixed with silver zeolitepowder as an antibacterial agent. The PET bottle container of the present invention is sanitary evenafter opening since the bottle body and the lid have antibacterial properties. It is also hygienic whendrinking leftover beverages. This PET bottle container is easy to clean after drinking. It can bewashed and reused as a PET bottle container. Unlike the photocatalyst, silver zeolite, which is anantibacterial agent, has antibacterial properties even in dark places where light does not shine. Themouth of the bottle body is antibacterial even when covered with a lid. Further, silver zeolite as anantibacterial agent is kneaded into polyethylene terephthalate or a synthetic resin, and is hard to falloff.

As shown in FIG. 1, the PET bottle container includes a bottle main body 1 of a blow molded productof polyethylene terephthalate and a lid 4 of an injection molded product of polyethylene orpolypropylene. The polyethylene terephthalate and the polyethylene or polypropylene are eachkneaded with silver zeolite powder as an antibacterial agent. The bottle body 1 and the lid 4 haveantibacterial properties on the inner surface, the outer surface, and the entire surface, respectively.

The bottle body I has a body portion 2, a mouth portion 3 formed at an upper end of the body portion2, and a screw formed on an outer peripheral surface of the mouth portion 3. The body 2 has a cylindrical shape with a bottom, and has dimensions suitable for being grasped by hand. The mouth 3has a cylindrical shape, and has dimensions suitable for being held by the mouth. The bottle body 1 islight and strong as a beverage container, and the body 2 having a thin structure is transparent. The lid4 is formed in a cap shape, and has a screw formed on the inner peripheral surface. The lid 4 isscrewed into the mouth 3 of the bottle body 1 and closes the upper end opening of the mouth 3.Themethod for manufacturing the bottle body 1 is to prepare a granular masterbatch of polyethyleneterephthalate mixed with silver zeolite powder as an antibacterial agent, form a preform using thegranular masterbatch as a raw material, and divide the preform into two parts. Blow molding using amold. The method of manufacturing the lid 4 is to prepare a polyethylene or polypropylene granularmasterbatch mixed with silver zeolite powder as an antibacterial agent, and to perform injectionmolding using the granular masterbatch as a raw material. Silver zeolite is an inorganic antibacterialagent in which silver, an antibacterial metal, is held on a porous synthetic zeolite as a carrier by ionexchange. The mixing ratio of the silver zeolite powder is 20 to 25% by weight.

In this PET bottle container, the bottle body 1 is filled with the beverage from the mouth 3, the lid 4 isscrewed into the threaded mouth 3, and the beverage is sealed and kept in an aseptic state. When drinking a beverage, the lid 4 is removed from the threaded mouth 3 and opened, and the person who drinks the threaded mouth 3 holds the mouth, tilts the bottle body 1 and drinks the beverage in thebottle body 1. If there is any drink left, the lid 4 is screwed into the threaded mouth portion 3 to savethe drink. Then, open and drink the remaining beverage. The bottle body 1 and the lid 4 that havebeen emptied after drinking can be washed and reused as a PET bottle container.FIG. 1 is alongitudinal sectional end view of a PET bottle container according to an embodiment of the presentinvention.

DESCRIPTION OF SYMBOLS 1 Bottle main body 2 Bottle main body part 3 Bottle main bodythreaded mouth 4 Cap-shaped lid.

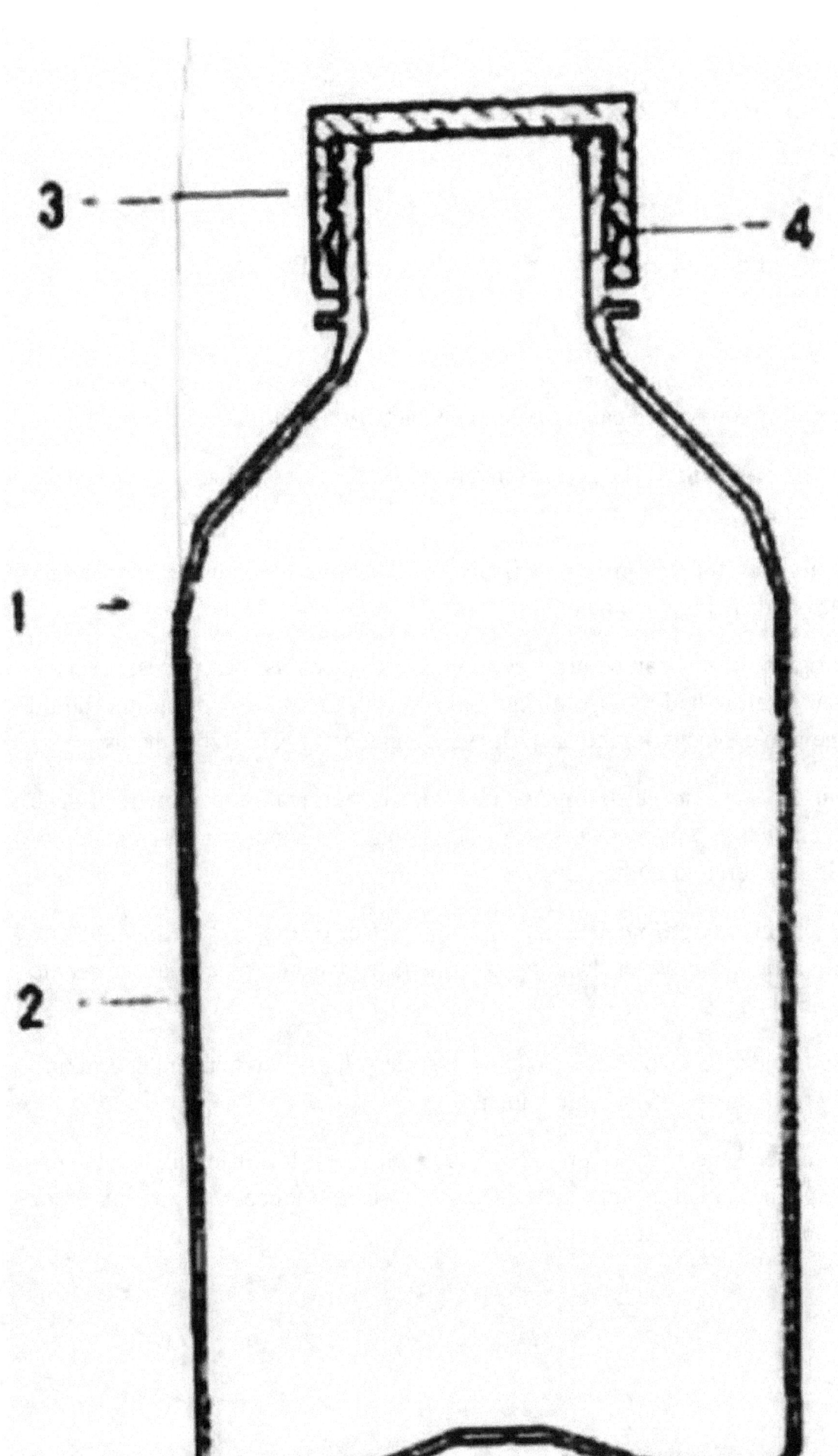

Ans.

Title -Antimicrobial Polyethelene Terephthalate closures for drinking containers

Or

Antibacterial PET Bottle Container with Silver Zeolite Powder

Abstract

A closure for a container for liquids made of a resin containing an inorganic antimicrobial agent which can come into contact with the liquid.

Field of the Invention: The present invention relates to containers, such as baby bottles and cups, used for drinking purposes and closures for these articles.

Background of the Invention: It is always desirable to improve the sanitary properties of drinking containers.

Bacterial growth sites can be produced by liquids, such as fruit juices, formula, and even water. When the user drinks liquid from the bottle or cup, the liquid can come into contact with the bacteria, which can be transferred to the user.

Accordingly, it would be desirable to attempt to eliminate the growth of such bacteria on such products, that is to make the sites incapable or less capable of supporting bacterial growth.

Objects of the Invention: It is therefore an object of the present invention to provide plastic closures for drinking containers which incorporate an inorganic antimicrobial agent.

A further object is to provide closures for baby bottle and juvenile drinking containers having an antimicrobial agent.

Still a further object is to provide plastic closures for drinking containers containing an inorganic antimicrobial agent which reduce the possibility of establishment of bacterial growth sites.

Brief Description of the Drawings Other objects and advantages of the present invention will become more apparent upon reference to the following specification and annexed drawings in which:

Description

Description: The present invention describes an improved PET bottle container for storing beverages with antibacterial properties. The bottle body is a blow-molded product of polyethylene terephthalate kneaded with silver zeolite powder as an antibacterial agent, while the cap-shaped lid is injection-molded of polyethylene or polypropylene kneaded with silver zeolite powder as an antibacterial agent. The bottle body and lid are antibacterial on both the inner and outer surfaces, making it hygienic and easy to clean after drinking. The manufacturing process involves preparing a granular masterbatch with silver zeolite powder, forming a preform, and blow-molding the preform into a bottle body. The granular masterbatch is also used to injection-mold the lid into a cap-shape. The invention provides a cost-effective way of creating PET bottle containers that can be reused, reducing waste and promoting sustainability.

Claims (18)

I Claim:

1. A closure for a container for holding a liquid, said closure formed to cover at least a part of the opening of the container and having a surface area which can be contacted by the liquid, said closure surface area comprising a resin containing an inorganic antimicrobial agent.

2. A closure as in claim 1 wherein the entirety of said closure is formed of said resin containing said inorganic antimicrobial agent.

3. A closure as in claim 1 wherein said closure comprises a collar to be attached to the open end of a bottle, said collar having a top wall with a central opening through which a nipple is to project, said surface to be contacted by the liquid being the inner surface of said top wall.

4. A closure as in claim 3 wherein said surface to be contacted comprises a disk of said resin containing said inorganic antimicrobial agent opposing said top wall inner surface.

5. A closure as in claim 1 wherein said closure comprises a lid to be attached to the open end of a container with said lid having a top wall with an opening, said surface to be contacted being the inner surface of said lid top wall.

6. A closure as in claim 5 wherein said lid top wall opening comprises a spout and said surface to be contacted further comprises the interior of said spout.

7. A closure as in claim 6 wherein said closure and spout are of integral one piece construction of said resin containing said inorganic antimicrobial agent.

8. A closure as in claim 1 wherein said agent is an antibiotic metal containing composition that imparts substantial antimicrobial action.

9. The closure of claim 8 wherein said inorganic antibiotic metal comprises antibiotic ceramic particles comprising said metal.

10. The closure of claim 9 wherein said ceramic particles are selected from the group consisting of zeolite, hydroxy apatite, and zirconium phosphate.

11. The closure of claim 8 wherein said inorganic antibiotic metal containing composition comprises a silver salt.

12. The closure of claim 11 wherein said silver salt is selected from the group consisting of silver iodate, silver iodide, silver nitrate, and silver oxide.

13. The closure of claim 12 wherein said silver salt is silver nitrate.

14. The closure of claim 9 wherein said antibiotic ceramic particles comprise antibiotic zeolite prepared by replacing all or part of the ion-exchangeable ions in zeolite with an antibiotic metal ion.

15. The closure of claim 8 wherein said antibiotic metal is selected from the group consisting of silver, copper, zinc, and gold.

16. The closure of claim 8 wherein said antibiotic metal is silver.

17. The closure of claim 1 wherein said inorganic antimicrobial agent comprises from 0.25% to 10.0% by total weight of the resin and agent.

18. The closure of claim 1 wherein said antibiotic agent is in particleform and the size of said particles is from 0.25 to 10.0 microns.

or

Claim 1: A PET bottle container comprising a bottle body of a blow-molded product of polyethylene terephthalate kneaded with silver zeolite powder as an antibacterial agent, and a cap-shaped lid injection-molded of polyethylene or polypropylene kneaded with silver zeolite powder as an antibacterial agent, wherein the bottle body and lid are both antibacterial on the inner surface, the outer surface, and the entire surface.

Claim 2: A method for manufacturing an antibacterial PET bottle container, comprising preparing a granular masterbatch of polyethylene terephthalate mixed with silver zeolite powder as an antibacterial agent, forming a preform using the granular masterbatch as a raw material, blow-molding the preform into a bottle body, and preparing a granular masterbatch of polyethylene or polypropylene mixed with silver zeolite powder as an antibacterial agent, and injection-molding the granular masterbatch into a cap-shaped lid.

OR

Q11. A face mask having a band with car loop attachments as well as drop down support for when themask is not being worn. Face masks that cover the nose and mouth of the wearer to filter air and/orprevent the spread of germs are well known. Masks take on many forms, including disposable moldedmasks that substantially fit the contour over the bridge of the nose and around the mouth of thewearer, and flexible masks used for surgery. Masks typically include one or more bands forattachment around the back of the head to retain the mask over the wearer's nose and mouth.

Othermasks provide for an ear loop attachment wherein bands extending from the side of the mask looparound the back of the wearer's ears.

There are advantages associated with providing a mask that attaches over the wearer's ears rather thanlooping around the back of the head. The mask may be easier to don and doff. In addition, bandswhich extend around the back of the wearer's head may be less appealing to many wearers because thebands may become entangled in the wearer's hair or otherwise ruin the wearer's hair style.

In addition to providing a mask that is retained by ear loops, it is also known to provide a drop downband on the mask. A drop down band allows the mask to be retained around the wearer's neck whenthe mask is not being worn over the nose and mouth. In this manner, the mask is retained at thewearer's chest and does not need to be stored. This provides for quickly accessing the mask toreposition over the wearer's nose and mouth. The drop down feature also frees the wearer's hands toperform other tasks. If a mask is inconvenient to don and doff or is not readily available andaccessible when not worn, the wearer is less likely to put the mask on, creating health hazards.

The present invention is directed to a face mask that covers the nose and mouth of the wearer and thathas an ear loop support and a drop down band. Masks that cover the nose and mouth of the wearer and use a band for retaining the mask over the nose and mouth are well known. The masks may bemolded. made of a flexible fabric, or use other configurations for fitting over the nose and mouth thatrequire a retaining band. The present invention utilizes a band that is configured for extending aroundthe ears of the wearer to support the mask against the wearer's face over the nose and mouth.

The band attaches at each side of the mask near either the upper or the lower portion. An orifice orother retainer guide that provides for slidably retaining the band is located at each side of the maskand in spaced apart relationship to an attachment point for each end of the band. The band may becontinuous around the back of the neck or separate sections may tie or clip together. Thisconfiguration provides for four attachment points and comfortable and secure positioning of the maskagainst the face of the wearer. The band preferably includes an elastic end portion or may be entirelymade of elastic material. The band fits around the back of the ears of the wearer to retain the mask inposition and provides for adjusting to a variety of sizes. When not worn, the band extends around theback of the neck of the wearer and retains the mask in an accessible position at the front of the wearer.

FIG. 1 shows a perspective view of a first embodiment of a mask according to the principles of thepresent invention being worn;

FIG. 2 shows a perspective view of the mask shown in FIG. | having an alternate band mountingconfiguration dropped down and supported around the neck of a wearer;

FIG. 3 shows a front elevational view of a second embodiment of a mask according to the principlesof the present invention;

FIG. 4 shows a front elevational view of the mask shown in FIG. 1; and,

FIG. 5 shows a front elevational view of the mask shown in FIG. 2 having the alternate bandmounting configuration.

As shown in FIG. 1, a mask 10 includes a cup-like mask body 12 typically made of fibrous filtermaterial and molded to fit over the mouth and nose of a wearer, generally following the contour of thewearer's face. The mask body 12 includes an upper portion 16 and a lower portion 18 as well as sideportions 20, as shown more clearly in FIG. 4. A nose clip 22 is utilized to provide additional formingover the bridge of the wearer's nose. Fabric-type fibrous filtering material of the mask body 12removes particulates from the air, providing a breathable air supply.

As shown in FIG. 1, a band 24 attaches at an upper point by means of staple or other fastener 34 andloops around the ear of the wearer. After looping around the ear, the band 24 extends to the front ofthe mask 10 through a lower orifice 32 or other band guide in the mask body 12 and extends aroundthe back of the neck of the wearer. It can be appreciated that the band 24 should be sized for thewearer or may be adjustable or should include at least some elastic material to provide a snug fit. Inthe preferred embodiment, at least the end portions 26 extending between the upper fastener 34 andthe lower orifice 32 has elasticity. This elasticity of the band 24 also provides sufficient flexibility tofit a range of head sizes.

As shown in FIGS. 4 and 5, it can be appreciated that there are multiple mounting configurationspossible with the present invention that provide an ear loop attachment and a drop down band. In theembodiment shown in FIGS. 1 and 4, the band 24 is fixedly attached by staples 34 or other wellknown fastening devices at the sides 20 near the upper portion 16 of the mask body 12. The band 24extends through the orifices 32 at the sides 20 spaced apart from the staples 34 and near the loweredge 18. The band 24 extends around the back of the neck of the wearer and the mask 10 as shown inFIG. 1. The band 24 may be a continuous element or have two sections that may be clipped, tied orotherwise releasably fastened around the back of the neck. The band may also have a slidable lengthadjustment.

Referring to FIGS. 2 and 5, the band 24 can also be mounted in a reversed orientation using fastenerssuch as staples 36 near the lower portion 18. Orifices 30 or other guides are positioned at the sides 20near the upper portion 16 of the mask body 12 in spaced apart relationship to the lower fasteners 36.With this configuration, the band 24 fastens near the lower portion 18 and extends up through theorifices 30 near the upper portion 16. With this mounting configuration, the band 24 extends from thelower fastener 36 around the ears and through the upper orifice 30 when worn. When not worn overthe nose and mouth, the band 24 extends around the neck of the wearer from the upper portion of themask body 12 so that the drop down retention feature is maintained.

Referring now to FIG. 2, when not worn over the nose and mouth, the mask 10 is supported by theband 24 extending around the back of the neck of the wearer. The band 24 shown in FIG. 2 includestwo sections joined by a clip or other fastener 38 at the back of the neck. The mask body 12 generallyfalls onto the chest of the wearer so that the mask 10 is retained, thereby freeing the hands of thewearer. Depending on the band configuration, the mask body 12 may also flip over on the wearer'schest with the upper portion 16 extending downward, rather, than the position shown in FIG. 2.

As explained above, it can be appreciated that the mounting configurations of the band 24 can also beused with other types of masks, such as surgical masks 50, shown in FIG. 3. The mask 50 includes aflexible mask body 52, typically made of a fabric, for covering the nose and mouth of the wearer. Themask body includes a top edge 54, a bottom edge 56, and sides 58. A band 60 extends from the uppercorners of the mask body 52 and extends down through loops 66 at the sides 58 along the bottom edge56. The band 60 includes an end elastic portion 62 in the preferred embodiment. It can be appreciatedthat the band 60 extends from attachment point 64 over the ears of the wearer when worn and thenthrough the loop 66 and around the back of the neck of the wearer similar to the arrangement shownin FIG. 1. It can also be appreciated that the mask 50 can be reversed with the end attachment points64 located along the bottom edge and the loops 66 positioned near the top of the mask 60 when worn.The ear loop and drop down configurations of the band 60 are similar to those shown in FIG.

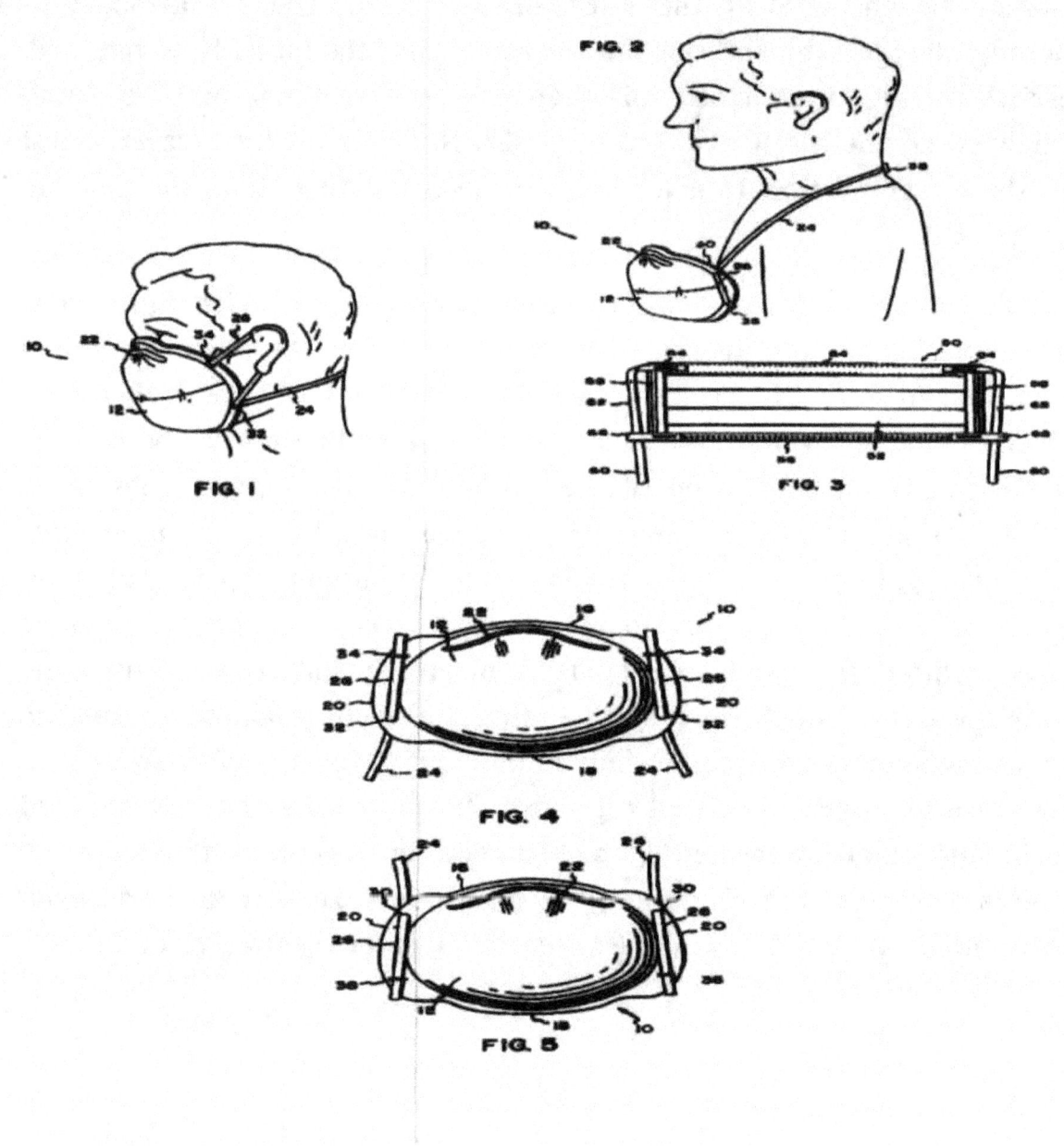

Ans. Please refer Patent No. WO1998028997A1

Face mask having a combination adjustable ear loop and drop down band

Or

Face Mask with Ear Loop Support and Drop Down Band

Abstract

A face mask (10) covers the nose and mouth of the wearer and includes a band (24) to retain the mask member (12) in position. The band attaches at the sides (20) of the mask and extends around the ears of the wearer and loops through orifices (32). The band (24) extends around the back of the neck and provides for retaining the mask (10) at the front of the wearer when not worn. Ends (26) of the band (24) are elastic to provide a snug fit for the mask (10).

TECHNICAL FIELD: The present invention relates to a face mask having a band with ear loop attachments as well as drop down support for when the mask is not being worn.

BACKGROUND: Face masks that cover the nose and mouth of the wearer to filter air and/or prevent the spread of germs are well known. Masks take on many forms, including disposable molded masks that substantially fit the contour over the bridge of the nose and around the mouth of the wearer, and flexible masks used for surgery. Masks typically include one or more bands for attachment around the back of the head to retain the mask over the wearer's nose and mouth. Other masks provide for an ear loop attachment wherein bands extending from the side of the mask loop around the back of the wearer's ears.

There are advantages associated with providing a mask that attaches over the wearer's ears rather than looping around the back of the head. The mask may be easier to don and doff. In addition, bands which extend around the back of the wearer's head may be less appealing to many wearers because the bands may become entangled in the wearer's hair or otherwise ruin the wearer's hair style.

In addition to providing a mask that is retained by ear loops, it is also known to provide a drop down band on the mask. A drop down band allows the mask to be retained around the wearer's neck when the mask is not being worn over the nose and mouth. In this manner, the mask is retained at the wearer's chest and does not need to be stored. This provides for quickly accessing the mask to reposition over the wearer's nose and mouth. The drop down feature also frees the wearer's hands to perform other tasks. If a mask is inconvenient to don and doff or is not readily available and accessible when not worn, the wearer is less likely to put the mask on, creating health hazards.

None of the masks, however, provide ear loop attachments to the wearer. It can then be seen that a new and improved mask is needed that provides both drop down retention as well as an ear loop attachment. Such a mask should provide for securely retaining the mask by attaching around the ears of the wearer with a single band. Moreover, a band should extend around the back of the wearer's neck and should retain the mask in an easily accessible location in front of the wearer when the mask is not being worn. The present invention addresses these as well as other problems associated with mask bands.

SUMMARY OF THE INVENTION

The present invention is directed to a face mask that covers the nose and mouth of the wearer and that has an ear loop support and a drop down band.

Masks that cover the nose and mouth of the wearer and use a band for retaining the mask over the nose and mouth are well known. The masks may be molded, made of a flexible fabric, or use other configurations for fitting over the nose and mouth that require a retaining band. The present invention utilizes a band that is configured for extending around the ears of the wearer to support the mask against the wearer's face over the nose and mouth.

The band attaches at each side of the mask near either the upper or the lower portion. An orifice or other retainer guide that provides for slidably retaining the band is located at each side of the mask and in spaced apart relationship to an attachment point for each end of the band. The band may be continuous around the back of the neck or separate sections may tie or clip together. This configuration provides for four attachment points and comfortable and secure positioning of the mask against the face of the wearer. The band preferably includes an elastic end portion or may be entirely made of elastic material. The band fits around the back of the ears of the wearer to retain the mask in position and provides for adjusting to a variety of sizes. When not worn, the band extends around the back of the neck of the wearer and retains the mask in an accessible position at the front of the wearer.

BRIEF DESCRIPTION OF THE DRAWINGS

In the drawings, like numerals and letters designate corresponding structure throughout the several views:

Figure 1 shows a perspective view of a first embodiment of a mask according to the principles of the present invention being worn;

Figure 2 shows a perspective view of the mask shown in Figure 1 having an alternate band mounting configuration dropped down and supported around the neck of a wearer;

Figure 3 shows a front elevational view of a second embodiment of a mask according to the principles of the present invention;

Figure 4 shows a front elevational view of the mask shown in Figure 1; and,

Figure 5 shows a front elevational view of the mask shown in Figure 2 having the alternate band mounting configuration.

DETAILED DESCRIPTION OF PREFERRED EMBODIMENT

As shown in Figure 1, a mask 10 includes a cup-like mask body 12 typically made of fibrous filter material and molded to fit over the mouth and nose of a wearer, generally following the contour of the wearer's face. The mask body 12 includes an upper portion 16 and a lower portion 18 as well as side portions 20, as shown more clearly in Figure 4. A nose clip 22 is utilized to provide additional forming over the bridge of the wearer's nose. Fabric-type fibrous filtering material of the mask body 12 removes particulates from the air, providing a breathable air supply. As shown in Figure 1, a band 24 attaches at an upper point by means of staple or other fastener 34 and loops around the ear of the wearer. After looping around the ear, the band 24 extends to the front of the mask 10 through a lower orifice 32 or other band guide in the mask body 12 and extends around the back of the neck of the wearer. It can be appreciated that the band 24 should be sized for the wearer or may be adjustable or should include at least some elastic material to provide a snug fit. In the preferred embodiment, at least the end portions 26 extending between the upper fastener 34 and the lower orifice 32 have elasticity. This elasticity of the band 24 also provides sufficient flexibility to fit a range of head sizes.

As shown in Figures 4 and 5, it can be appreciated that there are multiple mounting configurations possible with the present invention that provide an ear loop attachment and a drop down band. In the embodiment shown in Figures 1 and 4, the band 24 is fixedly attached by staples 34 or other well known fastening devices at the sides 20 near the upper portion 16 of the mask body 12. The band 24 extends through the orifices 32 at the sides 20 spaced apart from the staples 34 and near the lower edge 18. The band 24 extends around the back of the neck of the wearer and the mask 10 as shown in Figure 1. The band 24 may be a continuous element or have two sections that may be clipped, tied or otherwise releasably fastened around the back of the neck. The band may also have a slidable length adjustment.

Referring to Figures 2 and 5, the band 24 can also be mounted in a reversed orientation using fasteners such as staples 36 near the lower portion 18. Orifices 30 or other guides are positioned at the sides 20 near the upper portion 16 of the mask body 12 in spaced apart relationship to the lower fasteners 36. With this configuration, the band 24 fastens near the lower portion 18 and extends up through the orifices 30 near the upper portion 16. With this mounting configuration, the band 24 extends from the lower fastener 36 around the ears and through the upper orifice 30 when worn. When not worn over the nose and mouth, the band 24 extends around the neck of the wearer from the upper portion of the mask body 12 so that the drop down retention feature is maintained.

Referring now to Figure 2, when not worn over the nose and mouth, the mask 10 is supported by the band 24 extending around the back of the neck of the wearer. The band 24 shown in Figure 2 includes two sections joined by a clip or other fastener 38 at the back of the neck. The mask body 12 generally falls onto the chest of the wearer so that the mask 10 is retained, thereby freeing the hands of the wearer. Depending on the band configuration, the mask body 12 may also flip over on the wearer's chest with the upper portion 16 extending downward, rather than the position shown in Figure 2.

As explained above, it can be appreciated that the mounting configurations of the band 24 can also be used with other types of masks, such as surgical masks 50, shown in Figure 3. The mask 50 includes a flexible mask body 52, typically made of a fabric, for covering the nose and mouth of the wearer. The mask body includes a top edge 54, a bottom edge 56, and sides 58. A band 60 extends from the upper corners of the mask body 52 and extends down through loops 66 at the sides 58 along the bottom edge 56. The band 60 includes an end elastic portion 62 in the preferred embodiment. It can be appreciated that the band 60 extends from attachment point 64 over the ears of the wearer when worn and then through the loop 66 and around the back of the neck of the wearer similar to the arrangement shown in Figure 1. It can also be appreciated that the mask 50 can be reversed with the end attachment points 64 located along the bottom edge and the loops 66 positioned near the top of the mask 60 when worn. The ear loop and drop down configurations of the band 60 are similar to those shown in Figure 1.

It is to be understood, however, that even though numerous characteristics and advantages of the present invention have been set forth in the foregoing description, together with details of the structure and function of the invention, the disclosure is illustrative only, and the changes may be made in detail, especially in matters of shape, size and arrangement of parts within the principles of the invention to the full extent indicated by the broad general meaning of the terms in which the appended claims are expressed.

CLAIMS:

I claim:

1. A mask that comprises: a mask member configured to cover the mouth and nose of a wearer, the mask member having an upper portion, a lower portion and opposed side portions; a band attached at first locations at the opposed sides of the mask proximate one of the upper or lower portions; and guide means proximate each side portion of the mask in spaced apart relation to the first locations.

2. A mask according to claim 1, wherein the retaining means comprises orifices formed through the mask member.

3. A mask according to claim 1, wherein the retaining means comprises a loop at each side of the mask member.

4. A mask according to claims 1-3, wherein the band includes an elastic portion.

5. A mask according to claims 1-3, wherein the band includes an elastic portion proximate each first location.

6. A mask according to claims 1-3, wherein the band comprises two sections and a device joining the two sections.

7. A mask according to claims 1-6, wherein the band guide means slidably retains the band.

8. A mask according to claim 1, wherein the mask comprises a molded cup-type mask member, and wherein the band guide means comprises orifices formed through the mask member.

9. A mask according to claims 1-8, wherein the mask member comprises a fabric substantially rectangular element.

10. A mask according to claims 1-7, wherein the band guide means comprises a loop at each side portion of the mask member.

or

CLAIMS:

I claim:

Claim 1: A face mask comprising a mask body for covering the nose and mouth of the wearer, an elastic band configured to extend around the ears of the wearer for retaining the mask over the nose and mouth, and a drop down band attached to the mask body for retaining the mask in a convenient position when not being worn over the nose and mouth.

Claim 2: The face mask of claim 1, wherein the elastic band is made of an elastic material and provides for adjusting to a variety of sizes, and the drop down band is configured to extend around the back of the neck of the wearer.

PATENT AGENT EXAMINATION, 2018

[Under Section 126 of Patent Act, 1970}

Paper II

Total Marks: 100

Time: 2.30 p.m. to 5.30 p.n1. (Three Hours)

Instructions:

1. This paper consists of 3 parts —Part A (20 Marks), Part B(30 Marks) & Part C(50 Marks).

2. All questions in Part A and B are compulsory.

3. Part C comprises Part C1 of 20 Marks and C2 of 30 Mark. Part C1 consists of 2 questions and the candidate is required to answer any 1 of them, Part C2 consists of 2 questions and the candidate is required to answer any 1 of them.

4. In case a candidate answers more questions than required, the first attempted question shall be evaluated.

5. Candidates should read the questions very carefully before answering,

6. No clarification shall be provided during the course of the examination.

7. There is no negative marking.

PART A

4x5 Marks = 20 Marks (4 questions)

Q.1. **Write a short note on Non patentable inventions within the provision of The Patent Act, 1970.**

Ans. Non-patentable inventions are those that do not meet the requirements for patentability under the Patent Act, 1970. These include inventions that are not novel, or that are obvious to a person skilled in the relevant field. In addition, certain subject matter is specifically excluded from patent protection, such as scientific principles, mathematical methods, and computer programs per se. Furthermore, methods of treatment of the human or animal body by surgery or therapy, and diagnostic methods practiced on the human or animal body are also not patentable. Finally, inventions that are contrary to public order or morality, or those that are harmful to human, animal, or plant life or health, are also excluded from patent protection.

Section 3 of Indian Patent Act: What are not inventions;

The following are not inventions within the meaning of this Act,--

(a) an invention which is frivolous or which claims anything obviously contrary to well established natural laws;

[(b) an invention the primary or intended use or commercial exploitation of which would be contrary to public order or morality or which causes serious prejudice to human, animal or plant life or health or to the environment;]

(c) the mere discovery of a scientific principle or the formulation of an abstract theory [or discovery of any living thing or non-living substance occurring in nature];

[(d) the mere discovery of a new form of a known substance which does not result in the enhancement of the known efficacy of that substance or the mere discovery of any new property or new use for a known substance or of the mere use of a known process, machine or apparatus unless such known process results in a new product or employs at least one new reactant.

Explanation.--For the purposes of this clause, salts, esters, ethers, polymorphs, metabolites, pure form, particle size, isomers, mixtures of isomers, complexes, combinations and other derivatives of known substance shall be considered to be the same substance, unless they differ significantly in properties with regard to efficacy;]

(e) a substance obtained by a mere admixture resulting only in the aggregation of the properties of the components thereof or a process for producing such substance;

(f) the mere arrangement or re-arrangement or duplication of known devices each functioning independently of one another in a known way;

 (h) a method of agriculture or horticulture;

(i) any process for the medicinal, surgical, curative, prophylactic [diagnostic, therapeutic] or other treatment of human beings or any process for a similar treatment of animals to render them free of disease or to increase their economic value or that of their products.

[(j) plants and animals in whole or any part thereof other than micro-organisms but including seeds, varieties and species and essentially biological processes for production or propagation of plants and animals;

(k) a mathematical or business method or a computer programme per se or algorithms;

(l) a literary, dramatic, musical or artistic work or any other aesthetic creation whatsoever including cinematographic works and television productions;

(m) a mere scheme or rule or method of performing mental act or method of playing game;

(n) a presentation of information;

(o) topography of integrated circuits;

(p) an invention which, in effect, is traditional knowledge or which is an aggregation or duplication of known properties of traditionally known component or components.]

Q.2 A psychiatrist of Mumbai develops a music therapy for his schizophrenic patients which has tremendous impact on them and helps

them to get rid of many of the symptoms of schizophrenia. The doctor attended one awareness program for patent filing and being motivated approached you for advice. As a registered Patent agent what do you suggest him?

Ans. As a registered Patent agent, I would not advise the psychiatrist to consider filing a patent application for his music therapy invention. Methods of treatment are generally not patentable under Section 3(i) of the Patent Act, 1970. It is also not patentable under Section 3(i) of the Patent Act, 1970, the music therapy can be considered as a literary, musical or artistic work.

3(i) any process for the medicinal, surgical, curative, prophylactic [diagnostic, therapeutic] or other treatment of human beings or any process for a similar treatment of animals *** to render them free of disease or to increase their economic value or that of their products.

3(l) a literary, dramatic, musical or artistic work or any other aesthetic creation whatsoever including cinematographic works and television productions;

Q.3 One client 'A' has come to your office for seeking advice regarding assignment for a "solarcooktop" which 'B' has already patented. As a practicing Patent Agent brief him about the applicable issues as per the Patent Act and Rules to your client A?

Ans: As a practicing Patent Agent, I would advise client A regarding the assignment of a patented "solar cooktop". Here are the applicable issues as per the Patent Act and Rules:

1. Section 68 and 69 of the Patent Act 1970 - According to this section, the owner of a patent can assign, transfer, or grant licenses to any other party to use, make, and sell the patented invention for a certain period. The owner or assignee must record the transfer or assignment of ownership with the Controller of Patents to establish the assignee's title to the invention.

2. Rule 90 of the Patent Rules 2003 - A request for the assignment of a patent must be filed with the Controller of Patents accompanied by payment of a fee of INR 1600. A statement in writing setting forth the terms and conditions of the assignment and proof of the right to the property of the patent must be provided.

Section 68 of Patents Act: Assignments, etc., not to be valid unless in writing and duly executed;

[68. Assignments, etc., not to be valid unless in writing and duly executed.--An assignment of a patent or of a share in a patent, a mortgage, licence or the creation of any other interest in a patent shall not be valid unless the same were in writing and the agreement between the parties concerned is reduced to the form of a document embodying all the terms and conditions governing their rights and obligations and duly executed.]

Section 69 of Patents Act: Registration of assignments, transmissions, etc;

(1) Where any person becomes entitled by assignment, transmission or operation of law to a patent or to a share in a patent or becomes entitled as a mortgagee, licensee or otherwise to any other interest in a patent, he shall apply in writing in the prescribed manner to the Controller for the registration of his title or, as the case may be, of notice of his interest in the register.

(2) Without prejudice to the provisions of sub-section (1), an application for the registration of the title of any person becoming entitled by assignment to a patent or a share in a patent or becoming entitled by virtue of a mortgage, licence or other instrument to any other interest in a patent may be made in the prescribed manner by the assignor, mortgagor, licensor or other party to that instrument, as the case may be.

(3) Where an application is made under this section for the registration of the title of any person the Controller shall, upon proof of title to his satisfaction,--

(a) where that person is entitled to a patent or a share in a patent, register him in the register as proprietor or co-proprietor of the patent, and enter in the register particulars of the instrument or event by which he derives title; or

(b) where that person is entitled to any other interest in the patent, enter in the register notice of his interest, with particulars of the instrument, if any, creating it:

Provided that if there is any dispute between the parties whether the assignment, mortgage, licence, transmission, operation of law or any other such transaction has validly vested in such person a title to the patent or any share or interest therein, the Controller may refuse to take any action under clause (a) or, as the case may be, under clause (b), until the rights of the parties have been determined by a competent court.

(4) There shall be supplied to the Controller in the prescribed manner for being filed in the patent office copies of all agreements, licences and other documents affecting the title to any patent or any licence thereunder authenticated in the prescribed manner and also such other documents as may be prescribed relevant to the subject-matter:

Provided that in the case of a licence granted under a patent, the Controller shall, if so requested by the patentee or licensee, take steps for securing that the terms of the licence are not disclosed to any person except under the order of a court.

(5) Except for the purposes of an application under sub-section (1) or of an application to rectify the register, a document in respect of which no entry has been made in the register under sub-section (3) shall not be admitted by the Controller or by any court as evidence of the title of any person to a patent or to a share or interest therein unless the Controller or the court, for reasons to be recorded in writing, otherwise directs.

Rule 90 of Patent Rules: Registration of title and interest in patents.—(1) An application referred to in sub-section (1) or sub-section (2) of section 69 shall be made in Form 16.

(2) An application for an entry in the register of patents of any other document purporting to affect the proprietorship of the patent by the person benefiting under the document shall be made in **Form 16**.

Fee: 1600, 8000

Q.4 The grant of Patent is based on certain conditions as stipulated in section 47 of The Patent Act. Briefly explain those conditions.

Ans: Section 47 of the Indian Patents Act, 1970 outlines the conditions that must be met for the grant of a patent. These conditions are as follows:

The grant of a patent under this Act shall be subject to the condition that any machine, apparatus, or other article in respect of which the patent is granted or any article made by using a process in respect of which the patent is granted shall be available to the public at a reasonably affordable price.

The grant of a patent shall be subject to following conditions:

(1) any machine, apparatus or other article in respect of which the patent is granted or any article made by using a process in respect of which the patent is granted, may be imported or made by or on behalf of the Government for the purpose merely of its own use;

(2) any process in respect of which the patent is granted may be used by or on behalf of the Government for the purpose merely of its own use;

(3) any machine, apparatus or other article in respect of which the patent is granted or any article made by the use of the process in respect of which the patent is granted, may be made or used, and any process in respect of which the patent is granted may be used, by any person, for the purpose merely of experiment or research including the imparting of instructions to pupils; and

(4) in the case of a patent in respect of any medicine or drug, the medicine or drug may be imported by the Government for the purpose merely of its own use or for distribution in any dispensary, hospital or other medical institution maintained by or on behalf of the Government or any other dispensary, hospital or other medical institution which the Central Government may, having regard to the public service that such dispensary, hospital or medical institution renders, specify in this behalf by notification in the Official Gazette.

In addition to above, the grant of a patent is subject to further conditions, such as the availability of the patented invention at a reasonably affordable price, working of the patented invention in India on a commercial scale, and not using the patented invention in a manner that is prejudicial to public interest, essential public health needs, public order, or morality.

PART B

3X10M=30Marks (3 questions}

Q.5 Explain briefly the different Provisions of The Patent Act for the following:

a. Role of a Patent Agent.

b. Criteria for disqualification of Patent Agent.

Ans: A Patent Agent is a person who has the qualification to act as an agent or legal representative for any person applying for or granted a patent. The Patent Act 1970 defines the role of a Patent Agent under Section 125 to 146. Some of the roles of a Patent Agent are:

1. Preparation and filing of patent applications on behalf of clients.

2. Advise clients on all matters of patent law and prosecution, including patentability, infringement, and licensing.

3. Provide legal representation and advocacy before the Patent Office, Intellectual Property Appellate Board (IPAB), and courts.

4. Assist clients in drafting and reviewing patent-related agreements, such as licensing agreements and technology transfer agreements.

5. Conduct patent searches and provide opinions on the validity and infringement of patents.

Section 127 of Patents Act: Rights of patent agents;

Subject to the provisions contained in this Act and in any rules made thereunder, every patent agent whose name is entered in the register shall be entitled:--

(a) to practice before the Controller; and

(b) to prepare all documents, transact all business and discharge such other functions as may be prescribed in connection with any proceeding before the Controller under this Act.

Criteria for disqualification of Patent Agent:

Ans. 5(b): Section 130 of Patents Act: Removal from register of patent agents and restoration;

(1) The [Controller] may remove the name of any person from the register when [he] is satisfied, after giving that person a reasonable opportunity of being heard and after such further inquiry, if any, as [he] thinks fit to make--

(i) that his name has been entered in the register by error or on account of misrepresentation or suppression of material fact;

(ii) that he has been convicted of any offence and sentenced to a term of imprisonment or has been guilty of misconduct in his professional capacity which in the opinion of the [Controller] renders him unfit to be kept in the register.

(2) The [Controller] may, on application and on sufficient cause being shown, restore to the register the name of any person removed therefrom.

If any of the above criteria apply to a Patent Agent, then they can be disqualified from practicing as a Patent Agent. Additionally, the Patent Office may remove the name of the Patent Agent from the Register of Patent Agents if they are found guilty of unethical or unprofessional conduct.

Q.6 Explain the various provisions in the prevailing Patent Rules for 'Expedited Examination', 'Smallentity' and 'Startup'.

Ans.A. Provisions for expedited examination under Rule 24C:

Under Rule 24C of the Patent Rules, 2003, the provision for expedited examination of patent applications is provided. The following are the provisions of expedited examination:

1. The application for expedited examination shall be made on Form-18A along with the prescribed fees.

2. The applicant shall furnish a request for expedited examination along with the application in Form 18A.

3. The Patent Office shall examine the application within twelve months from the date of the request.

4. The applicant shall submit the required documents, including the search report, if conducted, and the relevant patent specifications along with the application.

5. The applicant shall have to satisfy the Patent Office with appropriate reasons why their application deserves expedited examination.

6. The examination report shall be issued within two months from the date of acceptance of the request for expedited examination.

B. Provisions for small entity under Rule 2(f)(a):

The Patent Rules have introduced a new category of applicants called Small Entities, which is defined as any individual, partnership firm, or a company. The following are the provisions under the Patent Rules for small entities:

1. The application fee and official fee payable by a small entity shall be one fifth the fees as prescribed for other entities.

2. A small entity has to submit a declaration in Form-28 to claim the status of a small entity.

3. A small entity can also get the benefit of expedited examinations as provided in Rule 24C by paying a prescribed fee.

C. Provisions for startup under Rule 2(f)(b):

The Startup Patent Rules, enables startups to access the patent registration system in a more streamlined and efficient way. The following are the provisions under the Patent Rules for startups:

1. The application fee and official fee payable by a startup shall be one fifth the fees as prescribed for other entities.

2. A startup shall submit a declaration in Form-28 in support of their startup status, which should be self-attested by the authorized signatory.

3. The provision of expedited examination for startups is provided under the scheme 'Startup Intellectual Property Protection' (SIPP).

4. Startups can avail a rebate of 80% on the official fee for filing of patent application over the normal fee.

5. Startups can also file a request for expedited examination by paying the prescribed fee.

Therefore, the Patent Rules provide various provisions and relaxations for expedited examination, small entities, and startups to encourage innovation and promote growth in the Patent industry.

Q.7 Mr. Dutta, a research scholar of an Indian University invented one watch which acts as an alarmfor senior citizen and patients to respective call centers of registered hospitals for emergency support. Inthe meantime Mr. Dutta has approached Central government to approve a financial grant for his inventionand had a discussion with concerned official of the said department. Mr. Dutta exhibited his invention inIndustrial fair organized by Government in Pragati Maidan, Delhi on 15th February, 2015. One of his colleague in the same laboratory published his invention in leading newspaper on 2nd March, 2015without his consent. Meanwhile, he has attended one awareness program in Patent in Delhi on 5th March2015. Immediately on 10th March, 2015 he has filed a Provisional Specification before The Patent Office,Delhi and subsequently filed Complete Specification on 10th December, 2015. Mr. Dutta is not sure whether the exhibition and publication in newspaper or communication with Govt. official would hamper his patent protection or not, hence he seeks your advice. Give the appropriate advice in writings to yourclient as a practicing Patent Agent quoting the relevant sections of Patent Act, 1970.

Ans.

Dear Mr. Dutta,

I am writing to advise you regarding the patent protection of your invention, which acts as an alarm for senior citizens and patients to respective call centers of registered hospitals for emergency support.

As per the facts mentioned in your case, you have exhibited your invention in an industrial fair organized by the government, and your colleague has published the invention in a leading newspaper without your consent, before filing a Provisional Specification before The Patent Office in Delhi.

Regarding the exhibition or publication of your invention, Section 31 of The Patent Act, 1970, provides An invention claimed in a complete specification shall not be deemed to have been anticipated by reason only of--

(a) the display of the invention with the consent of the true and first inventor or a person deriving title from him at an industrial or other exhibition to which the provisions of this section have been extended by the Central Government by notification in the Official Gazette, or the use thereof with his consent for the purpose of such an exhibition in the place where it is held; or

(b) the publication of any description of the invention in consequence of the display or use of the invention at any such exhibition as aforesaid; or

(c) the use of the invention, after it has been displayed or used at any such exhibition as aforesaid and during the period of the exhibition, by any person without the consent of the true and first inventor or a person deriving title from him; or

(d) the description of the invention in a paper read by the true and first inventor before a learned society or published with his consent in the transactions of such a society,

if the application for the patent is made by the true and first inventor or a person deriving title from him [not later than twelve months] after the opening of the exhibition or the reading or publication of the paper, as the case may be.

Regarding the communication with government officials, Section 30 of The Patent Act, 1970, provides that An invention claimed in a complete specification shall not be deemed to have been anticipated by reason only of the communication of the invention to the Government or to any person authorised by the Government to investigate the invention or its merits, or of anything done, in consequence of such a communication, for the purpose of the investigation.

In conclusion, it is advised that the exhibition and publication in newspaper or communication with Govt. official would not hamper his patent protection as the application for the patent is made by the true and first inventor or a person deriving title from him not later than twelve months after the opening of the exhibition or the reading or publication of the paper.

I hope this advice is helpful to you. Please feel free to contact me for any further clarification or assistance.

Sincerely,

[Your Name]

[Your Designation]

[Your Contact Information]

PART C1

After reading the specification

i. Provide an appropriate title

ii. Draft an abstract (maximum of 150 words)

iii. Draft at least two claims 1X20Marks =20Marks

This invention relates to a garden sprinkler hose to deliver water to restricted areas and in selecteddirections. The extent of the area to which water is delivered by the hose is controlled by the waterpressure. The objects of the invention are achieved by providing a hose construction which is generallytriangular in transverse cross section, two of its three wall sections being relatively firm and thicker thanits third wall section which is relatively thin and flexible. Only the flexible wall is provided with aperturesfor passage of water out of the hose. This invention permits either of the imperforate, firm relatively thickwalls to serve as a base on which the hose may rest, while the flexible wall responds to water pressure inthe hose by curving outwardly, causing the water streams to flow in predetermined directions and to coverlawn and garden areas to a selected extent. The hose may be placed adjacent a wall or sidewalk edge, withits flexible wall facing away from the wall or walk edge, to

deliver water without waste to cover an area of selected width. In the drawings:
FIG. 1 depicts a portion of a garden sprinkler hose embodying the invention.
FIG. 2 is a transverse sectional view showing the hose as it appears when delivering water streams in response to limited water pressure in the hose. FIG. 3 is similar to FIG. 2 showing the hose as it appears when delivering water streams in response to increased water pressure in the hose as compared to FIG. 2. In the embodiment of the invention shown in the drawings, the hose comprises two imperforate, relatively firm and thick wall sections 11 and 12, either of which may provide a base on which the hose rests in use. The walls 11 and 12 are joined together at one of their longitudinal edges to extend at divergent angles. The other longitudinal edges of the walls 11 and 12 are joined to a relatively thin and flexible wall 13 provided with apertures 14 for passage of water out of the hose. The junctions between each of the walls 11 and 12 and the flexible wall 13 are curved continuations of the flexible wall which merge into the thicker walls 11 and 12 as indicated at 15. The flexible wall 13 responds to the water pressure in the hose by curving outwardly to varying degrees, as illustrated in FIG. 2 where the water pressure is less than maximum, and in FIG. 3 where the water pressure has been increased as compared to FIG. 2. Thus the width of the area covered by the water is less in FIG. 2 than in FIG. 3, due to the degree of curvature of the wall 13. By placing the hose on either of its walls, 11 or 12, adjacent a wall or walk or patio edge, the water is directed away from the not-to-be watered area, and the extent of the area to be watered can be controlled as to direction and width. The hose may be made of rubber or any other suitable material which permits automatic curvature of the apertured wall in response to water pressure. The walls preferably are molded or formed integrally.

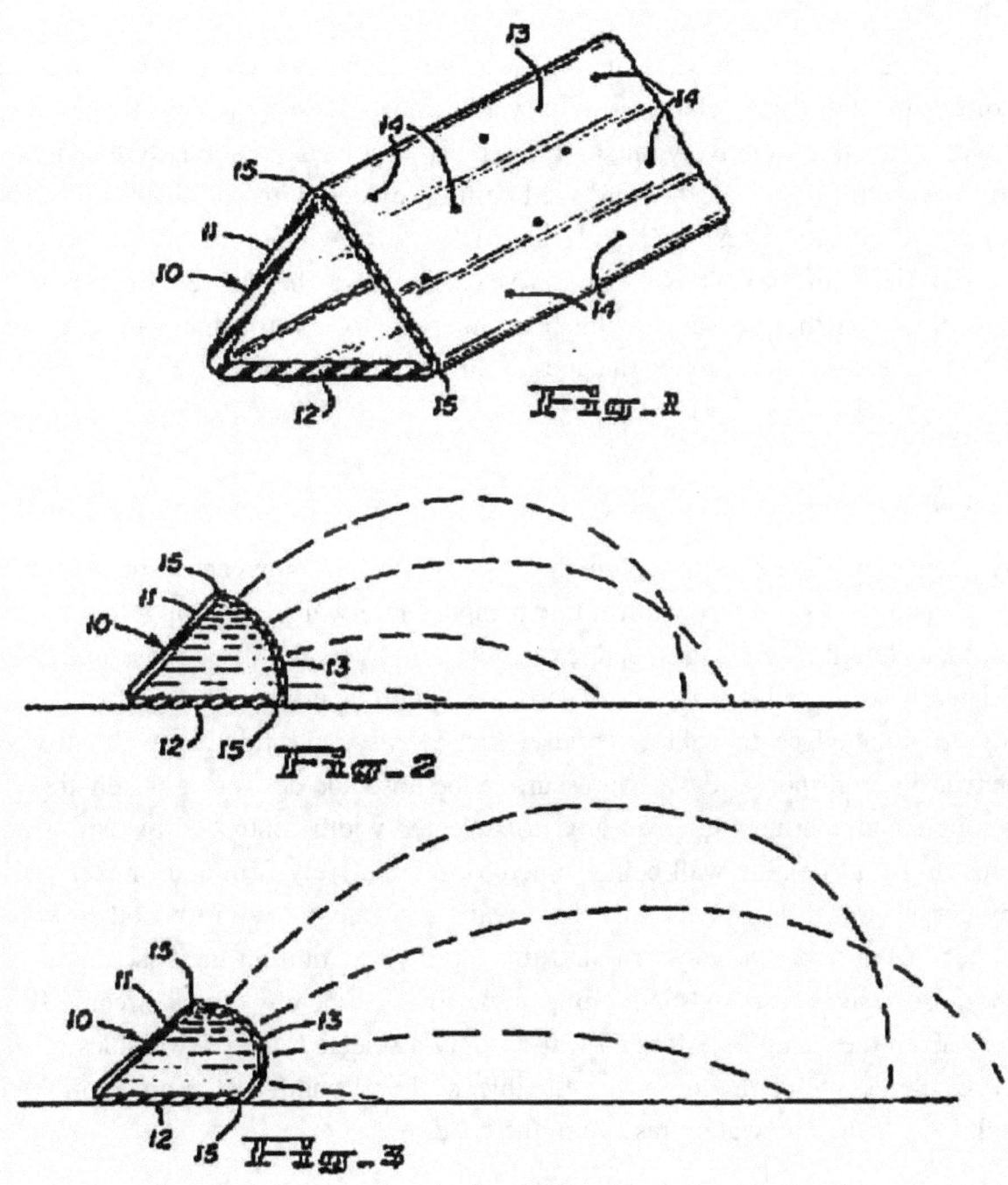

Ans: Please refer to US Patent No. US3727845A

Title- Garden sprinkler hose

Or

Garden Sprinkler Hose with Directional Water Delivery

Abstract

A garden sprinkler hose generally triangular in transverse cross section, comprising two firm relatively thick walls joined at one of their longitudinal edges, and a third relatively thin and flexible wall joined at its longitudinal edges to the two thicker walls, the third wall being provided with sprinkler holes. The hose is designed to rest on one of its thick walls. Water pressure in the hose causes the thin flexible wall to curve outwardly, the degree of curvature depending on the pressure in the hose, thereby to control and vary the area which receives water through the aperture in the flexible wall.

CLAIMS:

I claim:

1. A garden sprinkler hose which is triangular in transverse cross section comprising a. two relatively firm thick imperforate walls joined together at one of their longitudinal edges and extending in divergent directions, and b. a relatively thin and flexible wall provided with apertures and joined at its longitudinal edges to said relatively thick walls, said flexible wall curving outwardly in response to water pressure in the hose and delivering water streams through said apertures to cover areas of selected width controlled by said water pressure, said flexible wall being joined to the relatively firm and thicker walls by curved joints thinner than the firm walls and integral with said other walls, either of the two relatively firm and thick walls constituting the base on which the hose rests in use and both being imperforate, whereby water streams flow only from the flexible perforated wall to only a selected one of two sides of the hose, the degree of flexing of the flexible wall and width of the area sprinkled being controlled by water pressure in the hose.

Or

Claim 1: A flexible garden sprinkler hose comprising two imperforate, firm and thick walls joined together at one of their longitudinal edges to extend at divergent angles and a flexible wall provided with apertures for the passage of water out of the hose that responds to water pressure by curving outwardly to control the width and direction of water delivery.

Q.9

This invention relates to a hair conditioning product and process for producing a hair conditioner capable of increasing the gloss, softness, elasticity, and the tendency to maintain the desirable shape of the hair. Hair conditioners improve sensibly the aspect and the physical form of the hair treated with them. There exists a great variety of formulas for conditioning the hair. The available formulas leave much to be desired in the way of cost, ease of use and ingredients which may have an objectionable odor. Further, none of them attains the efficiency of the formulas and processes described in this invention. It is anobject of the present invention to provide a hair conditioning product having a low price and a pleasantodor. Yet another object of this invention is to provide a hair conditioning product that is easy to use. Stillanother object of the present invention is to provide a hair conditioning product that enhances the naturalshine and sofiness of the hair and which maintains the shape of the hair over extended periods of time. Itis another object of the present invention to provide a product that can remain in contact with the hair forlong periods of time without damage to the hair.

This invention relates to a hair conditioner and a process for producing an entirely new conditioneremploying ascorbic acid and cupric and/or cuprous salts. Ascorbic acid is vitamin C, found inmany fruits, especially in the citric, and in some vegetables with green leaves. The hair conditioner, madeaccordingly to this process, is presented to the user packaged as powder, which besides the activeingredients (which bring about the desired effects), contains also a thickening agent. This powder ismixed with water by the user, before application. Another form of the conditioner from this invention isas a convenient gel, paste or cream, which is applied directly by the user who intends to shape his or herhair. The formulations of the present invention may also include, without altering the basic concepts ofthe present patent application: tensoactives, hunectants, and their functional equivalents or similar,besides the other compounds used in the treatment of hair shaping and conditioning, like quaternary salts,certain dyes, relaxers, etc. In order to provide a perfect and complete idea of the invention, there will bepresented some examples of formulations which can be realized to attain the objectives of this invention,that is to produce an efficient hair conditioner, The following is an example of formulation of the present invention.

EXAMPLE NO.1 - 1 g of cuprous chloride, 3 g of ascorbic acid, 5 g of ammonium chloride and 15 g ofsoluble starch are milled. The powder is mixed with water and applied to hair, which acquires permanentgloss, softness and elasticity noticeably superior to other conditioners used by present art.

EXAMPLE NO.2 - 0.5 g ammonium chloride are dissolved in 150 ml of water, 25 g of carboxymethylcellulose are added and the mixture agitated until obtaining a homogenous paste, which isapplied to the hair. The gloss, softness and elasticity of the hair are superior to the results obtained with common conditioners on the market.

EXAMPLE NO.3 - 3 grams of pyrogallol, 1 g of cupric oxide, 12 ml of N-hydrochleric acid, 3 g ofascorbic acid, and 5 g of ammonium chloride are dissolved in 140 ml of water, 20 g of pre-gellified starch is added and agitated until homogenous. The hair which is treated with the resulting cream, after beingwashed and dried in the desired shape, undulated or stretched shows the characteristic gloss, softness andelasticity, besides maintaining permanently its shape. Independently from these results, the hair is alsotinted by the dye precursor (pyrogallol) included in the formula.

EXAMPLE NO4 - 1.6 g of pentahydrated cupric sulfate, 2.2 g of ascorbic acid, 1.3 g of ammonium chloride, and 35 g of sodium lauryl ether sulfate of 30% are dissolved in 60 ml of water, The solution, thus, obtained was used as conventional shampoo to wash hair. The washed hair, besides being clean, is glossy and soft and exhibits great tendency to keep permanently the shape in which it was dried.

Ans. Please refer to US Patent No. US5472688A

Title- Process for producing a hair conditioner

Abstract

Patent of invention "process for obtaining an hair conditioner," comprising a process for obtaining an hair conditioner which imparts gloss, softness and elasticity to the hair and augments its tendency to maintain the desired shape of the hairdo; the active ingredients of the conditioner being ascorbic acid and cupric and/or cuprous salts: the conditioner in one version being presented in powder form, containing besides the active ingredients, thickening agents, being mixed with water before use and in another version presented in form of a cream, gel or paste, to be used on hair, in both cases containing, optionally, other ingredients of specific action.

Claims (2)

I claim:

1. The process of producing a hair conditioner consisting of the steps of mixing cuprous chloride, ascorbic acid, ammonium chloride and a soluble starch and milling the mixture to produce a powder soluble in water.

2. The process of conditioning hair consisting of preparing a hair conditioner of ascorbic acid and at least one copper compound dissolved in water, adding ammonium chloride to the hair conditioner, and shampooing the hair with the hair conditioner so prepared.

PART C2

A Client meets you and provides technical information regarding his invention. Draft a complete specification with at least two claims and a title for the following description for filing before the Indian Patent office. While preparing the complete specification, do not redraw the figures, however you may refer to the figures in the specifications.

1x30Marks = 30marks

Q.10. This invention relates to apparatus and method for collecting liquids and, in particular, to liquid collectionapparatus and methods of the type employed in printing devices to collect unused ink. Traditional liquidcollection devices collect liquid (in the case of printing ink) for reuse in the process in which the liquid isbeing employed. Such liquid collection devices do, however, have problems associated with them. One significant problem is that air can be collected with the liquid and mixed with it by the collection device.

The air can contain contaminants, which are drawn into the liquid, reducing the quality of the recycledliquid. A further problem, particular to printing inks, is that mixing of the inks with air can lead to ink solvent evaporation into the air, increasing the viscosity of the ink. The present invention is directed towards the provision of a liquid collection apparatus which collects liquid without collecting air trappedtherein. According to the present invention there is provided a liquid collection apparatus comprising: means for collecting liquid; liquid conduit means for transferring liquid from the liquid collection means; porous liquid absorption means positioned between the liquid collection means and the liquid conduit; and pump means for pumping liquid from the liquid conduit, the pump means generating a pressure in liquid in the conduit that is sufficient to draw liquid through liquid collection means but is insufficient to draw a gas/liquid surface through the liquid absorption means. Because the pressure generated by the pump means is not sufficient to draw a gas/liquid surface through the porous liquid absorption means against surface tension forces in the absorption means, any gas contained within The liquid will not be drawn through the liquid absorption means and into the liquid conduit. The apparatus may be arranged to be employed in an ink jet print head, in which case the liquid may be ink. The liquid absorption means may have pores of a diameter of one micron or less. The pore diameters may be in the range of 0.2 to micron. Alternatively, it may be formed from a plurality of narrow capillaries. The material from which the liquid absorption means is formed will be dependent upon the type of liquid being collected, but may formed from cellulose, nylon, mixed esters or polypropylene. The liquid collecting means may be arranged so that the surface of the liquid absorption means is not in direct contact with the atmosphere to reduce the possibility of liquid retained by the absorption means drying due to contact with the atmosphere. The liquid collection means may be formed from a plurality of ribs or of an absorbent material containing pores/capillarics of larger diameter than those in the liquid absorption means. Such an arrangement provides an apparatus which can be moved without liquid spilling out due to the effects of the motion and/or gravity. According to the present invention there is also provided a method of collecting liquid, the method comprising the steps of: collecting liquid in a liquid collection means; and drawing the liquid through a porous liquid absorption means at a pressure level which ensures liquid flow through the liquid collection means yet which is insufficient to draw liquid through the liquid absorption means. One example of the present invention will now be described with reference to the accompanying drawing, in which: Figure 1 shows a schematic diagram of a liquid collection apparatus according to the present invention. Referring to figure 1, a liquid collection apparatus according to the present invention has a liquid collection means 1 in the form of a gutter. A conduit 2 is connected to a pump (not shown). Positioned between the liquid collection means 1 and conduit 2 is a liquid absorption means 3. This liquid absorption means 3, in this example has a structure which consists of a plurality of pores of a diameter of 1 micron or less. In operation, the pump is operated to draw liquid collected by the liquid collection means | through the liquid absorption means 3 and into the conduit 2. The strength of the pump is such that it creates a sufficient pressure differentia! across the liquid absorption means 3 to ensure liquid flow there through. The operation of the pump is controlled, however, such that it does not generate a sufficient pressure differential to draw the gas/liquid surface through the absorption means 3. This ensures that, if air or any gas is draw into the liquid collection means I it is not drawn into the absorption means 3 because the constant presence of liquid at the interface between the liquid and the gas at the boundary 4 between the collection means 1 and liquid absorption means 3 prevents the gas being drawn into the conduit 2, As mentioned above, the material from which the porous liquid absorption means 3 is formed will be dependent upon the type of liquid being collected, and should be selected so that it does not react with the collection liquid. As also mentioned above, the liquid collection means may include a plurality of ribs 5 to retain the liquid in use, and prevent spillage. Alternatively, it may be formed from absorbent material (not shown) of a density lower than that of the absorption means 3. In this example, the arrangement shown is employed to collect ink from a continuous in jet print head. It will be appreciated, however, that the collection device of the invention has applications in many other fields.

Fig. 1.

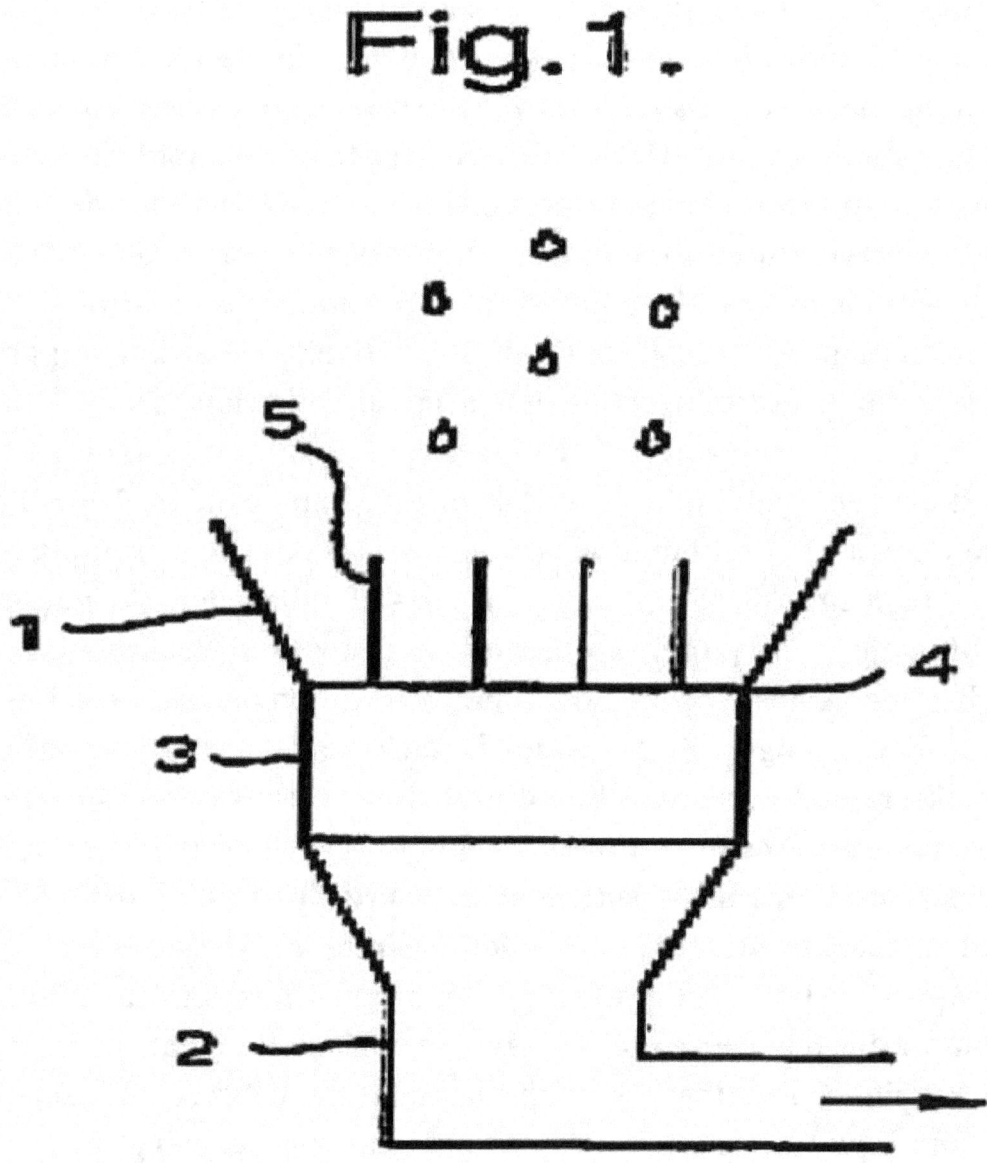

Ans: Please refer to **Patent No. 2947-del-1997**

Title- "Apparatus And Method For Collecting Liquids"

A liquid collection apparatus comprises means (1) for collecting liquid and liquid conduit means (2) for transferring liquid from the liquid collection means (1). Porous liquid absorption means (3) is positioned between the liquid collection means (1) and the liquid conduit (2). Pump means pump liquid from the liquid conduit (2), the pump means generating a pressure in liquid in the conduit (2) that is sufficient to draw liquid through liquid collection means (1) but is insufficient to draw a gas/liquid surface through the liquid absorption means (3).

Abstract: A liquid collection apparatus comprises means (1) for collecting liquid and liquid conduit means (2) for transferring liquid from the liquid collection means (1). Porous liquid absorption means (3) is positioned between the liquid collection means (1) and the liquid conduit (2). Pump means pump liquid from the liquid conduit (2), the pump means generating a pressure in liquid in the conduit (2) that is sufficient to draw liquid through liquid collection means (1) but is insufficient to draw a gas/liquid surface through the liquid absorption means (3).

Field of the Invention

This invention relates to apparatus and method for collecting liquids and, in particular, to liquid collection apparatus and methods of the type employed in printing devices to collect unused ink.

Background of Invention

Traditional liquid collection devices collect liquid (in the case of printing, ink) for reuse in the process in which the liquid is being employed. Such liquid collection devices do, however, have problems associated with them.

One significant problem is that air can be collected with the liquid and mixed with it by the collection device. The air can contain contaminants, which are drawn into the liquid, reducing the quality of the recycled liquid. A further problem, particular to printing inks, is that mixing of the inks with air can lead to ink solvent evaporation into the air, increasing the viscosity of the ink.

The present invention is directed towards the provision of a liquid collection apparatus which collects liquid without collecting air trapped therein.

Summary of the invention

A liquid collection apparatus comprises means for collecting liquid and liquid conduit means for transferring liquid from the liquid collection means. Porous liquid absorption means is positioned between the liquid collection means and the liquid conduit. Pump means pump liquid from the liquid conduit, the pump means generating a pressure in liquid in the conduit that is sufficient to draw liquid through liquid collection means but is insufficient to draw a gas/liquid surface through the liquid absorption means.

Detailed Description

According to the present invention there is provided a liquid collection apparatus comprising:

means for collecting liquid;

liquid conduit means for transferring liquid from the liquid collection means;

porous liquid absorption means positioned between the liquid collection means and the liquid conduit; and

pump means for pumping liquid from the liquid conduit, the pump means generating a pressure in liquid in the conduit that is sufficient to draw liquid through liquid collection means but is insufficient to draw a gas/liquid surface through the liquid absorption means.

Because the pressure generated by the pump means is not sufficient to draw a gas/liquid surface through the porous liquid absorption means against surface tension forces in the absorption means, any gas contained within

the liquid will not be drawn through the liquid absorption means and into the liquid conduit.

The apparatus may be arranged to be employed in an ink jet printhead, in which case the liquid may be ink. The liquid absorption means may have pores of a diameter of one micron or less. The pore diameters may be in the range of 0.2 to 1 micron. Alternatively, it may be formed from a plurality of narrow capillaries.

The material from which the liquid absorption means is formed will be dependent upon the type of liquid being collected, but may formed from cellulose, nylon, mixed esters, or polypropylene.

The liquid collecting means may be arranged so that the surface of the liquid absorption means is not in direct contact with the atmosphere, to reduce the possibility of liquid retained by the absorption means drying due to contact with the atmosphere. The liquid collection means may be formed from a plurality of ribs or of an absorbent material containing pores/capillaries of larger diameter than those in the liquid absorption means. Such an arrangement provides an apparatus which can be moved without liquid spilling out due to the effects of the motion and/or gravity.

According to the present invention there is also provided a method of collecting liquid, the method comprising the steps of:

collecting liquid in a liquid collection means; and drawing the liquid through a porous liquid absorption means at a pressure level which ensures liquid flow through the liquid collection means yet which is insufficient to draw liquid through the liquid absorption means.

One example of the present invention will now be described with reference to the accompanying drawing, in which:

Figure 1 shows a schematic diagram of a liquid collection apparatus according to the present invention.

Referring to figure 1, a liquid collection apparatus according to the present invention has a liquid collection means 1 in the form of a gutter. A conduit 2 is connected to a pump (not shown). Positioned between the liquid collection means 1 and conduit 2 is a liquid absorption means 3. This liquid absorption means 3 has, in this example, a structure such that it has a plurality of pores of a diameter of 1 micron or less.

In operation, the pump is operated to draw liquid collected by the liquid collection means 1 through the liquid absorption means 3 and into the conduit 2. The strength of the pump is such that it creates a sufficient pressure differential across the liquid absorption means 3 to ensure liquid flow therethrough. The operation of the pump is controlled, however, such that it does not generate a sufficient pressure differential to draw the gas/liquid surface through the absorption means 3. This ensures that, if air or any gas is draw into the liquid collection means I it is not drawn into the absorption means 3 because the constant presence of liquid at the interface between the liquid and the gas at the boundary 4 between the collection means 1 and liquid absorption means 3 prevents the gas being drawn into the conduit 2.

As mentioned above, the material from which the porous liquid absorption means 3 is formed will be dependent upon the type of liquid being collected, and should be selected so that it does not react with the collection liquid.

As also mentioned above, the liquid collection means may include a plurality of ribs 5 to retain the liquid in use, and prevent spillage. Alternatively, it may be formed from absorbent material (not shown) of a density lower than that of the absorption means 3.

In this example, the arrangement shown is employed to collect ink from a continuous ink jet printhead. It will be appreciated, however, that the collection device of the invention has applications in many other fields.

CLAIMS:

I claim:

1. A liquid collection apparatus comprising:

means for collecting liquid;

liquid conduit means for transferring liquid from the liquid collection means;

porous liquid absorption means positioned between the liquid collection means and the liquid conduit; and pump means for pumping liquid from the liquid conduit, the pump means generating a pressure in liquid in the conduit that is sufficient to draw liquid through liquid collection means but is insufficient to draw a gas/liquid surface through the liquid absorption means.

2. An apparatus according to claim 1, wherein the liquid absorption means has pores of a diameter of one micron or less.

3. An apparatus according to claim 2, wherein the pore diameters are in the range of 0.2 to 1 micron.

4. An apparatus according to claim 1, wherein the liquid absorption means is formed from a plurality of narrow capillaries.

5. An apparatus according to any of the preceding claims, wherein the material from which the liquid absorption means is formed is one of cellulose, nylon, mixed esters, or polypropylene.

6. An apparatus according to ant of the preceding claims, wherein the liquid collecting means is arranged so that the surface of the liquid absorption means is not in direct contact with the atmosphere.

7. An apparatus according to any of the preceding claims, wherein the liquid collection means is formed from a plurality of ribs.

8. An apparatus according to any of claims 1 to 6, wherein the liquid collection means is formed from an absorbent material containing pores/capillaries of larger diameter than those in the liquid absorption means.

9. An apparatus according to any of the preceding claims arranged to be employed in an ink jet printhead.

10. A method of collecting liquid, the method comprising the steps of:

collecting liquid in a liquid collection means;

and drawing the liquid through a porous liquid absorption means at a pressure level which ensures liquid flow through the liquid collection means.

Q.11

Noise filter such as herein disclosed is intended for use in desk computers, office machines and medical equipment and the like. Their main function of noise filter is the reduction of the line related noise levels. Since these filters, due to their application, are subjected to high electrical and magnetic field strength levels because of the environment in which they operate, it must be ensured that their suppression effectiveness is not reduced through unintended coupling of electrical and magnetic interferences to the wiring or the components of the filter circuit. Especially when used in electrical equipment with combined power supplies and/or microprocessor systems which have long bus runs, these problems are encountered frequently. Such filters have become known, as example, as filters with integrated cold appliance plugs in which the connections from the net side ave made via this cold appliance plug usually a so called power outlet and the contact to the equipment to be provided with the filter via flat plugs, soldering lugs. The terminals and the carriers of the electrical components are tightly cemented into a half round cup of nickel silver sheet. In this noise filter, the electrical components per se are mounted, insulated and manually soldered into the half round cup. Subsequently, the electrical components are fixed with a soft epoxy resin compound from the open side of the half round cup and then mechanically protected by a hard sealing compound, Other commercially available noise filters employ a deep-drawn nickel silver housing in place of the half round nickel silver cup. The components are then mounted and soldered in an auxiliary frame with flat plugs. Cementing the components and flat plug parts located in the filter housing is accomplished through a hole in the nickel silver housing which must be tightly sealed to plugs and frame by adding sealing rings. The cementing hole is covered up by a glued-on name plate. Many noise filters also available in market a soldered jacket tube of tin plate, the electrical components being mounted to a base plate which is subsequently riveted to the plug. The ground connection is soldered on through a hole in the jacket tube which must be pushed over the plug first. The soldering point is covered up by a name plate. The electrical components are cemented in from the open backside of the jacket tube.

The noise filter according to FIG. 1, which shows a partially sectioned top view comprises of a filter housing 1, such as of extruded aluminum tubing, which is reduced in section at its one face 15 in the manner of a shaft and closed by a connector socket 2 at its other face. Inserted into the filter housing 1 is an insulating material housing 7 which may be subdivided, e.g. by separating walls not detailed, into chambers.

Mounted in these chambers are electrical components, e.g. an electrical resistor 3, not preassembled electrical capacitors 4, 5 Y-capacitors 12, 13, and a radio noise suppression inductor 6 slid on a potential separating web 8 which is integrally molded to the insulating material housing 7. As shown in partial sectioned view in FIG. 2, the winding ends 31-34 of the inductor 6 are wound around appropriately bent ends of flat plugs 10, 11, 19 20 are soldered. The same applies to the capacitors 4, 5 and 12, 13 of FIG. 2 which are connected to the appropriate ends of the flat plugs via webs 21, 22, 23 24.To the face area of the insulating material housing 7 facing the face end 15 is integrally molded a shaft 14 whose outside surfaces rest against the inside surfaces of the filter housing. The electrical components and the fiat plugs 10, 11, 19, 20 connected to these components are embedded in epoxy resin 30, only the outwardly facing parts of the flat plugs being left free.

A grounded conductor 9 is provided, extending over the entire length of the insulating material housing 7. For contact between this ground wire and the filter housing a copper plate is welded ultrasonically to the filter housing 1 in the area where the ground wire penetrates the face wall of filter housing 1. The direct contact between ground wire 9 and this copper plate is established by the solder point indicated at 16.

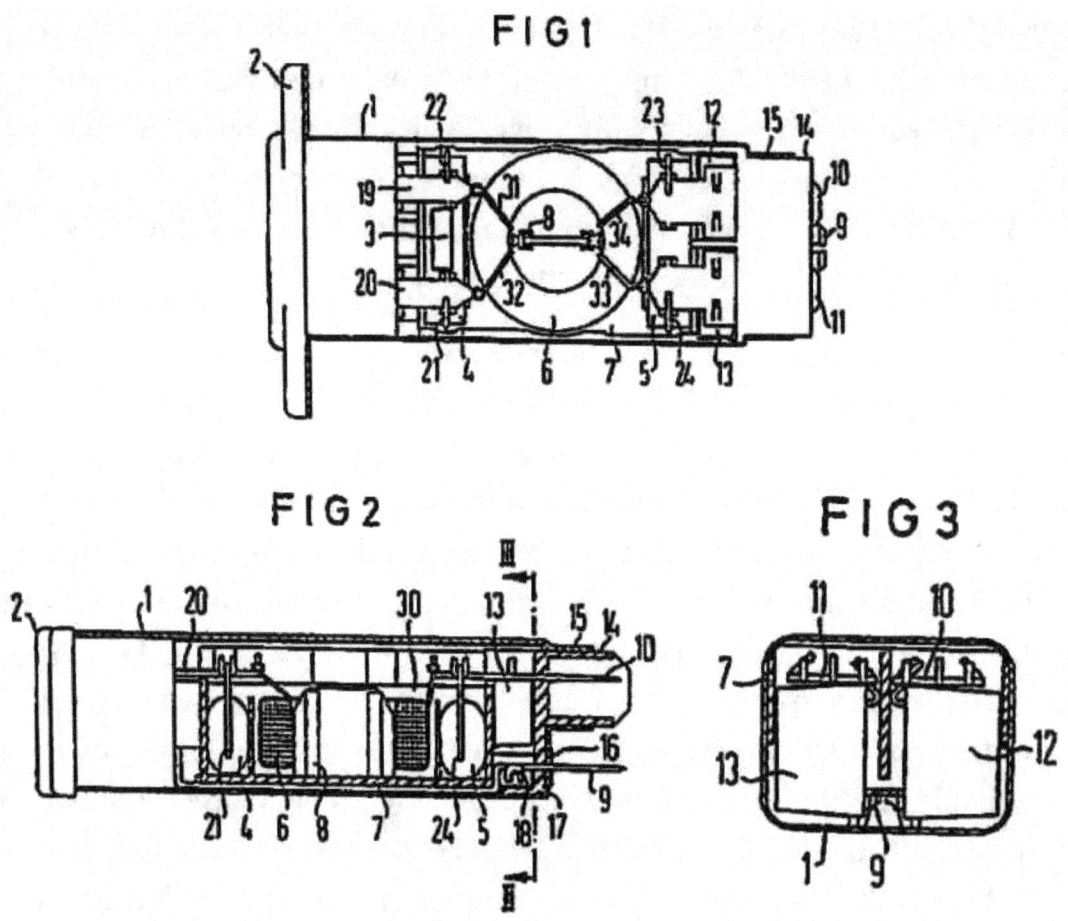

FIG 1

FIG 2

FIG 3

Ans: Please refer to **Patent No. US4611185A**

Electrical noise filter

Abstract

Electrical noise filter with a filter housing, with electrical terminals led out at open face ends, in particular flat plugs, litz wires, plug pins, and with electrical components, in particular inductances and capacitances which, embedded in sealing compound, are installed in the filter housing and connected to the terminals. The filter housing is extended so that the terminal elements facing outwardly are disposed within the filter housing and shielded.

BACKGROUND OF THE INVENTION

Noise filter of the above mentioned kind are intended for use in desk computers, office machines and medical equipment and the like. Their principal function is the reduction of the line related noise levels. Since these filters, due to their application, are subjected to high electrical and magnetic field strength levels because of the environment in which they operate, it must be ensured that their suppression effectiveness is not reduced through unintended coupling of electrical and magnetic interferences to the wiring or the components of the filter circuit. Especially when used in electrical equipment with combined power supplies and/or microprocessor systems which have long bus runs, these problems are encountered frequently.

SUMMARY OF THE INVENTION

It is an object of the present invention to provide a noise filter of the kind described above which is characterized by effective magnetic shielding and improved high-frequency properties and which can be produced at the least possible cost to meet national and international specifications for such filters.

Other features and advantages of the invention will be apparent from the following description of the preferred embodiments, and from the claims.

For a full understanding of the present invention, reference should now be made to the following detailed description of the preferred embodiments of the invention and to the accompanying drawings.

BRIEF DESCRIPTION OF THE DRAWINGS

FIG. 1 shows a partially sectioned top view of a noise filter according to the invention.

FIG. 2 shows a partially sectioned view of the noise filter according to FIG. 1.

FIG. 3 is a section along line 3--3 of FIG. 2.

FIG. 4 shows another embodiment of the subject of the invention in the view according to FIG. 2 (identical parts have the same reference symbols).

DETAILED DESCRIPTION

The noise filter according to FIGS. 1 to 3 has a filter housing 1, such as of extruded aluminum tubing, which is reduced in section at its one face 15 in the manner of a shaft and closed by a connector socket 2 at its other face. Inserted

108

into the filter housing 1 is an insulating material housing 7 which may be subdivided, e.g. by separating walls not detailed, into chambers. Mounted in these chambers are electrical components, e.g. an electrical resistor 3, not preassembled electrical capacitors 4, 5 Y- capacitors 12, 13, and a radio noise suppression inductor 6 slid on a potential separating web 8 which is integrally molded to the insulating material housing 7. As shown in FIG. 2, the winding ends 31-34 of the inductor 6 are wound around appropriately bent ends of flat plugs 10, 11, 19 20 are soldered. The same applies to the capacitors 4, 5 and 12, 13 of FIG. 2 which are connected to the appropriate ends of the flat plugs via webs 21, 22, 23 24.

To the face area of the insulating material housing 7 facing the face end 15 is integrally molded a shaft 14 whose outside surfaces rest against the inside surfaces of the filter housing. The electrical components and the flat plugs 10, 11, 19, 20 connected to these components are embedded in epoxy resin 30, only the outwardly facing parts of the flat plugs being left free.

In addition, a grounded conductor 9 is provided, extending over the entire length of the insulating material housing 7. For contact between this ground wire and the filter housing a copper plate is welded ultrasonically to the filter housing 1 in the area where the ground wire penetrates the face wall of filter housing 1. The direct contact between ground wire 9 and this copper plate is established by the solder point indicated at 16.

The Y- capacitors 12, 13 are disposed directly between phase and ground wire housing and contacted to the ground wire at 18. A very low inductance connection is obtained by these extremely short leads.

In FIG. 3, a sectional view as indicated in FIG. 2, the organization of internal components of the filter are illustrated. The short lead connections for the Y-capacitors 12 and 13 is clearly illustrated connecting respectively between flat plugs 11 and 12 and grounded connector 9.

There has thus been shown and described a novel electrical line noise filter which fulfills all the objects and advantages sought therefor. Many changes, modifications, variations and other uses and applications of the subject invention will, however, become apparent to those skilled in the art after considering this specification and the accompanying drawings which disclose preferred embodiments thereof. All such changes, modifications, variations and other uses and applications which do not depart from the spirit and scope of the invention are deemed to be covered by the invention which is limited only by the claims which follow.

Claims (4)

Claims

I claim:

1. An electrical interference filter of the type having an external filter housing of highly conductive metal containing an additional insulating material housing filled with a sealing compound of insulating material, the insulating material housing being inserted into the external filter housing and having embedded electrical filter components therein interconnected in circuit relationship to form the filter circuit, the filter comprising:

plug connectors having outer connection elements extending from one end of the insulating material housing serving as ports of the filter circuit, the external filter housing being shaped to include a partially closed face end having an apertured portion of reduced cross section for containing the outer connection elements arranged in the interior of the filter housing;

a ground conductor extending over the entire length of the insulating material housing in the external filter housing having an external connection part extending through a closed area of the face end of the external filter housing and electrically connected with the external filter housing at one location in a conducting manner; and

the apertured portion of the external filter housing being extended beyond the face end in the form of a rectangular shaft and encircling the outer connection elements located within this rectangular shaft portion of the external filter housing section and shielded electromagnetically.

2. An electrical interference filter according to claim 1, wherein the inner wall of the external filter housing is electrically insulated in the apertured portion area of its partially closed face end.

3. An electrical interference filter according to claim 1, wherein there is inserted in the shaft-like portion of the external filter housing a shaft-like insulating material section through which the outer connection elements are over their entire length electrically insulated from the external filter housing.

4. An electrical interference filter according to claim 2, wherein there is inserted in the shaft-like portion of the external filter housing a shaft-like insulating material section through which the outer connection elements are over their entire length electrically insulated from the external filter housing.

PATENT AGENT EXAMINATION, 2016

(Under Section 126 of the Patents Act, 1970)

PAPER II

Total Marks: 100

Time: 2.30 p.m. to 5.30 p.m.

Three hours

Instructions:

1. This paper consists of 3 parts- Part A (20 marks), Part B (30 Marks) & Part C (50 marks).

2. ALL questions in Part A and B are compulsory.

3. Part C comprises Part C1 (20 Marks) and C2 (30Marks). Part C1 consists of 2 questions and the candidate is required to answer any 1 of them. Part C2 also consists of 2 questions and the candidate is required to answer any 1 of them.

4. In case a candidate answers more questions than required, the first attempted question will be evaluated.

5. Candidates should read the questions very carefully before answering.

6. No clarification will be provided during the course of the examination.

7. There is no negative marking.

PART A

4 x5 M =20 marks (4 questions)

Q.1. Aand B are co-inventors of a tracking device. Later A files an application for a patent in his own name. B comes to know about this fact from the Journal of the Patent office. What action B can take to redress this injustice inflicted upon him by A?

Ans.B can file a petition under Section 28 and Rule 67 of the Indian Patents Act, 1970. This section deals with the right to apply for a patent by an inventor or his legal representative. Rule 67 states that A claim under sub-section (3) of section 28 shall be made in Form 8, and shall be accompanied by a statement setting out the circumstances under which the claim is made. A copy of the claim and the statement shall be sent by the Controller to every applicant for the patent (not being the claimant) and to any other person whom the Controller may consider to be interested.

Section 28 of Patents Act: Mention of inventor as such in patent;

(1) If the Controller is satisfied, upon a request or claim made in accordance with the provisions of this section,--

(a) that the person in respect of or by whom the request or claim is made is the inventor of an invention in respect of which application for a patent has been made, or of a substantial part of that invention; and

(b) that the application for the patent is a direct consequence of his being the inventor, the Controller shall, subject to the provisions of this section, cause him to be mentioned as inventor in any patent granted in pursuance of the application in the complete specification and in the register of Patents:

Provided that the mention of any person as inventor under this section shall not confer or derogate from any rights under the patent.

(2) A request that any person shall be mentioned as aforesaid may be made in the prescribed manner by the applicant for the patent or (where the person alleged to be the inventor is not the applicant or one of the applicants) by the applicant and that person.

(3) If any person [other than a person in respect of whom a request in relation to the application in question has been made under sub-section (2)] desires to be mentioned as aforesaid, he may make a claim in the prescribed manner in that behalf.

[(4) A request or claim under the foregoing provisions of this section shall be made before the grant of patent.]

* * * * *

(6) [Where] a claim is made under sub-section (3), the Controller shall give notice of the claim to every applicant for the patent (not being the claimant) and to any other person whom the Controller may consider to be interested; and before deciding upon any request or claim made under sub-section (2) or sub-section (3), the Controller shall, if required, hear the person in respect of or by whom the request or claim is made, and, in the case of a claim under sub-section (3), any person to whom notice of the claim has been given as aforesaid.

(7) Where any person has been mentioned as inventor in pursuance of this section anyother person who alleges that he ought not to have been so mentioned may at any time apply to the Controller for a certificate to that effect, and the Controller may, after hearing, if required, any person whom he may consider to be interested, issue such a certificate, and if he does so, he shall rectify the specification and the register accordingly.

In this case, B can claim that he is the co-inventor of the tracking device and therefore has the right to apply for a patent. He can request the Controller to revoke the patent granted to A and grant the patent to both of them jointly.

Q.2 Y owns an Indian Patent. X requests for a licence under the patent from Y.Y imposes certain conditions such that X cannot acquire such articles which are not covered by the Patent from any person other than Y. Y also imposes a condition of exclusive grant back in the licence. As an agent do you think these conditions are appropriate? Please give your answer vis-a-vis the relevant provisions of the Patents Act.

Ans. No, the conditions imposed by Y for granting a license under the Indian Patent are not appropriate under Section 140 of the Indian Patents Act, 1970.

Section 140 of Patents Act: Avoidance of certain restrictive conditions;

(1)It shall not be lawful to insert--

(i) in any contract for or in relation to the sale or lease of a patented article or an article made by a patented process; or

(ii) in a licence to manufacture or use a patented article; or

(iii) in a licence to work any process protected by a patent, a condition the effect of which may be--

(a) to require the purchaser, lessee, or licensee to acquire from the vendor, lessor, or licensor, or his nominees, or to prohibit him from acquiring or to restrict in any manner or to any extent his right to acquire from any person or to prohibit him from acquiring except from the vendor, lessor, or licensor or his nominees, any article other than the patented article or an article other than that made by the patented process; or

(b) to prohibit the purchaser, lessee or licensee from using, or to restrict in any manner or to any extent the right of the purchaser, lessee or licensee, to use an article other than the patented article or an article other than that made by the patented process, which is not supplied by the vendor, lessor or licensor or his nominee; or

(c) to prohibit the purchaser, lessee or licensee from using or to restrict in any manner or to any extent the right of the purchaser, lessee or licensee to use any process other than the patented process; or

[(d)to provide exclusive grant back, prevention to challenges to validity of patent and coercive package licensing,]

and any such condition shall be void.

(2) A condition of the nature referred to in clause (a) or clause (b) or clause (c) of sub-section (1) shall not cease to be a condition falling within that sub-section merely by reason of the fact that the agreement containing it has been entered into separately, whether before or after the contract relating to the sale, lease or licence of the patented article or process.

(3) In proceedings against any person for the infringement of a patent, it shall be a defence to prove that at the time of the infringement there was in force a contract relating to the patent and containing a condition declared unlawful by this section:

Provided that this sub-section shall not apply if the plaintiff is not a party to the contract and proves to the satisfaction of the court that the restrictive condition was inserted in the contract without his knowledge and consent, express or implied.

(4) Nothing in this section shall--

(a) affect a condition in a contract by which a person is prohibited from selling goods other than those of a particular person;

(b) validate a contract which, but for this section, would be invalid;

(c) affect a condition in a contract for the lease of, or licence to use, a patented article, by which the lessor or licensor reserves to himself or his nominee the right to supply such new parts of the patented article as may be required or to put or keep it in repair.

Q.3 An inventor/applicant has filed an application for patent in India and approaches you immediately thereafter for filing international application under PCT with specific questions on following:

a) Whether he can claim priority of his application filed in India and within what time.

b) When he can file a national phase application from PCT route.

c) After filing of national phase application, what would be fate of his previous application? Please advise him as per provisions of PCT and Indian Patents Act.

Ans.

The applicant can file a national phase application in India from the PCT route within 31 months from the priority date. The Indian national phase application must be filed under Section 135 of the Indian Patents Act, 1970.

Section 135 of Patents Act: Convention applications;

(1) Without prejudice to the provisions contained in section 6, where a person has made an application for a patent in respect of an invention in a convention country (hereinafter referred to as the "basic application"), and that person or the legal representative or assignee of that person makes an application under this

Act for a patent within twelve months after the date on which the basic application was made, the priority date of a claim of the complete specification, being a claim based on matter disclosed in the basic application, is the date of making of the basic application.

Explanation.--Where applications have been made for similar protection in respect of an invention in two or more convention countries, the period of twelve months referred to in this sub-section shall be reckoned from the date on which the earlier or earliest of the said applications was made.

(2) Where applications for protection have been made in one or more convention countries in respect of two or more inventions which are cognate or of which one is a modification of another, a single convention application may, subject to the provisions contained in section 10, be made in respect of those inventions at any time within twelve months from the date of the earliest of the said applications for protection:

Provided that the fee payable on the making of any such application shall be the same as if separate applications have been made in respect of each of the said inventions, and the requirements of clause (b) of sub-section (1) of section 136 shall, in the case of any such application, apply separately to the applications for protection in respect of each of the said inventions.

1[(3) In case of an application filed under the Patent Cooperation Treaty designating India and claiming priority from a previously filed application in India, the provisions of sub-sections (1) and (2) shall apply as if the previously filed application were the basic application:

Provided that a request for examination under section 11B shall be made only for one of the applications filed in India.]

Section 45 of Patents Act: Date of patent;

[(1) Subject to the other provisions contained in this Act, every patent shall be dated as of the date on which the application for patent was filed.]

(2) The date of every patent shall be entered in the register.

(3) Notwithstanding anything contained in this section, no suit or other proceeding shall be commenced or prosecuted in respect of an infringement committed before [the date of publication of the application].

Q.4 Write a short note on the benefits provided for startups and small entities under the Patents Rules.

Part B

3X10 M=30 Marks (3 questions)

Benefits for start ups and small entities

The first set of amendments – the Patents (Amendment) Rules, 2020, notified on 19 October 2020 – simplify the procedure relating to the submission of priority applications and their translations, as well as the filing of working statements (Form 27). These amendments will reduce both compliance and prosecution costs for applicants.

The second set of amendments – the Patents (Second Amendment) Rules, 2020 ("2020 Second Rules"), notified on 04 November 2020 – further reduce the filing and prosecution costs for applicants that are startups and small entities. These amendments will cumulatively make intellectual property protection affordable as well as accessible to various classes of business, and will likely also boost patent filings.

Fees for Small Entities

The Patent Rules, 2003 previously allowed almost 80% reduction in the fees payable by a small entity, compared to that payable by other entities. The amendments reduce this further: now, the fee payable by a small entity is down to 20% of that payable by other entities. This makes the fee payable by a small entity at par with that payable by a natural person and a startup.

Change in the status of startups

The Patent Rules, 2003 previously provided that an entity would no longer be able to claim the status of a startup after a period of "five years" from the date of its incorporation or registration. The amendments substitute this period of five years by a "period during which it is recognised by the competent authority".

In an important procedural clarification, the 2020 Second Rules clarify that even if applicant's status of startup/ small entity ceases after filing a request for expedited examination, the request made for expedited examination will not be questioned.

Q.5 Section 3(d) of Indian Patents Act, 1970 was amended which includes an explanation as follows:

"For the purposes of this clause, salts, esters, ethers, polymorphs, metabolites, pure form, particle size, isomers, mixtures of isomers, complexes, combinations and other derivatives of known substance shall be considered to be the same substance, unless they differ significantly in properties with regard to efficacy;Explain the term "efficacy" in the light of the judgment of Supreme Court and other relevant orders by different courts in the matter of Novartis vs Union of India involving an anti-cancer compound.

Ans: Novartis v Union of India (1 April 2013)

What is "efficacy"? Efficacy means "the ability to produce a desired or intended result". Hence, the test of efficacy in the context of section 3(d) would be different, depending upon the result the product under consideration is desired or intended to produce. In other words, the test of efficacy would depend upon the function, utility or the purpose of the product under consideration. Therefore, in the case of a medicine that claims to cure a disease, the test of efficacy can only be "therapeutic efficacy". The question then arises, what would be the parameter of therapeutic efficacy and what are the advantages and benefits that may be taken into account for determining the enhancement of therapeutic efficacy? With regard to the genesis of section 3(d), and more particularly the circumstances in which section 3(d) was amended to make it even more constrictive than before, we have no doubt that the "therapeutic efficacy" of a medicine must be judged strictly and narrowly.

Whether or not an increase in bioavailability leads to an enhancement of therapeutic efficacy in any given case must be specifically claimed and established by research data. In this case, there is absolutely nothing on this score apart from the adroit submissions of the counsel. No material has been offered to indicate that the beta crystalline form of Imatinib Mesylate will produce an enhanced or superior efficacy (therapeutic) on molecular basis than what could be achieved with Imatinib free base in vivo animal model.

Q.6 A invents a medicine which is a combination of components A, B and C. Component C is a powder of herb which occurs in hilly terrain of Assam and adjoining areas. As a Patent agent advise him regarding the essential procedural and substantial aspects of patenting of such combinations.

Ans.

Section 3 of the Patents Act lists what are not considered to be inventions and are therefore not eligible for patent protection. One of the subsections under Section 3 specifically deals with the patentability of combinations. According to Section 3(d) of the Patents Act, "the mere discovery of a new form of a known substance which does not result in the enhancement of the known efficacy of that substance" is not considered an invention. This means that if the combination of components A, B, and C does not result in an enhanced efficacy compared to the known substances individually, it may not be eligible for a patent. To assess the essential procedural and substantial aspects of patenting such combinations, the following considerations should be taken into account:

1. Novelty: Confirm if the combination of components A, B, and C is truly novel and not previously known or disclosed. Conduct a thorough search for existing patents, scientific articles, and other prior art to ensure the novelty requirement is met.

2. Inventive step: Determine if the combination involves an inventive step that is not obvious to a person skilled in the field. The combination should not be an obvious or routine arrangement of known components. It must involve a non-obvious technical advancement.

3. Industrial applicability: Establish that the combination of components A, B, and C has a practical application and can be industrially manufactured or used. The invention should have a useful purpose and be capable of being produced or implemented on an industrial scale.

Section 3 of Patents Act: What are not inventions;

(e) a substance obtained by a mere admixture resulting only in the aggregation of the properties of the components thereof or a process for producing such substance;

(p) an invention which, in effect, is traditional knowledge or which is an aggregation or duplication of known properties of traditionally known component or components.]

Q.7 A patent was granted to X on a communication system. After getting the patent X serves a notice of infringement upon Y on the ground that he was infringing the patent granted to X. Y approaches you for suitable advice. Please explain to Y the remedies under the Patents Act.

Ans: Under Section 107 of the Patents Act, there are several defenses available to Y in the event of infringement claims made by X. The following are the potential remedies and defenses that Y can consider:

1. Invalidity of the patent: Y can challenge the validity of X's patent by filing for revocation. If Y can successfully prove that the patent is invalid due to lack of novelty, inventive step, or industrial applicability, the patent can be revoked, and the infringement claim would no longer be valid.

2. Non-infringement: Y can argue that their communication system does not infringe upon the claims of X's patent. It is essential to thoroughly analyze the claims made in X's patent and compare them with the features and functionalities of Y's system. If there are key differences or distinctions between the two, Y may have a defense of non-infringement.

3. Prior use: Y can assert that they have been using the communication system in question before X filed their patent application. Prior use can act as a defense against infringement claims under certain circumstances. Y must be able to substantiate this claim with evidence that demonstrates their prior commercial use or development of the identical or substantially equivalent communication system.

4. License agreement: If Y has obtained a license from X or any other authorized party to use the patented communication system, they can rely on the license agreement as a defense. Y must ensure that the scope of the license covers the allegedly infringing activities.

Section 107: Defences, etc., in suit for infringement;

(1) In any suit for infringement of a patent, every ground on which it may be revoked under section 64 shall be available as a ground for defence.

(2) In any suit for infringement of a patent by the making, using or importation of any machine, apparatus or other article or by the using of any process or by the importation, use or distribution of any medicine or drug, it shall be a ground for defence that such making, using, importation or distribution is in accordance with any one or more of the conditions specified in section 47.

Part C

Part C1 consists of 2 questions and the candidate is required to answer any 1 of them. Part C2 also consists of 2 questions and the candidate is required to answer any 1 of them. In case a candidate answers more questions than required, the first attempted question will be evaluated.

Part C1

After reading the specification:

i. Provide an appropriate title,

ii. Draft an abstract (maximum of 150 words) and

iii. Draft 5 claims

1X20 M = 20 marks

Q.8 The invention is generally related to the field of formulation and use of fertilizer compositions for agricultural use. More specifically, the invention

relates to fertilizer compositions that contain viable Bacillus bacteria and decontaminated animal manure. It is well understood that nitrogen (N), the single most important plant nutrient, has been over used in modern agriculture in an effort to encourage maximum plant yields. Nitrogen in the form of soluble nitrates is particularly harmful to the environment since nitrates readily leach out of soil and cause pollution of ground and surface waters. One of the principal goals of agricultural science has been to invent a perfect fertilizer composition that is capable of optimizing food plant production when used at minimum application rates and that, subsequently, will not degrade or adversely affect the soil ecosystem. The present invention attains this goal.

Prior art X, claims a biochemical fertilizer but no mention is made of using decontaminated manure as a source of the organic ingredients. Other non-manure organics are indicated. A broad list of microorganisms, listed by genera, is claimed in claim 10, which includes Bacillus, but this claim simply lists all the genera that may contain beneficial microorganisms, not novel as they are listed as such in numerous textbooks, and does not give any specific examples of species with performance data. The need for microbial nutrients is mentioned in claim 14 but these must be part of the microorganism ingredient, not the bulk organic ingredient as in my invention (where decontaminated manure feeds the Bacillus).There is a great but heretofore unmet need worldwide for technology that permits lower use rates of N while maintaining plant yields. The present invention provides such technology by combining unique ingredients and processing them in such a way as to arrive at potentiated fertilizer compositions capable of effecting substantial benefits in plant production. The novelty of the present invention relates to specific synergisms between the various ingredients and to the processing technology that renders such ingredients functional. In accordance with the present invention, fertilizer compositions that contain viable Bacillus bacteria and decontaminated animal manure are presented. Optionally, these formulations preferably also contain humic acid and N—P—K substances, where N means nitrogenous or nitrogen-containing compounds (organic or inorganic), P indicates phosphorous-containing (organic or inorganic compounds), and K indicates potassium-containing (organic or inorganic compounds). More specifically, the invention concerns compositions comprising at least one species of probiotic Bacillus bacteria that exert a positive effect on the yield of agricultural plants and/or reduce the nitrogen requirements of agricultural plants, and animal manure that has been decontaminated to reduce the concentration of undesirable microorganisms.Thus, a first aspect of the invention is a fertilizer composition for plant production comprised of decontaminated manure and Bacillus spores, and preferably humic acid and, optionally, one or more of N compounds, P compounds, K compounds, and combinations of two or more of these compounds (for example two N compounds, an N compound with a P compound, two K compounds, or one each of N compound, P compound, and K compound). Preferred compositions are those wherein the ingredients are blended into an admixture resulting in a granular product. Other preferred compositions are those blended into an admixture resulting in a powdered product. Preferably, the ingredients are formed into hardened pellets. The decontaminated manure is preferably derived from manure selected from the group consisting chicken or swine manure, particularly produced without litter or bedding, and produced from animals not receiving growth-promoting antibiotics in their feed. Other preferred compositions of the invention are those wherein the Bacillus spores are from strains of probiotic Bacillus bacteria capable of enhancing beneficial microbial populations within the rhizosphere. Preferably, the decontaminated manure has a total aerobic/facultative viable plate count reduced by 2-4 logs (100 to 10,000 times) compared to raw manure. Yet other preferred compositions of the invention are those wherein the humic acid is derived from lignite.

As used herein, "humic acid" means a polymeric compound typically containing the brownish-black pigment melanin, and can be obtained from lignite. It is soluble in bases, but insoluble in mineral acids and alcohols. It is not a well-defined compound, but a mixture of polymers containing aromatic and heterocyclic strictures, carboxyl groups, and nitrogen, and is used in drilling fluids, printing inks, and plant growth. See Hawley's Condensed Chemical Dictionary, 12th Edition, (1 993), page 608. As seen in the examples herein, not all humic acids behave in similar fashion. Still other preferred compositions of the invention are those wherein the N compounds are selected from the group consisting of urea, ammonium sulfate, ammonium nitrate, ammonium phosphate, calcium nitrate, potassium nitrate, sodium nitrate; the P compounds are selected from the group consisting of ammonium phosphate, superphosphate, Ca(H2P04)2, tricalcium phosphate, phosphate salts of sodium or potassium, including orthophosphate salts; and the K compounds are selected from the group consisting of KCl, potassium sulfate, potassium nitrate, and phosphate salts of potassium, including orthophosphate salts.

Preferred compositions of the invention are those wherein the decontaminated manure has a total aerobic/facultative viable plate count reduced by 2-4 logs (100 to 10,000 times) compared to raw manure. Still other preferred compositions of the invention are those wherein the N compounds are selected from the group consisting of urea, ammonium sulfate, ammonium nitrate, ammonium phosphate, calcium nitrate, potassium nitrate, sodium nitrate; the P compounds are selected from the group consisting of ammonium phosphate, superphosphate, Ca(H2P04)2, tricalcium phosphate, phosphate salts of sodium or potassium, including orthophosphate salts; and the K compounds are selected from the group consisting of KCl, potassium sulfate, potassium nitrate, and phosphate salts of potassium, including orthophosphate salts.

Decontaminated manures are prepared by methods known in US patent zzzz. The fertilizer is prepared by mixing decontaminated manures and other ingredients as discussed above and a suitable amount Bacillus spores. Preferred compositions of the invention are those wherein the decontaminated manure has a total aerobic/facultative viable plate count reduced by 2-4 logs (100 to 10,000 times) compared to raw manure.

Ans. Please refer to Patent No. US20050235717A1

Fertilizer compositions and methods of making and using same

Abstract

Fertilizer compositions for plant production are described, comprised of decontaminated manure and Bacillus spores, preferably a humic acid derived from lignite and, optionally, one or more of N compounds, P compounds, K compounds, and combinations of two or more of these compounds. Preferred compositions are those wherein the ingredients are blended into an admixture resulting in a granular product. Other preferred compositions are those blended into an admixture resulting in a powdered product. Preferably, the ingredients are formed into hardened prills or pellets. Processes for production and use are also presented.

Claims (5)

I claim:

1. A method of making a fertilizer composition comprising decontaminated manure and Bacillus spores, humic acid and one or more of N, P, K compounds and combinations thereof.

2. A fertilizer composition as claimed in claim 1 where ingradients are treated resulting in granular or powdered product.

3. A fertilizer composition as claimed in claim 1 where ingradients are treated resulting preferably in hardened pellets.

4. A fertilizer composition as claimed in claim 1 where decontaminated manure is derived from animals not receiving growth promoting antibiotics in their feed.

5. A fertilizer composition as claimed in claim 1 where bacillus spores are from strains of probiotic bacillus bacteria capable of enhancing beneficial microbial populations within rhizosphere.

OR

Q.9

This invention relates to new and useful improvements in lawn sprinklers, and has as its principal object. The provision of a lawn sprinkler com prising a sprinkler head mounted on a wheeled frame and attached to a

pressure water supply; and having means operable by the pressure of the supply water to propel said wheeled frame over the ground.

Another object is the provision in a lawn sprinkler of the character described wherein the sprinkler head rotates to distribute water evenly over a wide area, and wherein said propelling means operates mechanically from the rotation of said head.

A further object is the provision of a lawn sprinkler of the class described wherein said propelling means operates by traction in an elongated member, which may be the water supply hose; laid out on the ground. The frame is steerable, so as to follow the elongated member around curves. Other objects are simplicity and economy of construction, efficiency and dependability of operation, and adaptability for uses other than the watering of lawns.

With these objects in view, as well as other objects which will appear in the course of the specification, reference will be to the drawing, wherein:

Fig. 1 is a side elevational view of a lawn sprinkler embodying the present invention, shown in operative relationship to a water supply hose,

Fig. 2 is a plan view of the parts as shown in Fig. 1,

Fig. 3 is an enlarged plan view of the sprinkler,

Numerals 22,26,28,34,36,50,52,54,56,58 &60 mentioned in the description are not shown in the figures.

Like reference numerals apply to similar parts throughout the several views, and the numeral 2 applies to a frame formed of sheet metal and having generally the form of a hollow rectilinear box. It has a top wall 4 and depending side walls 6, front wall 8, and rear wall 10, and is open at the bottom. It is supported at each of its forward corners by a ground engaging wheel 12 rotatably mounted on a stub axle 14 fixed in the adjacent side wall 6, and at each of its rearward corners by a caster wheel 16, whereby the frame is rendered steerable.

Carried on top wall 4 of the frame, adjacent the forward edge thereof, is a sprinkler head 18. Said sprinkler head includes a vertical tubular body member 20 closed at its upper end and threaded at its lower end to a pipe 22, extending upwardly through said wall. Said body and pipe are fixed relative to the frame by a nut 24 threaded on said pipe below wall 4. Body member 20 is provided adjacent its upper end with a plurality of apertures 26, and at its upper end with a threaded axial extension 28, mounted rotatably on said extension and secured thereon by nut 30, is an inverted cup-shaped member 32 the depending skirt of which is disposed concentrically about body 20 and is of larger diameter than said body member whereby to form a chamber 34 there between. At its lower end member 32 is provided with a sealing ring 36 which engages body member 20 to seal chamber 34, and with an external circular flange 38 which is disposed eccentrically to the axis of body member 20. Flange 38 serves as a cam as will be fully described below. Fixed in the skirt portion of member 32, in communicating relation with chamber 34, are a plurality of upwardly and outwardly inclined tubes 40; at the outer end of each of which is mounted a nozzle 42. It will be noted in Figs. 2 and 3 that the nozzles are angled to direct streams of water substantially tangentially to the orbit of the nozzles, in the same relative angular direction. Hence when water under pressure is delivered to sprinkler head 18 through pipe 22, it passes outwardly through holes 26 of body 20 into chamber 34 and hence through tubes 40 to nozzles 42. There active force of the streams leaving the nozzles causes cup 32 of the head to rotate, this rotation being clockwise as shown although the direction of rotation is immaterial. This rotation distributes the water evenly over a relatively large ground area, and also causes rotation of cam flange38, which operates the frame propelling mechanism to be described below. Pipe 22 extends horizontally and rearwardly just below frame wall 4 and extends through rear wall 10, being secured therein by a pair of nuts 44. A flexible water supply hose 46 is secured to the outwardly extended end of said pipe by a suitable coupling 48; the hose is then looped as shown in Figs. 1 and 2 and passed beneath the frame 2 parallel to the line of travel thereof. The hose is then lifted from the ground and laid over a pair of rollers and 52 carried rotatably at the inner face of rear wall 10 and front wall 8 respectively, said rollers being mounted on axles fixed to said frame walls by brackets 54. Said rear and front frame walls are each provided with an inverted J-shaped notch 56 through which the hose may be moved transversely to engage the associated roller, and which serves to hold the hose centered over said roller. Intermediate rollers 50 and 52, the hose is gripped between a pair of drive wheels 58, each of said wheels having a thick soft rubber facing 60 whereby to grip the hose frictionally. The drive wheel faces AES Aan TRE Chita llon ML. on He DER Ae Rb are concave whereby to conform closely to the hose. However, the wheel facings are sufficiently yieldable that the hose may be crowded there between. Each of the drive wheels is fixed on a vertical shaft 62 which extends upwardly through top frame wall 4 and is journal led in a bearing member 64 affixed to said frame wall. To the upper end of each of shafts 62, above wall 4, is affixed a ratchet wheel 66. Ratchet wheels 66 are operated by a cam follower mechanism including a bar 68 disposed horizontally above frame wall 4 and carried slidably in a pair of brackets 70 fixed to said frame wall. Said bar is movable longitudinally along a line intersecting the axis of sprinkler head 18 and passing between ratchet wheels 66. It is provided at its forward end with an upright finger 72 which bears slidably against the rim of flange cam 38 of the sprinkler head, and which is urged slildably against said cam by a coil spring 74 encircling bar 68. Said spring bears at one end against one of brackets 70, and at its opposite end against a pin 76 inserted transversely through bar 68. At its rearward end, a pair of leaf springs 78 is affixed to bar 68, and extend rearwardly therefrom. Said springs extend between ratchet wheels 66, and are tensioned outwardly so that each spring engages in the teeth of one of the ratchet wheels, as best shown in Fig. 3.

Thus it will be seen that as sprinkler head 18 rotates as previously described, cam 38 thereof will rotate and urge cam follower bar 68 rearwardly against spring 74, and leaf springs 78, acting as pawls, will turn ratchet wheels 66 in the direction indicated by the arrows in transversely to ride over the ratchet teeth as the bar 68 is moved rearwardly by spring 74. The rotation of ratchet wheels 66 of course also turns drive wheels 58, and since the drive wheels are in frictional engagement with the hose, the frame is pulled forwardly along the hose. The hose may be laid out on the ground ahead of the sprinkler in any desired pattern, so long as any curves therein are of sufficiently large radius, and the frame will follow the hose. In this manner, even an irregularly shaped lawn may be watered thoroughly and evenly without necessity of attendance on the sprinkler.

It has been found that the work which must be performed by the frame in lifting the hose from the ground applies a braking force to the frame sufficient to prevent the frame from coasting forwardly by gravity, which could occur if the ratchet wheels overran the pawls 78, on any slope usually encountered in lawns. The ratchet wheels are secured against following pawls 78 on their retracting stroke, which could otherwise occur particularly on up slopes, by a pair of dogs 80 pivotally mounted on a bolt 82 fixed in frame wall 4 and engaging respectively the two ratchet wheels 66 (Fig. 3). Said dogs are urged yieldably into engagement with said ratchet wheels by a coil spring 84 disposed on bolt 82 and having its end portions extended to engage said dogs intermediate their ends.

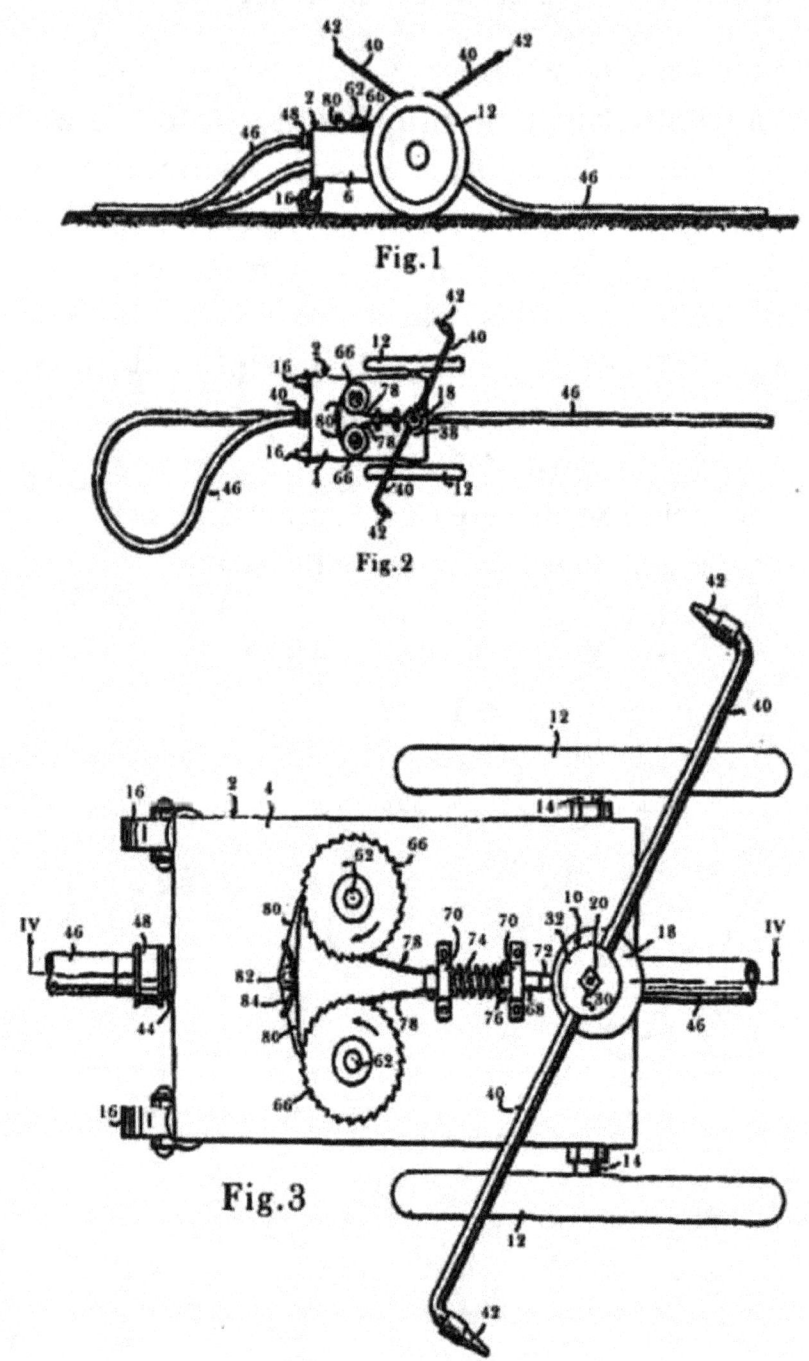

Fig.1

Fig.2

Fig.3

Ans. Please refer to Patent no. US2795459A.

Title: Lawn Sprinkler with Self-Propelling Mechanism

Abstract: A lawn sprinkler comprising a sprinkler head mounted on a wheeled frame and attached to a pressure water supply. The sprinkler head rotates to distribute water evenly over a wide area, and its rotation propels the wheeled frame over the ground by means of a mechanical mechanism that operates from the pressure of the supply water. The sprinkler is designed to follow a flexible water supply hose laid out on the ground, and is steerable to negotiate curves. The hose is also used for the sprinkler's propulsion, and its lifting from the ground by the frame results in a braking force that prevents the sprinkler from coasting downhill.

CLAIMS:

I claim:

Claim 1: A lawn sprinkler comprising a sprinkler head, a wheeled frame, and a flexible water supply hose laid out on the ground.

Claim 2: The lawn sprinkler of claim 1, wherein the mechanical mechanism is a pair of ratchet wheels operated by a cam follower bar and a pair of pawls.

Claim 3: The lawn sprinkler of claim 1, wherein the sprinkler head comprises an inverted cup-shaped member with a concentrically disposed depending skirt that forms a chamber with a plurality of upwardly and outwardly inclined tubes.

Claim 4: The lawn sprinkler of claim 1, wherein the frame is formed of sheet metal and has a hollow rectilinear box shape with a top wall and depending side walls, a front wall, and a rear wall.

Claim 5: The lawn sprinkler of claim 1, wherein the water supply hose is passed over a pair of rollers mounted on axles fixed to the front and rear frame walls, which are each provided with an inverted J-shaped notch through which the hose may be moved transversely to engage the associated roller and to hold the hose centered over it.

Part C2

A client meets you and provides technical information regarding his invention. Draft a complete specification (with at least one claim and title) for any one of the following descriptions, for filing in the Indian Patent Office. While preparing the complete specification, do not redraw the figures. However, you may refer to the figures in the specification as Fig. 1, Fig. 2 and Fig. 3 etc.

1X30 M =30 marks

Q.10. **This invention relates to a composition and oral pharmaceutical dosage form for selective delivery of drugs to the colon. More particularly, the invention relates to compositions and oral pharmaceutical dosage forms for release of biologically active ingredients in the colon while avoiding or minimizing release into the upper gastrointestinal tract, such the stomach and small intestine. Numerous drug entities based on oral delivery have been successfully commercialized, but many others are not readily available by oral administration, which are incompatible with the physical and/or chemical environments of the upper Gl tract and/or demonstrate poor uptake in the upper Gl tract. Due to the lack of digestive enzymes, colon is considered a suitable site for the absorption of various drugs. However, colon drug delivery is hardly achieved in that the oral dosage form should pass through the stomach and small intestine, where many drugs are deactivated by their digestive materials. Ideally, a colon specific drug delivery system is designed such that it remains intact in stomach and small intestine but releases encapsulated drugs only in colon. CSDS system is useful in administering a drug that is an irritant to the upper Gl tract, such as non-steroidal anti-inflammatory agents, or drugs that are degraded by gastric juice or an enzyme present in the upper Gl tract, such as peptide or protein. Further, the colonic drug delivery system allows local, direct treatment of colonic disease, e.g., ulcerative colitis, Crohn's disease, or colon cancer, thus reducing the dosage of the drugs and minimizing undesirable or harmful side effects. Similarly, colonic drug delivery is useful for administering drugs, e.g. non-steroidal anti-inflammatory drugs (NSAIDS), which are irritants to the mucosa of the upper gastrointestinal tract such as the stomach or small intestine. Recently, it is believed that colonic drug delivery systems maintain the efficacy of drugs for a longer time and increase the bioavailability of the drugs as compared to other oral routes of** administration. As the colon has a longer retention time, drug absorption is prolonged, and total bioavailability is increased. The present invention comprises a mixture, prepared at a pH of about 7 or above, without use of a cross-linking agent, of a galactomannan and a polysaccharide, preferably pectin, selected from the group consisting of pectin, derivatives of pectin, and mixtures thereof. The composition forms a strong elastic gel that is not appreciably dissolved or disintegrated in gastric or intestinal fluids, thus protecting drugs from being released in the upper GI tract. When the composition arrives in the colon, the composition is easily degraded by synergic effect of pectinolytic enzymes and glactomannanase, thus releasing drugs rapidly in the colon. The ratio of the two polysaccharides determines the rate of enzymatic degradation of the composition and disintegration of dosage form through GI tract, which in turn enables the composition to release the drug site specifically in the colon.

The pharmaceutical composition of the present invention comprises an effective amount of a drug, diagnostic reagent, or mixture thereof, and a polysaccharide mixture formed in an aqueous medium at a pH of about 7 or above of (a) a polysaccharide selected from the group consisting of pectin, derivatives of pectin, and mixture thereof, and (b) galactomannan, without use of a cross-linking agent. The drug is an antimigraine, antinauseant, antineoplastic, antiparkinsonism, antipruritic, antipsychotic, antipyretic, antispasmodic, anticholinergic, sympathomimetic, xanthine derivative, potassium channel blocker, calcium channel blocker, beta-blocker, alpha-blocker or other drugs. The weight ratio of polysaccharide: galactomannan is from about 50:50 to about 99.9:0.1 in the composition. The weight ratio of polysaccharide:galactomannan is from about 66.6:33.4 to about 90:10.

The drug as used in the pharmaceutical composition may be selected from the group consisting of mesalamine, balsalazide, olsalazine, ibuprofen, prednisolone, dexamethasone, budesonide, beclomethasone, flucticasone, tioxocortal, hydrocortisone, metronidazole, cyclosporin, methotrexate, domperidone, 5-fluorouracil, bisacodyl, senna, insulin, vasopressin, growth hormones, colony stimulating factors, calcitonin, immunoglobulin, glibenclimide, diltiazem, verapamil, nifedipine, captopril, benazepril, enalapril, theophylline, naxopren, diclofenac, acyclovir, omeprazole, lovastatin, alendronate, desmopressin, metformin, metoprolol, cisapride, tacrine, mixtures thereof and probiotics.

In the pharmaceutical composition of the invention the drug, diagnostic reagent, of mixture thereof may be used in the form of a tablet, a pill, a seed, or a capsule formulation and may be coated coated with said polysaccharide mixture to form a coated formulation. The coating may be 1-100 mg/cm2in size. In a preferred embodiment the coating is 1-40 mg/cm2 in size.

The drug, diagnostic reagent, or mixture thereof is encapsulated with a shell composed of said polysaccharide mixture to form a hard capsule formulation. The said shell is 1-100 pm in thickness. Most desired thickness of the shell is 1-40 um in thickness. A method for preparing the colon selective pharmaceutical composition for oral delivery of a drug, diagnostic reagent, or mixture thereof comprising forming a polysaccharide mixture in an aqueous medium at a pH of about 7 or above of (a) a polysaccharide selected from the group consisting of pectin, derivatives of pectin, and mixtures thereof, and (b) galactomannan, without use of a cross- linking agent, and contacting the polysaccharide mixture with a drug, diagnostic regent or mixture thereof.

Ans. Please refer to Patent no. US6413494B1

Title - Composition and pharmaceutical dosage form for colonic drug delivery using polysaccharides

Abstract : A colonic drug delivery composition contains a first polysac charide and a Second polysaccharide wherein both polysac charide are degradable by colonic enzymes and are mixed at a environmental pH of about 7 or above, without use of a croSS-linking agent. A colon Selective pharmaceutical com position and dosage form for oral delivery of a drug, diagnostic reagent, or mixture thereof includes the drug, diagnostic reagent, or mixture thereof in contact with the polysaccharide composition. A method of preparing Such a colonic drug delivery composition and the colon Selective pharmaceutical composition and dosage from are also dis closed.

FIELD OF THE INVENTION

This invention relates to a composition and oral pharmaceutical dosage form for selective delivery of drugs to the colon. More particularly, the invention relates to compositions and oral pharmaceutical dosage forms for release of biologically active ingredients in the colon while avoiding or minimizing release into the upper gastrointestinal tract, such the stomach and small intestine.

BACKGROUND OF THE INVENTION

Numerous drug entities based on oral delivery have been successfully commercialized, but many others are not readily available by oral administration, which are incompatible with the physical and/or chemical environments of the upper GI tract and/or demonstrate poor uptake in the upper GI tract. Due to the lack of digestive enzymes, colon is considered a suitable site for the absorption of various drugs. However, colon drug delivery is hardly achieved in that the oral dosage form should pass through the stomach and small intestine, where many drugs are deactivated by their digestive materials. Ideally, a colon specific drug delivery system is designed such that it remains intact in stomach and small intestine but releases encapsulated drugs only in colon. CSDS system is useful in administering a drug that is an irritant to the upper GI tract, such as non-steroidal anti-inflammatory agents, or drugs that are degraded by gastric juice or an enzyme present in the upper GI tract, such as peptide or protein. Further, the colonic drug delivery system allows local, direct treatment of colonic disease, e.g., ulcerative colitis, Crohn's disease, or colon cancer, thus reducing the dosage of the drugs and minimizing undesirable or harmful side effects. Similarly, colonic drug delivery is useful for administering drugs, e.g. non-steroidal anti-inflammatory drugs (NSAIDS), which are irritants to the mucosa of the upper gastrointestinal tract such as the stomach or small intestine. Recently, it is believed that colonic drug delivery systems maintain the efficacy of drugs for a longer time and increase the bioavailability of the drugs as compared to other oral routes of administration.

BRIEF SUMMARY OF THE INVENTION

An object of the present invention is to provide a composition and pharmaceutical dosage form for delivering a drug, wherein such dosage form is orally-administered for specifically delivering the drug to the colon of a subject in need thereof.

Another object of the invention is to provide a composition and pharmaceutical dosage form for colonic drug delivery that is not degraded or disintegrated in the upper GI tract.

Still another object of the invention is to provide a composition and pharmaceutical dosage form for delivering an orally-administered drug is that is inactivated in the upper GI tract, wherein the dosage form is in a form that passes through the upper GI tract and then releases the drug in the colon of a human subject in need thereof.

Yet another object of the invention is to provide a composition and pharmaceutical dosage form for colonic drug delivery that releases the drug rapidly and effectively at the target site, the colon, and minimizes adverse systemic effects to a subject being treated.

Another object of the invention is to provide a composition and pharmaceutical dosage form for colonic drug delivery that is easy to formulate in a form suitable for loading the drug to be delivered.

One aspect of this invention is a composition and pharmaceutical dosage form designed for delivering an orally administered drug to the colon. The composition passes through the upper GI tract without releasing the drug, but the drug is rapidly and effectively released at the target site in the colon, more especially in the ascending colon, minimizing adverse systemic effects to a human subject being treated. The composition comprises a mixture, prepared at a pH of about 7 or above, without use of a cross-linking agent, of a galactomannan and a polysaccharide, preferably pectin, selected from the group consisting of pectin, derivatives of pectin, and mixtures thereof. The composition forms a strong elastic gel that is not appreciably dissolved or disintegrated in gastric or intestinal fluids, thus protecting drugs from being released in the upper GI tract.

DETAILED DESCRIPTION OF THE INVENTION

Before the present composition and method for colonic drug delivery are disclosed and described, it is to be understood that this invention is not limited to the particular configurations, process steps, and materials disclosed herein as such configurations, process steps, and materials may vary somewhat. It is also to be understood that terminology employed herein is used for the purpose of describing particular embodiments only and is not intended to be limiting since the scope of the present invention will be limited only by the appended claims and equivalents thereof.

In must be noted that, as used in this specification and the appended claims, the singular forms "a," "an," and "the" include plural referents unless the context clearly dictates otherwise. Thus, for example, reference to a composition containing "a galactomannan" includes a mixture of one or more galactomannans, reference to "a pectin salt" includes reference to one or more of such pectin salts, and reference to "a coating" includes reference one or more of such coatings.

In describing and claiming the present invention, the following terminology will be used in accordance with the definitions set out herein.

As used herein, "colon-specific drug delivery system" and similar terms mean devices and methods for oral administration that release biologically active ingredients in the colon without substantial release into the upper gastrointestinal tract, e.g. stomach and intestine.

As used herein, the term "drug" or "pharmacologically active agent" or any other similar term means any chemical or biological material or compound suitable for administration by the methods previously known in the art and/or by the methods taught in the present invention, that induces a desired biological or pharmacological effect, which may include but is not limited to (1) having a prophylactic effect on the organism and preventing an undesired biological effect such as preventing an infection, (2) alleviating a condition caused by a disease, for example, alleviating pain or inflammation caused as a result of disease, and/or (3) either alleviating, reducing, or completely eliminating the disease from the organism. The effect may be local, such as providing for a local anaesthetic effect, or it may be systemic. This invention is not drawn to novel drugs or to new classes of active agents. Rather it is limited to the mode of delivery of agents of drugs that exist in the state of the art or that may later be established as active agents and that are suitable for delivery by the present invention. Such substances include broad classes of compounds normally delivered into the body. In general, this includes but is not limited to: antiinfectives such as antibiotics and antiviral agents; analgesics and analgesic combinations; antimigraine preparations; antinauseants ;antineoplastics; antiparkinsonism drugs; antipruritics; antipsychotics; antipyretics; antispasmodics; anticholinergics; sympathomimetics; xanthine derivatives; cardiovascular preparations including potassium and calcium channel blockers, beta-blockers, alpha-blockers, and antiarrhythmics;

As used herein, "nutrient" means a substance that affects the nutritive or metabolic processes of the body. Nutrients include essential nutrients, i.e. those nutrients such as proteins, minerals, carbohydrates, fats, and vitamins necessary for growth, normal functioning, and maintaining life, and secondary nutrients, i.e. substances that stimulate the intestinal microflora to synthesize other nutrients.

As used herein, "diagnostic reagent" means a substance used to produce a chemical reaction so as to detect or measure another substance.

As used herein, 'derivatives of pectin' and similar terms includes cation salts of pectin such as sodium pectinate, potassium pectinate, and ammonium pectinate, and the like.

As used herein, 'effective amount' means an amount of a drug or pharmacologically active agent that is nontoxic but sufficient to provide the desired local or systemic effect and performance at a reasonable benefit/risk ratio attending any medical treatment. An effective amount of a nutrient is an amount sufficient to provide a selected nutritive benefit. An effective amount of a diagnostic reagent is an amount sufficient to be efficacious in a selected diagnostic test or assay.

The present invention relates to a colonic drug delivery composition comprising a mixture of (a) a polysaccharide selected from the group consisting of pectin, derivatives of pectin, and mixtures thereof, and (b) galactomannan. The mixture is made by combining the ingredients in an aqueous medium at a pH of about 7 or above.

In a preferred embodiment of the invention, the composition comprises (a) pectin or a derivative of pectin or a mixture thereof and (b) galactomannan. The composition is prepared at a pH of about 7 or above. The ratio of ingredients is limited only by functionality. Preferably, however, the composition has a polysaccharide: galactomannan weight ratio of about 50:50 to about 99.9:0.01, more specifically, about 2:1 to about 5:1. A coating prepared with the instantly claimed composition will generally have a mass to area ratio in the range of about 1-100 mg/cm2, and preferably about 1-40 mg/cm2. A hard capsule shell will generally have a thickness of about 1-100 μm, preferably 1-40 μm.

Illustrative example of drugs is a member Selected from the group consisting of Salamine, balsala Zide, olSalazine, ibuprofen, prednisolone, dexamethasone, budeSonide, beclomethasone, flucticasone, tioXocortal, hydrocortisone, metronidazole, cycloSporin, methotrexate, domperidone, 5-fluorouracil, bisacodyl, Senna, insulin, Vasopressin, growth hormones, colony Stimulating factors, calcitonin, immunoglobulin, glibenclimide, diltiazem, Verapamil, nifedipine, captopril, benazepril, enalapril, theophylline, naxopren, diclofenac, acyclovir, omeprazole, lova Statin, a lendronate, deSmopressin, metformin, metoprolol, cisapride, tacrine, mixtures thereof and probiotics.

The composition and the dosage form of this invention is not limited to the above mention embodiments, and modification may be made thereto by a person skilled in the art. The invention may be explained by the representative examples, which are provided only for the purpose of illustrating certain aspects of the present invention. Therefore, they are not to be construed as limiting the scope of the present invention in any way.

Claims

I claim:

1. A pharmaceutical composition comprising an effective amount of a drug, diagnostic reagent, or mixture thereof, and a polysaccharide mixture formed in

an aqueous medium at a pH of about 7 or above of (a) a polysaccharide selected from the group consisting of pectin, derivatives of pectin, and mixture thereof, and (b) galactomannan, without use of a croSS-linking agent, wherein the drug is an antiinfective, analgesic, anotexic, helminthic, antimigraine, antinauseant, antineoplastic, antiparkinsonism, antipruritic, antipsychotic, antipyretic, antiSpaS modic, anticho linergic, Sympathomimetic, Xanthine derivative, potassium channel blocker, calcium channel blocker, beta-blocker, alpha blocker, antiarrhythmic or a combination thereof.

2. The composition of claim 1 wherein Said polysaccha ride is pectin. 3. The composition of claim 1 wherein the weight ratio of polysaccharide:galactomannan is from about 50:50 to about 99.9:0.1

4. The composition of claim 3 wherein the weight ratio of polysaccharide:galactomannan is from about 66.6:33.4 to about 90:10.

5. A pharmaceutical composition comprising an effective amount of a drug, diagnostic reagent, or mixture thereof in contact with a composition consisting essentially of a polysaccharide mixture formed in an aqueous medium at a pH of about 7 or above of (a) a polysaccharide selected form the group consisting of pectin, derivatives of pectin, and mixtures thereof, and (b) galactomannan, without use of a croSS-linking agent, wherein the drug is an antiinfective, analgesic, anorexic, helminthic, antimigraine, antinauseant, antineoplastic, antiparkinsonism, antipruritic, antipsychotic, antipyretic, antiSpaS modic, anticho linergic, Sympathomimetic, Xanthine derivative, potassium channel blocker, calcium channel blocker, beta-blocker, alpha blocker, antiarrhythmic, antihypertensive, diuretic, antidiuretic, or a combination thereof.

6. The pharmaceutical composition of claim 5 wherein Said polysaccharide is pectin.

7. The pharmaceutical composition of claim 5 wherein the weight ratio of polysaccharide:galactomannan is from 50:50 to 99.9:0.1.

8. The pharmaceutical composition of claim 7 wherein the weight ratio of polysaccharide:galactomannan is from 66.6:33.4 to 90:10.

9. The pharmaceutical composition of claim 5 wherein Said drug is a member Selected from the group consisting of Salamine, balsala Zide, olSalazine, ibuprofen, prednisolone, dexamethasone, budeSonide, beclomethasone, flucticasone, tioXocortal, hydrocortisone, metronidazole, cycloSporin, methotrexate, domperidone, 5-fluorouracil, bisacodyl, Senna, insulin, Vasopressin, growth hormones, colony Stimulating factors, calcitonin, immunoglobulin, glibenclimide, diltiazem, Verapamil, nifedipine, captopril, benazepril, enalapril, theophylline, naxopren, diclofenac, acyclovir, omeprazole, lova Statin, a lendronate, deSmopressin, metformin, metoprolol, cisapride, tacrine, mixtures thereof and probiotics.

OR

Q.11. The present invention relates to a cycle tyre tool and more specifically to a tool for removing tyres from the wheels of cycles namely monocycles, bicycles and tricycles . Tyres are normally removed from cycle wheels by means of three tyre levers which are used to lever the bead of the tyre over the rim of the cycle wheel. A problem arises in the use of tyre levers for this purpose in that there is a very real danger of trapping the inner tube between the lever and the bead of the tyre and thus damaging the inner tube. The object of the present invention is to provide a tool that enables tyres to be removed very readily while assisting in avoiding damage to the inner tube.

Fig. 1 is a perspective view of a tool according to the invention;

Fig. 2 is a longitudinal section thereof showing the parts of the tool; and

Figs. 3 and 4 illustrate the manner in which the tool is used.

The tool, in a preferred form, consists of a handle 10 into which fits a shaft 11. The shaft 11 is free to rotate in the handle 10 but is restrained against axial movement by the press-on claw clip 12. At the free end of the shaft is a roller member 13 that is fixed at the end of the shaft 11. On the portion of the shaft 11 projecting from the handle 10 is a sleeve 14 that is rotatable on the shaft 11.

In an alternative construction (not illustrated) the sleeve 14 is omitted and the roller member 13 is rotatably mounted on the shaft 11. In use for removing a tyre the tool is held in the hand of the user and the roller 13 is inserted between the rim of the wheel and the bead of the tyre, as shown in Fig. 3, after the inner tube 15 has been fully deflated. The blunt end presented by the roller 13 serves to push the inner tube 15 out of the path of the tool as it enters between the rim and the bead. Once the tool is fully entered the handle is depressed, as shown in Fig. 4, so that the bead 17 is forced upwardly and outwardly in relation to the rim. The tool is then rolled around the circumference of the rim 16 with the sleeve 14 resting on the rim 16 and the roller 13 resting against the inside of the tyre 19 adjacent the bead 17 (as shown in Fig. 4). It will, however, be appreciated that the sleeve 14 and the roller 13 will be rotating at different speeds due to their making contact respectively with the rim 16 and the tyre 19 at different distances from the centre of the wheel 20. It is thus necessary that the sleeve shall be rotatable relative to the handle and the roller 13 rotatable relative to the sleeve. The tool may also be used for replacing the tyre by reversing the steps described above after slightly inflating the inner tube 15.

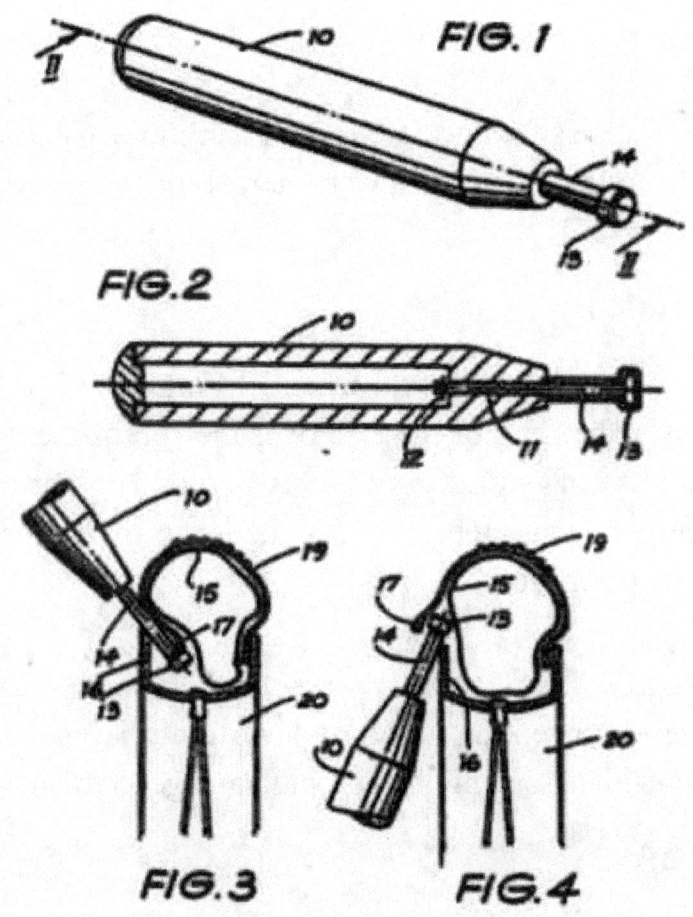

FIG. 1

FIG.2

FIG.3   FIG.4

Ans. Please refer to **Patent No. WO1990012697A1.**

Title- Cycle tyre tool

Abstract

A cycle tyre tool for removing tyres from cycle wheels consisting of a handle, a shaft or sleeve rotatable relative to the handle and projecting therefrom and, at the free end of the shaft or sleeve, a roller member shaped and constructed for insertion between the bead of a cycle tyre and the rim of a cycle wheel and

144

engagement with the bead, the roller member being freely rotatable in relation to both the sleeve and the handle.

Technical Field

The present invention relates to a cycle tyre tool and more specifically to a tool for removing tyres from the wheels of cycles namely monocycles, bicycles and tricycles.

Background of Invention:

Tyres are normally removed from cycle wheels by means of three tyre levers which are used to lever the bead of the tyre over the rim of the cycle wheel. A problem arises in the use of tyre levers for this purpose in that there is a very real danger of trapping the inner tube between the lever and the bead of the tyre and thus damaging the inner tube.

Object of invention:

The object of the present invention is to provide a tool that enables tyres to be removed very readily while assisting in avoiding damage to the inner tube.

Detailed Description:

The present invention consists in a cycle tyre tool for removing tyres from cycle wheels consisting of a handle, a shaft or sleeve rotatable relative to the handle and projecting therefrom and, at the free end of the shaft or sleeve, a roller member shaped and constructed for insertion between the bead of a cycle tyre and the rim of a cycle wheel and engagement with the bead, the roller member being freely rotatable in relation to both the sleeve and the handle. In order that the nature of the invention may be better understood a preferred embodiment thereof is hereinafter described by way of example with reference to the accompanying drawings in which:-

Brief Description of Drawings:

Fig. 1 is a perspective view of a tool according to the invention;

Pig. 2 is a longitudinal section thereof showing the parts of the tool; and

Figs. 3 and 4 illustrate the manner in which the tool is used. The tool, in a preferred form, consists of a handle 10 into which fits a shaft 11. The shaft 11 is free to rotate in the handle 10 but is restrained against axial movement by the press-on claw clip 12.

At the free end of the shaft is a roller member 13 that is fixed at the end of the shaft 11. On the portion of the shaft 11 projecting from the handle 10 is a sleeve 14 that is rotatable on the shaft 11.

In an alternative construction (not illustrated) the sleeve 14 is omitted and the roller member 13 is rotatably mounted on the shaft 11.

In use for removing a tyre the tool is held in the hand of the user and the roller 13 is inserted between the rim of the wheel and the bead of the tyre, as shown in Fig. 3, after the inner tube 15 has been fully deflated. The blunt end presented by the roller 13 serves to push the inner tube 15 out of the path of the tool as it enters between the rim and the bead.

Once the tool is fully entered the handle is depressed, as shown in Fig. 4, so that the bead 17 is forced upwardly and outwardly in relation to the rim. The tool is then rolled around the circumference of the rim 16 with the sleeve 14 resting on the rim 16 and the roller 13 resting against the inside of the tyre 19 adjacent the bead 17 (as shown in Fig. 4). It will, however, be appreciated that the sleeve 14 and the roller 13 will be rotating at different speeds due to their making contact respectively with the rim 16 and the tyre 19 at different distances from the centre of the wheel 20. It is thus necessary that the sleeve shall be rotatable relative to the handle and the roller 13 rotatable relative to the sleeve.

The tool may also be used for replacing the tyre by reversing the steps described above after slightly inflating the inner tube 15.

The construction described is given by way of example only as constituting a preferred form of the invention within the broad scope thereof as defined in the succeeding claims.

CLAIMS:

I claim:

1. A cycle tyre tool for removing tyres from cycle wheels consisting of a handle, a shaft or sleeve rotatable relative to the handle and projecting therefrom and, at the free end of the shaft or sleeve, a roller member shaped and constructed for insertion between the bead of a cycle tyre and the rim of a cycle wheel and engagement with the bead, the roller member being freely rotatable in relation to both the sleeve and the handle.

PATENT AGENT EXAMINATION, 2013

(Under Section 126 of the Patents Act, 1970)

4th May 2013

PAPER II

Total Marks: 100

Time: 2.30 p.m. to 5.30 p.m.

Three hours

Instructions:

ALL questions in Part A are compulsory.

This paper consists of 2 parts — Part A (40 marks) & Part B (60 marks).

Part A consists of 4 questions of 10 marks each.

Part B comprises two sections - Part B1 and B2, of 30 marks each. Part B1 consists of 2 questions and you are required to answer any 1 of them. Part B2 also consists of 2 questions and you are required to answer any 1 of them. In case a candidate answers more questions than required, the first attempted question will be evaluated.

Candidates should read the questions very carefully before answering.

No clarification will be provided during the course of the examination.

There is no negative marking.

PART A

4 x 10 =40 marks

Rupa, a textile designer with a 'Design House' in Mumbai having branch offices in various parts of the world, wishes to obtain patent protection in 50 different countries for smart textiles invented by her. Foreign buyers prefer

to deal with inventor/applicants who have filed their patent applications in Europe as basic applications i.e. the first application to be filed on the subject matter. She also wishes to file a set of patent applications in Europe with varying priority dates. Rupa has approached you as her Patent Agent in India to help her in her mission. Provide a note to her outlining the strategy she ought to follow alongwith information on various processes / routes involved and the timelines involved. How would you also deal with the multiple priorities?

Ans.1.

To file patent applications for smart textiles in 50 different countries with different priority dates, Rupa can consider the following strategy:

File a PCT application: Rupa can file an international patent application under the Patent Cooperation Treaty (PCT). This application will have a uniform filing date (priority date) and will provide protection in over 150 countries.

Or alternatively, she may opt for Convention Application:

Section 137 of Patents Act: Multiple priorities;

(1) Where two or more applications for patents in respect of inventions have been made in one or more convention countries and those inventions are so related as to constitute one invention, one application may be made by any or all of the persons referred to in sub-section (1) of section 135 within twelve months from the date on which the earlier or earliest of those applications was made, in respect of the inventions disclosed in the specifications which accompanied the basic applications.

(2) The priority date of a claim of the complete specification, being a claim based on matters disclosed in one or more of the basic applications, is the date on which that matter was first so disclosed.

(3) For the purposes of this Act, a matter shall be deemed to have been disclosed in a basic application for protection in a convention country if it was claimed or disclosed (otherwise than-by way of disclaimer or acknowledgment of a prior art) in that application, or any documents submitted by the applicant for

protection in support of and at the same time as that application, but no account shall be taken of any disclosure effected by any such document unless a copy of the document is filed at the patent office with the convention application or within such period as may be prescribed after the filing of that application.

2.Korobi Sen in Kolkata has worked on the development of special sweet compositions for diabetic patients. These compositions also contain some herb extracts. The sweets developed by her have very special properties in that the blood sugar levels do not rise when these sweets are consumed. She has filed a patent application in the Patent Office, Kolkata claiming the compositions for her sweets and the method of making them. The Controller issued an examination report objecting to the grant of the patent by citing Sections 3(e), 3(i) and 3(p) of the Indian Patents Act. Korobi has approached you to respond to the first examination report (FER) and also to attend a hearing at the Patent Office in due course. Draft a response to the objections raised in the FER.

Ans.2. [Your Name]

[Your Address]

[City, State, ZIP]

[Email Address]

[Phone Number]

[Date]

Controller of Patents

Patent Office, Kolkata

[Address]

Subject: Response to First Examination Report for Patent Application No. [Application Number]

Dear Sir/Madam,

I am writing to respond to the objections raised in the First Examination Report (FER) issued in relation to the above-mentioned patent application filed by Korobi Sen. As Ms. Sen's authorized representative, I would like to address the objections cited in the FER under Sections 3(e), 3(i) and 3(p) of the Indian Patents Act.

1.   Objection based on Section 3(e) - Admixtures:

The objection raised under Section 3(e) of the Indian Patents Act stating that the claimed sweet composition does not fall under patentable subject matter. The objection states that the claimed "compositions" consisting of the special sweet compositions and herb extracts do not fulfill the patentability requirements. We believe that sweet composition developed by Ms. Sen has no similarity to traditional sweets compositions as it comprises several herb extracts. It cannot be considered a mere admixture but requires innovative and non-obvious steps for the composition of the said sweet.

2. Objection raised under Section 3(i) - Medical Process:

The FER also raises issues under Section 3(i) of the Indian Patents Act, stating that the invention is a medical process which cannot be patented. However, we believe that the process claimed by Ms. Sen is not related to a medical process but rather emphasizes a non-medical product, i.e. the sweet composition. Specifically, the process mainly involves creating a sweet composition that is safe for consumption by patients with diabetes. Therefore, the invention is not a medical process but an innovative product, fulfilling the patentability criteria.

3. Objection based on Section 3(p) - Traditional Knowledge:

The objection raised under Section 3(p) of the Indian Patents Act, stating that the claimed compositions and method of making them consist of traditional knowledge which is not patentable. However, we would like to clarify that the invention is not based on traditional knowledge. The sweet compositions developed by Ms. Sen are a product of continuous research, experimentation, and innovation to create a novel composition that has properties that do not elevate blood sugar levels. We respectfully submit that this inventive process is distinct from traditional knowledge and should not be considered non-patentable.

In light of the above, we strongly believe that the claimed sweet compositions and method of making them satisfy the requirements of patentability under the Indian Patents Act. Furthermore, we request an opportunity to discuss and attend a hearing at the Patent Office, Kolkata, to provide further information and clarification regarding the objections raised in the FER.

Thank you for your consideration. I look forward to a positive resolution to this matter. Please acknowledge receipt of this response. Should you require further information or have any additional questions, please do not hesitate to contact me.

Sincerely,

[Your Name]

[Patent Agent]

[Contact Information]

Section 3 of Patents Act: What are not inventions;

The following are not inventions within the meaning of this Act,--

(i) any process for the medicinal, surgical, curative, prophylactic [diagnostic, therapeutic] or other treatment of human beings or any process for a similar treatment of animals *** to render them free of disease or to increase their economic value or that of their products.

(p) an invention which, in effect, is traditional knowledge or which is an aggregation or duplication of known properties of traditionally known component or components.]

3. Anjan has been involved in the development of drainage systems. He thought it necessary to conduct tests in the compound of his large housing society to assess the scalability of his newly developed drainage system on 30" March 2009. On 1st September 2009, Anjan applied for a patent in the Mumbai Patent Office. Anjan was very confident that there was no prior art that could come in way of the grant of his patent application. Praful who lives in the same housing society and had seen the testing of the invention in their society, came to know about the patent application when it was published in the Journal of the Patent Office and opposed the patent application on the ground that he had witnessed the use of the invention in a public place in India before the patent application was filed. Please draft the statement in reply that is required to be submitted to the Patent Office.

Ans. 3.

[Your Name]

[Your Address]

[City, State, ZIP]

[Email Address]

[Phone Number]

[Date]

Controller of Patents

Mumbai Patent Office

[Address]

Subject: Response to Patent Opposition for Application No. [Application Number]

Dear Sir/Madam,

I am writing in response to the patent opposition filed by Praful against the above-mentioned patent application filed by Anjan in the Mumbai Patent Office. As Anjan's authorized representative, I would like to address the grounds of opposition cited by Praful.

Praful has cited Section 32 of the Indian Patents Act, claiming that the invention was used in a public place in India before the patent application was filed. We acknowledge that the testing of the drainage system was conducted in the compound of a large housing society in March 2009, which could be considered a public place.

However, we would like to point out that the testing of the invention was done only to assess the scalability of the newly developed drainage system. The testing was not for commercial purposes and was not open to the public. Besides, the testing of the invention on 30th March 2009 was not done in good faith, as the obvious intention was not to disclose the invention to the public. It was done in a limited and controlled manner, and nobody could have inferred or disclosed the invention from the testing of the system.

Furthermore, we are confident that the invention is novel and not anticipated by any prior art. We would like to emphasize that the invention has been developed through a series of innovative steps and fulfills the requirements of being a new and inventive product or process.

In light of the above, we respectfully submit that the opposition raised by Praful be dismissed, and our patent application be allowed. We would be happy to provide additional information or clarification if needed.

Please acknowledge receipt of this response.

Sincerely,

[Your Name]

[Patent Agent]

[Contact Information]

Section 32 of Patents Act: Anticipation by public working;

An invention claimed in a complete specification shall not be deemed to have been anticipated by reason only that at any time within one year before the priority date of the relevant claim of the specification, the invention was publicly worked in India--

(a) by the patentee or applicant for the patent or any person from whom he derives title; or

(b) by any other person with the consent of the patentee or applicant for the patent or any person from whom he derives title, if the working was effected for the purpose of reasonable trial only and if it was reasonably necessary, having regard to the nature of the invention, that the working for that purpose should be effected in public.

4. A ship named 'Voyager' registered in Panama and operated by 'White Waterlines from Brunei accidentally entered the territorial waters of India in the Bay of Bengal. The Indian Coast Guard confiscated the ship and brought it to the Chennai Port. Upon inspection, it was found that Voyager had an 'Under Water Exploration Robot Arm' for its actual needs. The said equipment contains many features that are claimed in a patent granted to the Indian Maritime University (IMU). IMU files an infringement case against the owners of the vessel. White Waterlines approaches you for advice.

Draft a note for your client suitably advising them in accordance with the provisions of the Patents Act, 1970?

Ans. 4.

[Your Name]

[Your Address]

[City, State, ZIP]

[Email Address]

[Phone Number]

[Date]

White Waterlines, Brunei

[Address]

Subject: Advice on Patent Infringement Case

Dear Sir/Madam,

I am writing to provide legal advice concerning the infringement case filed by the Indian Maritime University (IMU) against White Waterlines for the unauthorized use of their patented technology in the 'Under Water Exploration Robot Arm' found on board the ship 'Voyager'.

As per the provisions of the Indian Patents Act, 1970, Section 49 states that patent rights are not considered to be infringed when the patented invention is used on foreign vessels temporarily or accidentally in India. In this case, the ship 'Voyager' registered in Panama and operated by White Waterlines from Brunei accidentally entered the territorial waters of India in the Bay of Bengal.

Given this provision, it can be argued that the use of the 'Under Water Exploration Robot Arm' on 'Voyager' falls within the exception for temporary or accidental use of a patented invention on a foreign vessel in Indian waters. Consequently, there might be a valid defense for White Waterlines against the infringement claim filed by IMU.

Should you require further guidance or have any questions, please do not hesitate to contact us.

Sincerely,

[Your Name]

[Patent Agent]

[Contact Information]

Section 49. Patent rights not infringed when used on foreign vessels etc., temporarily or accidentallyin India.—(1) Where a vessel or aircraft registered in a foreign country or a land vehicle owned by a person ordinarily resident in such country comes into India (including theterritorial waters thereof) temporarily or accidentally only, the rights conferred by a patentfor an invention shall not be deemed to be infringed by the use of the invention—(a) in the body of the vessel or in the machinery, tackle, apparatus or other accessoriesthereof, so far as the invention is used on board the vessel and for its actual needsonly; or(b) in the construction or working of the aircraft or land vehicle or of the accessoriesthereof,as the case may be.

(2) This section shall not extend to vessels, aircrafts or land vehicles owned by persons ordinarily resident in a foreign country the laws of which do not confer corresponding rights with respect to the use of inventions in vessels, aircraft or land vehicles owned by persons ordinarily resident in India while in the ports or within the territorial waters of that foreign country or otherwise within the jurisdiction of its courts.

Part B (60 Marks)

Part B1

For any one of the two specifications (1 and 2) stated below,

I. draft 5 claims

II. draft an abstract (maximum of 150 words) and

IIL provide an appropriate title

1 X 30 = 30 marks

Specification No. 1

The invention generally relates to a device for cutting or cracking open nuts or hard fruits of variable size. The invention particularly relates to a device for cutting open coconuts of various shapes and sizes for domestic use and use in temples and in small-scale industries.

Coconuts find extensive use in domestic and industrial applications in various forms such as coconut shavings, coconut water, coconut-milk, coconut oil, desiccated coconut, coir etc. Coconut is also used in foods,

cosmetics, personal care products, neutraceuticals, etc. In many countries, coconuts falling from trees are wasted due to high costs involved in plucking and breaking coconuts. Breaking of coconuts is usually done manually. Holding a coconut in one hand and using a heavy metallic object in the other hand to break the coconut tends to damage the nerves and muscles of the operator over a period of time. A need therefore exists for a device that can be used in homes, temples, hotels, and restaurants, It should be simple, easy to operate and flexible enough to cater to different sizes and types of coconuts, with a capability of being automated.

Description;

As illustrated in Fig. 1, the coconut breaking device has a vertical stand (1) having grooves and notches (4), a coconut holder (2) having an adjustment knob (3) and a receptacle / container (5) placed over a base (6). The vertical stand (1) is connected to the base (6) at its one end and is connected to a rod, which has a fulcrum at the point where the said rod is connected to the vertical stand (1). This rod has a sharp edged laminar blade/knife (7) at its one end and a handle (8) at its other end. The base (6) can be mounted or attached rigidly to any flat surface for operation. The grooves and notches (4) on the vertical stand (1) allow appropriate vertical positioning of the coconut holder (2). The receptacle (5) is provided at the base (6) to collect coconut water. The prong like structure of the coconut holder (2) allows the coconut to be grasped firmly and thereby minimizes the risk of accidental slippage.

A coconut is held in between the prongs of the coconut holder (2). Vertical position of the coconut holder (2) is adjusted suitably, An operator moves the handle (8) in the upward direction causing the knife (7) to come into contact with the coconut, placed in the coconut holder (2) thereby slicing the coconut into two pieces, The motion can be as swift as the situation demands, i.e. depending on the outside crust of the coconut. The coconut water is collected in the receptacle (5), The handle (8) is made of a material that prevents injury to the hand of the operator e.g. leather, cloth etc,

In an embodiment of the invention, the process can be automated by using electrically operated parts. Any such embodiment will fall within the scope of this invention.

Ans: Title: Device for Cutting Open Coconuts

Abstract: The present invention discloses a device for cutting or cracking open nuts or hard fruits, particularly coconuts, of various shapes and sizes. The device is designed for domestic use, as well as in temples and small-scale industries. The invention aims to provide a simple, easy-to-operate, and flexible device that can cater to different sizes and types of coconuts.

The device comprises a vertical stand with grooves and notches, a coconut holder with an adjustment knob, and a receptacle/container placed over a base. A rod with a sharp-edged laminar blade/knife and a handle is connected to the vertical stand. The coconut holder allows for secure grip and minimizes the risk of accidental slippage. The operator adjusts the vertical position of the coconut holder and moves the handle in an upward motion to slice the coconut into two pieces. The coconut water is collected in the receptacle.

The invention also contemplates the possibility of automating the process using electrically operated parts.

CLAIMS:

I claim:

1. A device for cutting or cracking open nuts or hard fruits, comprising:

    a) a vertical stand with grooves and notches;

    b) a coconut holder with an adjustment knob;

    c) a receptacle/container for collecting coconut water;

    d) a base for mounting the device on a flat surface;

    e) a rod with a sharp-edged laminar blade/knife and a handle;

2. The device of claim 1, wherein the grooves and notches on the vertical stand allow for appropriate vertical positioning of the coconut holder.

3. The device of claim 1, wherein the coconut holder comprises a prong-like structure for secure grip of the coconut.

4. The device of claim 1, wherein the handle is made of a material that prevents injury to the operator's hand.

5. The device of claim 1, further comprising electrically operated parts for automating the cutting process.

Specification No. 2

The invention in general relates to substances for removing dirt from leather and/or for coloring the leather. In particular, the invention relates to a shoe polish.

The object of the invention is to provide a shoe polish which may be readily and easily applied to ordinary leather shoes to color them with any desired tint, or to match or harmonize them with the costume of the wearer. A further object of the invention is to provide a shoe polish as mentioned which may be readily removed from the shoes when it is desired to change the color thereof. A further object of the invention is to provide a shoe polish as mentioned which will not be deleterious to the leather but which on the contrary will serve to keep the leather soft and pliable. Other objects will appear hereinafter.

In carrying out the invention, preferably the shoe polish (or dressing) is applied to the leather

in the seven positive colors namely: yellow, red, blue, green, brown, black, and white. The user can also compound the desired tints therefrom as needed, without departing from the scope of the invention.

Description:

The composition of the shoe polish is as follows :—

Powdered coloring matter 4 parts by weight Water, containing a small quantity of salt, | 8 parts by weight sodium carbonate and an egg Lard oil 1 part by weight Syrup (corn or cane or mixture of both) 4 parts by weight Mucilage formed of gum arabic and water 8 parts by weightage 4 parts by weight of powdered coloring matter is ground well into 8 parts of a first mixture of salt, sodium carbonate and a well-beaten raw egg in 1 litre of warm water to form a second mixture. About 60 grams of salt, 15 grams of sodium carbonate and 60 grams of beaten egg will usually be sufficient. The coloring matter is preferably chrome yellow, chrome red, ultramarine blue, chrome green, burnt umber, bone black, and zinc white. To twelve parts of the said second mixture thus formed is added 1 part of lard oil with stirring after which are added four parts of syrup and eight parts of mucilage. The syrup used is preferably ninety per cent corn syrup and ten per cent cane syrup, although either may be used separately or in different proportions; and the mucilage is formed by dissolving 500 grams of gum arabic in 2.5 litres of water resulting in the final composition, which is allowed to stand for one week after which it is ready for use. Egg is added to the water for the color and it also helps to keep the leather soft and adds luster to the polish. The salt preserves the egg and the sodium carbonate neutralizes the acids in the color. The lard oil preserves the leather and keeps it soft and pliable and also prevents the polish from cracking. The syrup and mucilage are added for an adhesive and to give luster to the polish. In using the polish (or dressing) two or more of the colors may be mixed together to form a dressing of the desired tint. Usually two applications of the dressing will give an even color although sometimes three or more may be preferred. Unless the dressing has remained upon the leather for a great length of time it may be readily washed off to be replaced by another tint.

Title: Multi-Colored Shoe Polish Composition

Abstract: The present invention discloses a shoe polish composition specifically designed for coloring leather shoes with a variety of tints. The primary objective of the invention is to provide a shoe polish that can be easily applied and removed from shoes, utilizing a range of seven positive colors: yellow, red, blue, green, brown, black, and white. The composition includes powdered coloring matter, a mixture of salt and sodium carbonate in water, lard oil, syrup (such as corn or cane), and mucilage made from gum arabic and water. The shoe polish mixture is formed by grinding the coloring matter with the mixture of salt, sodium carbonate, and water, followed by the addition of lard oil, syrup, and mucilage. The final composition enhances the leather's softness, pliability, and luster. Different tints can be achieved by mixing two or more colors together. The polish can be easily washed off to allow for the application of a different tint.

CLAIMS:

I claim:

1. A shoe polish composition for coloring leather, comprising:

   a) powdered coloring matter;

   b) a mixture of salt, sodium carbonate, and water;

   c) lard oil;

   d) syrup (e.g., corn or cane); and

   e) mucilage formed from gum arabic and water.

2. The shoe polish composition of claim 1, wherein the powdered coloring matter includes chrome yellow, chrome red, ultramarine blue, chrome green, burnt umber, bone black, and zinc white.

3. The shoe polish composition of claim 1, wherein the mixture of salt, sodium carbonate, and water preserves the egg and neutralizes the acids in the color.

4. The shoe polish composition of claim 1, wherein the lard oil preserves the leather, maintains its softness and pliability, and prevents the polish from cracking.

5. The shoe polish composition of claim 1, wherein the syrup and mucilage serve as an adhesive and give luster to the polish.

Part B2

A client meets you and provides technical information regarding his invention. Draft a complete specification, for any one of the following descriptions, for filing in the Indian Patent Office. While preparing the complete specification, do not redraw the figures. However, you may refer to the figures in the specification as Fig. 1, Fig. 2 and Fig. 3.

1 X 30 = 30 marks

Question 1: This invention is about a down-flow drinking straw that delivers liquid below the water level of a drinking vessel, while eliminating siphoning after an individual has stopped drinking, to reduce the amount of liquid spilled. The invention finds application in hospitals, convalescent homes and private homes for use by bed-ridden individuals. We are familiar with the use of a straw that is used to sip liquid from a cup or a glass. A problem arrises when the delivery end of the straw is below the fluid level of the glass as a siphon is created due to which even after the person stops sucking the straw, fluid continues to flow out from the straw. This can be undesirable as liquid can spill on the person's face and clothes. There is a lot of prior art dealing with this problem but no straws with anti-siphoning features have been invented yet. Complicated straws with a variety of check valves to avoid back flows are however available. Straws with controlled pumping systems are also available. The present invention overcomes all the drawbacks of the known straws.

Figures 1 provides a schematic diagram of the construction of the straw of the present invention. Figure 2 provides a view of a patient using the straw in a hospital. Note the straw having a straight supply tube portion connected by an adjustable bend to another straight pickup tube portion with an increased diameter portion below the adjustable bend. Also note the nature of the adjustable bend so that the supply tube portion is above the increased diameter portion when the straw is released. Once the supply tube portion is above the increased diameter portion of the tube, the increased diameter portion provides a volume of liquid to reverse the siphon and pulls the remaining liquid in the supply tube portion back into the glass. The volume of liquid 'in the enlarged diameter portion of the

straw exceeds the volume of the entire supply tube portion. Several variants of the straw are possible. Figure 3 illustrates one such variant.

Fig.3 A side view of a glass containing a variant of the anti-spilling down flow drinking straw, having a spiraling pickup tube. In the variant illustrated in figure 3, the straw has a long straight supply tube portion connected by an adjustable bend to another straight pickup tube portion, with an increased diameter portion in the supply tube portion that extends from below the adjustable bend downwardly. In this case, the spiral sections of straw connect the increased diameter portion to the adjustable end. The spiral sections are most useful when a container having a cover with a small opening is used (such as aluminium can). The straw is rotated and the lower spiral sections of the straw are routed through the opening and below the cover. This results in the spiral sections of the straw gripping the cover from below and above thus supporting the straw on the container. By supporting the straw's pickup tube portion, the spring action of the adjustable bend is better able to lift the supply tube portion to the correct height for draining the straw. The spring action itself can be provided by the spiral sections. The increased diameter portion in this embodiment extends to the bottom of the pickup tube.

The actual material used to make the straw may be any of a number of available plastics, acrylics, polyurethanes, etc., as long as the material provides the spring function of the adjustable bend. Various colours and reservoir shapes may also be envisioned for aesthetic and entertainment purposes.

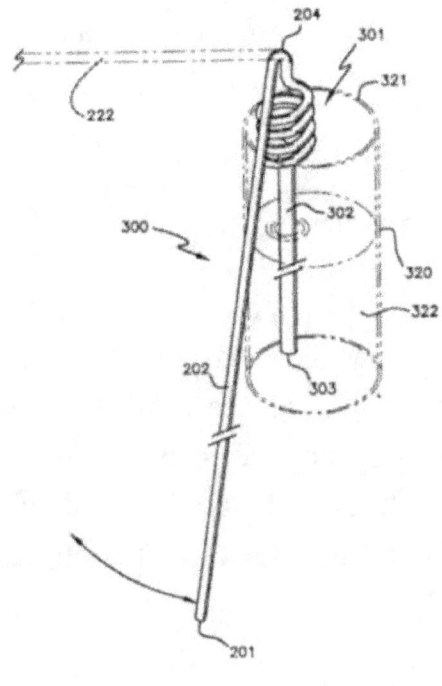

Fig.3

*A side view of a glass containing a variant of the anti-spilling down flow drinking straw,
having a spiraling pickup tube*

IN THE INDIAN PATENT OFFICE

COMPLETE SPECIFICATION

(Section 10; rule 13)

TITLE: Down-Flow Drinking Straw with Anti-Siphoning Feature

FIELD OF THE INVENTION:

The present invention relates to a drinking straw and more particularly to a
down-flow drinking straw that delivers liquid below the water level of a

drinking vessel while eliminating siphoning to reduce the amount of liquid spilled. The invention finds application in hospitals, convalescent homes, and private homes for use by bed-ridden individuals.

BACKGROUND OF THE INVENTION:

The use of a straw to sip liquid from a cup or a glass is well known. However, a problem arises when the delivery end of the straw is below the fluid level of the glass, creating a siphon effect that causes fluid to continue flowing out of the straw even after the person has stopped sucking. This can result in undesired liquid spillage on the person's face and clothes. While complicated straws with a variety of check valves to avoid backflows and controlled pumping systems are available, there is currently no straw with an anti-siphoning feature that is effective and easy to use.

SUMMARY OF THE INVENTION:

The present invention provides a down-flow drinking straw with an anti-siphoning feature that delivers liquid below the water level of a drinking vessel while eliminating siphoning after an individual has stopped drinking, reducing the amount of liquid spilled. The straw includes a straight supply tube portion connected by an adjustable bend to another straight pickup tube portion with an increased diameter portion below the adjustable bend. The adjustable bend is designed in such a way that the supply tube portion is above the increased diameter portion when the straw is released. Once the supply tube portion is above the increased diameter portion of the tube, the increased diameter portion provides a volume of liquid to reverse the siphon and pulls the remaining liquid in the supply tube portion back into the glass. The volume of liquid in the enlarged diameter portion of the straw exceeds the volume of the entire supply tube portion. The straw can also include a spiraling pickup tube variant for use with containers having a small opening.

DETAILED DESCRIPTION OF THE INVENTION:

The present invention provides a down-flow drinking straw with an anti-siphoning feature that delivers liquid below the water level of a drinking vessel while eliminating siphoning to reduce the amount of liquid spilled.

In one embodiment, the straw includes a straight supply tube portion connected by an adjustable bend to another straight pickup tube portion with an increased diameter portion below the adjustable bend. The adjustable bend is designed in such a way that the supply tube portion is above the increased diameter portion when the straw is released. Once the supply tube portion is above the increased diameter portion of the tube, the increased diameter portion provides a volume of liquid to reverse the siphon and pulls the remaining liquid in the supply tube portion back into the glass. The volume of liquid in the enlarged diameter portion of the straw exceeds the volume of the entire supply tube portion.

In another embodiment, the straw includes a spiraling pickup tube variant for use with containers having a small opening. The spiral sections of the straw connect the increased diameter portion to the adjustable bend. The spiral sections are most useful when a container having a cover with a small opening is used, such as an aluminum can. The straw is rotated and the lower spiral sections of the straw are routed through the opening and below the cover. This results in the spiral sections of the straw gripping the cover from below and above, thus supporting the straw on the container. By supporting the straw's pickup tube portion, the spring action of the adjustable bend is better able to lift the supply tube portion to the correct height for draining the straw. The spring action itself can be provided by the spiral sections. The increased diameter portion in this embodiment extends to the bottom of the pickup tube.

The straw may be made of any suitable material such as plastic, acrylic, polyurethane, etc. Various colors and reservoir shapes may be envisioned for aesthetic and entertainment purposes.

EXAMPLES:

Not Applicable.

CLAIMS:

I claim:

1. A down-flow drinking straw with an anti-siphoning feature that delivers liquid below the water level of a drinking vessel while eliminating siphoning to reduce the amount of liquid spilled, comprising a straight supply tube portion connected by an adjustable bend to another straight pickup tube portion with an increased diameter portion below the adjustable bend, wherein the adjustable bend is designed in such a way that the supply tube portion is above the increased diameter portion when the straw is released, forming a volume of liquid in the increased diameter portion to reverse the siphon and pull the remaining liquid in the supply tube portion back into the glass.

2. The straw of claim 1, wherein the volume of liquid in the enlarged diameter portion of the straw exceeds the volume of the entire supply tube portion.

3. The straw of claim 1, further comprising a spiraling pickup tube variant for use with containers having a small opening, wherein the spiral sections of the straw connect the increased diameter portion to the adjustable bend.

4. The straw of claim 1, wherein the spiral sections of the straw provide the spring action for the adjustable bend to lift the supply tube portion to the correct height for draining the straw.

5. The straw of claim 1, wherein the increased diameter portion in the spiraling pickup tube variant extends to the bottom of the pickup tube.

6. The straw of claim 1, wherein the straw is made of a suitable material such as plastic, acrylic, polyurethane, etc.

7. The straw of claim 1, having a reservoir shape for aesthetic or entertainment purposes.

8. The straw of claim 1, being color-coded for aesthetic purposes.

9. The straw of claim 1, wherein the adjustable bend is designed to fit comfortably and securely in a person's mouth to facilitate drinking.

10. The straw of claim 1, comprising a safety feature such as a split ring capable of disengaging the straw from the drinking vessel if subjected to an excessive load.

Question 2

Bilayer tableting technology has become popular in recent times. Bilayer tablets offer several advantages over conventional tablets. The standard generic dosage forms of Analgesic-Antipyretic drugs have maximum effectiveness only for a few hours, e.g. 4 to 6 hours. Therefore, a patient needs to take such medication as least 2 to 3 times a day, which is undesirable.

It is desirable to offer patient friendly dosage forms that need to be taken only once day and yet ensuring uniform concentration of the drug in the serum for a 12 to 24-hour period.nPatient compliance will be maximized when frequent dosing is avoided and relief is available for a longer period.Formulating oral dosage form of Aceclofenac has remained a challenge in view of its poor or lack of solubility. Aceclofenac being insoluble in water, needs to be combined with solubilizers to improve the bioavailability. The disease conditions where Aceclofenac is used requires immediate relief and effectiveness on a continued uniform level for a prolonged period of time.

By "immediate release core", it is meant for purposes of the present invention that the tablet core containing the therapeutically active agent(s) meets the disintegration and/or dissolution requirements for immediate release tablets of the particular therapeutically active agent(s) included in the tablet core, as set forth in the USP XXII, 1990 (The United States Pharmacopeia).

By "sustained release", it is meant for purposes of the present invention that the release of the therapeutically active agent occurs such that blood levels are maintained within a desired therapeutic range over an extended period of time, e.g., at least about 8 and preferably from about 12 to about 24 hours. The "dissolution requirements" and "disintegration requirements" referred to above are conducted using the equipment and tests specified in the USP XXII and conducted pursuant to the individual Official Monographs of USP XXII for the particular therapeutically active agent(s) included in the tablet core.

Prior art discloses analgesic composition with uniform bioavailability over a prolonged period. sustainable oral dosage forms of aceclofenac. The invention discloses oral dosage pharmaceutical composition of aceclofenac that provides uniform blood level concentrations over 12 hours to 24 hours a day. A bilayer oral dosage form of the water insoluble drug is formulated with a first layer which offers immediate release and a second layer which offers the drug from a sustained release matrix over 12 hours to 24 hours a day. The first layer for immediate release is formulated to release aceclofenac into the blood stream to initiate and achieve peak level concentrations as desired within 15 minutes.

The immediate release component is prepared by mixing 30% of total Aceclofenac in the composition with Betacyclodextrin along with pharmaceutically acceptable excipients. The sustained release component was prepared by mixing 70% of total Aceclofenac with pharmaceutically acceptable excipients selected from PVP, hydroxyl propyl methyl cellulose (HPMC), carboxy methyl cellulose (CMC), glyceryl monosterate poloxamer and surfactants, based on hydrogenated castor oil (PEG-60, PEG-40).

The Aceclofenac composition has following advantages :

(a) Rapid availability in bloodstream and hence early onset of relief.

(b) Uniform plasma level concentrations of aceclofenac over prolonged period.

(¢) Lower frequency of dosage and hence better patient compliances.

The bilayer tablet is prepared using the granules/pellets of immediate layer prepared by solvent/water based dissolution followed by dry granulation process and the sustained release granules/pellets prepared by the non-aqueous wet granulation process and compressing the two grades of granules/pellets using a C-300 or CTX IT A Catmark Rotary Tablet Press. The bilayer tablet can be prepared either as a tablet in tablet form or as a

171

conventional bilayer tablet using the above equipment. The tablet prepared by compression is thereafter subjected to standard evaluation procedures such as disintegration, dissolution as well as bioavailability studies to determine that the desired blood level concentrations over a 12 hour or 24 hour sustained release period is met as preset in the objective of the formulation.

Examples: Aceclofenac in the present invention is incorporated in a total quantity of 100mg for standard SR dosage from and 200mg for Forte dosage form.

Immediate Release layer

30gms Aceclofenac is dissolved in 50ml solvent selected from acetone or ethyl alcohol or a combination thereof and mixed with Betacyclodextrin (50gms) dissolved in 30ml de-ionized water. The mixture is stirred to evaporation with moderate heating (40 to 50°C) to form a uniform paste comprising aceclofenac-betacyclodextrin complex. The complex so obtained is subjected to dry granulation by precompression followed by granulation or pelletisation and blended with lubricants.

Sustained Release layer

70gms of aceclofenac is dissolved in 50ml of acetone or ethyl alcohol or a combination thereof. 50gms of HPMC and 30gms of Povidone is added followed by 0.5gms of sodium lauryl sulfate along with 50 ml of deionized water.

The resultant solution was spray dried to produce a solid powder using a standard spray dryer. The solid powder is subjected to dry granulation by blending with lubricants by precompression or roll compaction followed by granulation/pelletisation. The granules of the immediate release layer and the granules of the sustained release layer are directly fed into the tablet compression machine to obtain a standard bilayer tablet or a tablet in tablet dosage form. The tablet is subjected to standard tests such as disintegration, dissolution as well as compliance to the preset bioavailability parameters.

The immediate release layer composition is Aceclofenac — 30% of the total aceclofenac in the composition Betacyclodextrin — 5 to 10% of Aceclofenac in the immediate release layer. Pharmaceutical excipients for granulation — 2 to 3% of the Aceclofenac in the immediate release layer.

The sustained release layer composition is Aceclofenac — 70% of the total aceclofenac in the composition Hydroxy propyl methyl cellulose — 40 to 50% of Aceclofenac in the sustained release layer. 1-venyl 2-pyrrolidone — 50 to 60% of the Aceclofenac in the sustained release layer. Pharmaceutical excipients for granulation — 5 to 10% of the total weight of the sustained release layer.

IN THE INDIAN PATENT OFFICE

COMPLETE SPECIFICATION

(Section 10; rule 13)

TITLE: Bilayer Tablet Composition of Aceclofenac with Immediate Release and Sustained Release Layers

FIELD OF THE INVENTION:

The present invention relates to a bilaycr tablet composition of Aceclofenac with both immediate release and sustained release layers. The bilayer tablet provides uniform blood level concentrations of the drug over prolonged periods and lowers the frequency of dosage, enhancing patient compliance.

BACKGROUND OF THE INVENTION:

Conventional dosage forms of analgesic-antipyretic drugs have maximum effectiveness only for a few hours, resulting in patients having to take medication 2 to 3 times daily for continued relief. Aceclofenac, a commonly used analgesic-antipyretic drug, is also insoluble in water and requires solubilizers to improve bioavailability. Immediate relief and effectiveness on a continued uniform level are required for disease conditions where Aceclofenac is used, and prior art formulations have struggled to provide such a dosage form.

SUMMARY OF THE INVENTION:

The present invention provides a bilayer tablet composition of Aceclofenac that provides uniform blood level concentrations over 12 hours to 24 hours a day. The tablet comprises a first layer offering immediate release and a second layer offering sustained release of the drug from a matrix over the prolonged period. The immediate release layer releases Aceclofenac into the bloodstream to initiate and achieve peak level concentrations within 15 minutes, and the sustained release layer maintains the desired therapeutic range of blood levels for an extended period.

DETAILED DESCRIPTION OF THE INVENTION:

The present invention provides a bilayer tablet composition of Aceclofenac with both immediate release and sustained release layers. The immediate release component is formulated to achieve peak level concentrations within 15 minutes of ingestion, and the sustained release component ensures that blood levels of the drug are maintained within a therapeutic range for an extended period of time, e.g., at least about 8 hours and preferably from about 12 to about 24 hours. The dissolved material provides a clear solution for processing.

The immediate release component comprises Aceclofenac in a quantity of 30% of the total Aceclofenac in the composition, mixed with Betacyclodextrin (5 to 10% of Aceclofenac in the immediate release layer) and pharmaceutical excipients for granulation (2 to 3% of the Aceclofenac in the immediate release layer), such as magnesium stearate, colloidal silicon dioxide, and microcrystalline cellulose. The immediate release component of Aceclofenac is prepared by dissolving the Aceclofenac in a solvent such as acetone or ethyl alcohol or a combination thereof and mixing it with Betacyclodextrin dissolved in de-ionized water. The mixture is stirred and evaporated with moderate heating (40 to 50°C) to form a uniform paste comprising Aceclofenac-Betacyclodextrin complex. The complex is then dry granulated by compression or granulation or pelletization and blended with lubricants.

The sustained release component comprises Aceclofenac in a quantity of 70% of the total Aceclofenac in the composition, hydroxy propyl methyl cellulose (40 to 50% of Aceclofenac in the sustained release layer), 1-vinyl 2-pyrrolidone (50 to 60% of the Aceclofenac in the sustained release layer), and pharmaceutical excipients for granulation (5 to 10% of the total weight of the sustained release layer), such as polyvinyl pyrrolidine (PVP), carboxymethylcellulose (CMC), glyceryl monostearate, poloxamer and surfactants based on hydrogenated castor oil (PEG-60, PEG-40). The sustained release component of Aceclofenac is prepared by dissolving the Aceclofenac in a solvent such as acetone or ethyl alcohol or a combination thereof and adding HPMC, Povidone, sodium lauryl sulfate, and de-ionized water. The resultant solution is spray-dried to produce a solid powder using a standard spray dryer. The solid powder is then dry granulated by compression or roll compaction and blended with stable lubricants.

The bilayer tablet comprises a first layer of the immediate release component and a second layer of the sustained release component. The granules or pellets of the immediate layer are prepared by a solvent/water-based dissolution followed by dry granulation process. The granules or pellets of the sustained release layer are prepared by the non-aqueous wet granulation process. The two grades of granules or pellets are compressed using a C-300 or CTX IT A Catmark Rotary Tablet Press, resulting in a bilayer tablet with a clear demarcation between the two layers.

Standard evaluations are conducted on the tablet, such as disintegration, dissolution, and bioavailability studies, to determine that the desired blood level concentrations over a 12-hour or 24-hour sustained release period are met, as set forth in the USP XXII.

EXAMPLES:

Aceclofenac is incorporated in a total quantity of 100mg for the standard sustained release dosage form and 200mg for the forte dosage form.

Immediate Release layer:

30gms Aceclofenac is dissolved in 50ml solvent (acetone or ethyl alcohol or combination thereof) and mixed with Betacyclodextrin (50gms) dissolved in 30ml de-ionized water. The mixture is stirred and evaporated with moderate heating (40 to 50°C) to form a uniform paste comprising Aceclofenac-

Betacyclodextrin complex. The complex so obtained is subjected to dry granulation by precompression followed by granulation or pelletisation and blended with lubricants.

Sustained Release layer:

70gms of Aceclofenac is dissolved in 50ml of acetone or ethyl alcohol or a combination thereof. 50gms of HPMC and 30gms Povidone is added followed by 0.5gms of sodium lauryl sulfate along with 50 ml of de-ionized water. The resultant solution was spray dried to produce a solid powder using a standard spray dryer. The solid powder is subjected to dry granulation by blending with lubricants by precompression or roll compaction followed by granulation or pelletisation.

CLAIMS:

I claim:

1. A bilayer tablet composition of Aceclofenac, comprising a first layer of an immediate release component, comprising Aceclofenac in a quantity of 30% of the total Aceclofenac in the composition, mixed with Betacyclodextrin and pharmaceutical excipients, and a second layer of a sustained release component, comprising Aceclofenac in a quantity of 70% of the total Aceclofenac in the composition, hydroxy propyl methyl cellulose, 1-vinyl 2-pyrrolidone, and pharmaceutical excipients, wherein the immediate release layer releases Aceclofenac into the bloodstream to initiate and achieve peak level concentrations within 15 minutes, and the sustained release layer maintains the desired therapeutic range of blood levels for an extended period.

2. The bilayer tablet composition of claim 1, wherein the Betacyclodextrin is present in a quantity of 5 to 10% of the Aceclofenac in the immediate release layer.

3. The bilayer tablet composition of claim 1, further comprising magnesium stearate, colloidal silicon dioxide, and microcrystalline cellulose as pharmaceutical excipients for the immediate release layer, comprising 2 to 3% of the Aceclofenac in the immediate release layer.

4. The bilayer tablet composition of claim 1, further comprising HPMC, Povidone, sodium lauryl sulfate, polyvinyl pyrrolidine (PVP), carboxymethylcellulose (CMC), glyceryl monostearate, poloxamer and surfactants based on hydrogenated castor oil (PEG-60, PEG-40) as pharmaceutical excipients for the sustained release layer, comprising 5 to 10% of the total weight of the sustained release layer.

5. The bilayer tablet composition of claim 1, wherein the Aceclofenac is present in a total quantity of 100mg for the standard sustained release dosage form and 200mg for the forte dosage form.

6. The bilayer tablet composition of claim 1, wherein the immediate release component releases Aceclofenac into the bloodstream to initiate and achieve peak level concentrations within 15 minutes of ingestion.

7. The bilayer tablet composition of claim 1, wherein the sustained release component maintains the desired therapeutic range of blood levels for at least 8 hours and preferably from12 to 24 hours.

8. The bilayer tablet composition of claim 1, wherein the granules or pellets of the immediate layer are prepared by a solvent/water-based dissolution followed by dry granulation process, and the granules or pellets of the sustained release layer are prepared by the non-aqueous wet granulation process.

9. The bilayer tablet composition of claim 1, wherein standard evaluations are conducted on the tablet comprising disintegration, dissolution, and bioavailability studies to determine that desired blood level concentrations over a 12-hour or 24-hour sustained release period are met, as set forth.

PATENT AGENT EXAMINATION, 2011

(Under Section 126 of the Patents Act, 1970, as amended)

January 15, 2011

PAPER II

TOTAL MARKS: 100

Time: 2.30 PM to 5.30 PM (3 hours)

Total number of pages: 11

Instructions;

1. This paper consists of 2 parts

2. Part A of 40 marks requires you to answer all four questions of 10 marks each.

3. Part B has two sections (Part B! and B2).

4. Part B1 is compulsory of 30 marks.

5. Part B2 has two questions and you are required to answer any one of them for 30 marks

6. If there is a word limit in the question it should be followed strictly or else the answer can be rejected.

7. Read the questions carefully before answering them. No clarification or doubt can be sought on the questions to the invigilators and you need to interpret it from the questions given as it is.

PART A (4X10 = 40 MARKS)

Question 1. Rahman Roshan, a student of one of the [ITs came up with an invention which is acylindrical slide which can be installed in the balcony of high rise apartments. In case ofany emergency of fire or earthquake, the inmates roll the cylindrical slide to the groundfloor and can slide to safety.He shared his views with his brother in a private conversation who is

an editor of journal'Safe Houses' in February 2010.He conducted a trial of his invention from the ninth floor of his hostel to assess theeffectiveness in March 2010. He wanted to know the feedback of this invention and exhibited the same in anexhibition 'New Millennium Designs' at Raffles Centre in Singapore on July 2nd of 2010.In the meanwhile he learnt that his brother published the details he shared in "SafeHouses" journal issue dated August 2010.In September 2010 he filed a provisional application in the Indian Patent office and complete specification in January 2011.Rahman Roshan approaches you with the above facts and seeks your consultation onwhether any of these events will impact the granting of the patent. Give your written statement with the relevant sections of the Patent Act to this client and explain the position of the issues stated that will have an impact on granting of the patent.

Ans:1. Section 29:Anticipation by Previous Publication

This section provides that any publication of the invention made in India or abroad without the prior consent of the applicant or patentee is not considered anticipation and the ground for rejection of the patent. The patentee must establish that he filed an application for the patent as soon as he found out about the publication.

Section 30:Anticipation by previous communication to the Government

Any disclosure of the invention to the government prior to the filing date of a patent application for the purpose of the investigation is not considered anticipation.

Section 31:Anticipation by Public Display

if the invention is disclosed for private consumption of a peer group, which is formed for the purpose of promotion of knowledge and scholarship, solely for the benefit of the members of the society, it is not anticipation. A grace period is given to the original inventor to file an application within 12 months of the public display, to prevent labelling of his claim as an anticipated claim.

Section 32:Anticipation by Public Working

Anticipation by public working could be done by the importation of a patented product into India before the priority date the product would amount to public knowledge or public use, except where such importation was for the purpose of reasonable trial or experiment. To benefit from this exception, the application must be filed within 12 months after the invention has been publicly worked for the purpose of reasonable trial and considering the nature of the invention.

Question 2. Sumathy an R&D Scientist is married to Anand. After few years of marriage she found her husband snoring which disturbed her sleep. She found the anti-snoring devices in the market not very effective and convenient and came up with her own invention which is a mask which will transmit the noise to a small box kept under the bed, thereby reducing the snoring noise by about 90%. She filed apatent for the same and was granted in December 2007.Later, in July 2010 she came up with a new idea wherein the snoring noise is transmitted from the mask to the box which is now connected to a small electronic device with a key board which converts it as to soothing background music. She seeksyour advice on to how best to protect this improvisation. Based on the relevant sections of the Indian Patent Act, prepare a brief on the best strategies available to protect the invention of this client.

Ans: as per Section 54 of the Indian Patent Act, Sumathy can also consider filing for a patent of addition. This allows her to add any new improvements or modifications made to the original invention and obtain protection for the same without having to file a separate patent application.

Ans.2. Section 54: Patents of addition.

(1) Subject to the provisions contained in this section, where an application is made for a patent in respect of any improvement in or modification of an invention described or disclosed in the complete specification filed therefor (in this Act referred to as the "main invention") and the applicant also applies or has applied for a patent for that invention or is the patentee in respect thereof, the

Controller may, if the applicant so requests, grant the patent for the improvement or modification as a patent of addition.

(2) Subject to the provisions contained in this section, where an invention, being an improvement in or modification of another invention, is the subject of an independent patent and the patentee in respect of that patent is also the patentee in respect of the patent for the main invention, the Controller may, if the patentee so requests, by order, revoke the patent for the improvement or modification and grant to the patentee a patent of addition in respect thereof, bearing the same date as the date of the patent so revoked.

(3) A patent shall not be granted as a patent of addition unless the date of filing of the [application] was the same as or later than the date of filing of the [application] in respect of the main invention.

[(4) A patent of addition shallnot be granted before grant of the patent for the main invention].

Question 3. Raja and Radha did their PhD together in Indian Institute of Science Bangalore in thefield of Biotechnology. After completing their doctoral programme they planned to set uptheir own lab with a loan from a bank. They started working on a novel dermalapplication which will heal severe burn wounds and will grow the skin back in a shorttime and no such dermal application was known in the prior art.

In the course of their working together they also came to the view based on theircompatibility in professional interest and other issues they will get married. They jointlyfiled for patent and also received the patent in December 2009.Raja orally promised her that if they license the patent, Radha can take 75% of the profitas he cared for her and it is a pre-marriage gift to her in a private meeting with her. Theyhave an offer for a licence for this patent from a company for a hefty amount.In the course of next few months they developed differences in their relationship andeventually decided not to marry. After some time they bitterly quarreled and decided topart ways.Radha approaches you and complaints that Raja is retracting from his earlier promiseto give her the 75% as promised and says that he will give only 50% of the amount.Further she

states that Raja also wants it to be licensed to another friend of his who isoffering a lesser licence fee which is not acceptable to her. She approaches you for aconsultation on the above issues.You are required to give an advice based on the relevant sections of the PatentsAct and any remedy you can get by approaching the Controller.

Ans.3. Section 50 : Rights of co-owners of patents:

(1) Where a patent is granted to two or more persons, each of those persons shall, unless an agreement to the contrary is in force, be entitled to an equal undivided share in the patent.

(2) Subject to the provisions contained in this section and in section 51, where two or more persons are registered as grantee or proprietor of a patent, then, unless an agreement to the contrary is in force, each of those persons shall be entitled, by himself or his agents, to 1[the rights conferred by section 48] for his own benefit without accounting to the other person or persons.

(3) Subject to the provisions contained in this section and in section 51 and to any agreement for the time being in force, where two or more persons are registered as grantee or proprietor of a patent, then, a licence under the patent shall not be granted and a share in the patent shall not be assigned by one of such persons except with the consent of the other person or persons.

(4) Where a patented article is sold by one of two or more persons registered as grantee or proprietor of a patent, the purchaser and any person claiming through him shall be entitled to deal with the article in the same manner as if the article had been sold by a sole patentee.

(5) Subject to the provisions contained in this section, the rules of law applicable to the ownership and devolution of movable property generally shall apply in relation to patents; and nothing contained in sub-section (1) or sub-section (2) shall affect the mutual rights or obligations of trustees or of the legal representatives of a deceased person or their rights or obligations as such.

(6) Nothing in this section shall affect the rights of the assignees of a partial interest in a patent created before the commencement of this Act.

Section 51 of the Patents Act: Power of Controller to give directions to co-owners;

(1) Where two or more persons are registered as grantee or proprietor of a patent, the Controller may, upon application made to him in the prescribed manner by any of those persons, give such directions in accordance with the application as to the sale or lease of the patent or any interest therein, the grant of licences under the patent, or the exercise of any right under section 50 in relation thereto, as he thinks fit.

(2) If any person registered as grantee or proprietor of a patent fails to execute any instrument or to do any other thing required for the carrying out of any direction given under this section within fourteen days after being requested in writing so to do by any of the other persons so registered, the Controller may, upon application made to him in the prescribed manner by any such other person, give directions empowering any person to execute that instrument or to do that thing in the name and on behalf of the person in default.

(3) Before giving any directions in pursuance of an application under this section, the Controller shall give an opportunity to be heard--

(a) in the case of an application under sub-section (1), to the other person or persons registered as grantee or proprietor of the patent;

(b) in the case of an application under sub-section (2), to the person in default.

(4) No direction shall be given under this section so as to affect the mutual rights or obligation of trustees or of the legal representatives of a deceased person or of their rights or obligations as such, or which is inconsistent with the terms of any agreement between persons registered as grantee or proprietor of the patent.

Question 4. Brahma is a retired naval officer in Chennai. After his retirement he set up his own labfor research and development. He developed an ultrasonic device which can identifydolphins. This device if attached to the large fishing nets can identify if a dolphin isentrapped and the same can be released by the fishing vessels by a releasemechanism in the net. As dolphins are also a protected species, this invention has agreat potential for commercial interest. He applied for a patent and received it in

40countries in January 2009.In December 2009 he came to know that a fishing vessel from Lemuria was fishing inIndian territorial waters and was confiscated by the Indian Navy and brought to Chennaiport.The captain of the vessel pleaded that they lost their way due to failure of theirnavigation direction software and thus entered the territorial water. The Lemurianembassy at Delhi had taken up their case. He also learnt that they used fishing netswhich contained his patented ultrasonic device made in country Lemuria. Lemuria is anew nation state does not have any patent laws and are in the process of preparing one. Brahma approaches you to consult whether he can file a suit of infringement on the company owning the vessel for infringing the patent. Based on the abovefacts you are required to prepare a consultation note to your client based on therelevant provisions of the Indian Patent Act.

Ans.4. As per Section 48 of the Indian Patent Act, Brahma has the exclusive right to use, sell, or import his patented ultrasonic device, and therefore he can file a suit of infringement against the company owning the vessel.

However, in this case, the company owning the vessel might argue that the use of Brahma's patented invention in their fishing nets was unintentional and due to ignorance. Section 49 of the Indian Patent Act provides a defense to the infringement of a patent when the act was on foreign vessel and accidental. In this case, the company owning the vessel might claim good faith and state that they were unaware of Brahma's patent rights, and they used the device accidentally and did not have any commercial intent.

Section 111 of the Patents Act: Restriction on power of court to grant damages or account of profits for infringement;

(1)In a suit for infringement of a patent, damages or an account of profits shall not be granted against the defendant who proves that at the date of the infringement he was not aware and had no reasonable grounds for believing that the patent existed.

Explanation.--A person shall not be deemed to have been aware or to have had reasonable grounds for believing that a patent exists by reason only of the application to an article of the word "patent", "patented" or any word or words expressing or implying that a patent has been obtained for the article, unless the number of the patent accompanies the word or words in question.

(2) In any suit for infringement of a patent the court may, if it thinks fit, refuse to grant any damages or an account of profits in respect of any infringement committed after a failure to pay any renewal fee within the prescribed period and before any extension of that period.

(3) Where an amendment of a specification by way of disclaimer, correction or explanation has been allowed under this Act after the publication of the specification, no damages or account of profits shall be granted in any proceedings in respect of the use of the invention before the date of the decision allowing the amendment, unless the court is satisfied that the specification as originally published was framed in good faith and with reasonable skill and knowledge.

(4) Nothing in this section shall affect the power of the court to grant an injunction in any suit for infringement of a patent.

Therefore, it is not advisable to file a suit of infringement against the company.

Part B {60 Marks)

This part contains three questions of 30 (thirty marks each). The first part of B1 is compulsory and in B2 you need to answer one question.

Part B1 -Question |

After reading the specification stated below,

I. Draft 10 claims

II. Draft an Abstract (maximum of 140 words)

FIELD OF THE INVENTION

The present invention is device meant for dogs which is attached to a bicycle, tricycle orsimilar moving vehicle enabling the user to operate the vehicle and exercise the dog ina safe and efficient manner.BACKGROUND OF THE INVENTIONMany people exercise their dogs by taking them for

a walk. However, it is known thatwalking a dog does not provide the dog with sufficient exercise unless the dog is walkedfor extensive periods of time. However, most people do not take a dog for a lengthywalk because it is too exhausting or too boring.The alternative is to exercise the dog while riding a bicycle. This is done by pedaling inthe customary manner while holding the dog's leash in one hand or attaching the leashto the handle bars or other portion of the bicycle frame.While this manner of exercise provides the dog with an excellent workout, it doeshowever, subject both the dog and rider to possible serious injury. For example, therider and/or dog may be injured if the dog should accidentally suddenly pull away fromthe bicycle or bump into the wheels or pedals. It is obvious that even a minor tug by thedog can cause the rider to lose control of the bicycle. The dog may also be injured if either the dog or the bicycle comes to an abrupt halt.This can cause the leash to strangle the dog and topple the bicycle. In addition, if theleash should become entangled in the pedals, the dog may be strangled as well.It is thus apparent that despite the benefits of exercising a dog while riding a bicycle, thedangers of this form of exercise far outweigh the benefits. It is therefore an object of theinvention to provide a device for exercising a dog while riding a bicycle in which the dogcannot interfere with the rider. It is another object of the invention to provide a devicewhich is resilient and provides controlled resistance to the movement of the dog.

DETAILED DESCRIPTION OF THE INVENTION

The device according to the present invention includes a bracket adapted to beattached to the frame of the bicycle away from the pedals and preferably as close to theground as possible. Extending outward and essentially perpendicular from the frame isa first bar. The length of the first bar determines the distance between the dog and theframe of the bicycle when the exercising device is attached to the dog through a leash.The bar is attached to the bar through a resilient means such as a spring and afastening device. The fastening device is secured to the first bar through a bolt or othersuitable device and includes a block having grooves on the exterior surface for securelyretaining therein individual turns of the spring. A similar block is mounted to the secondbar for securing the spring thereto.The bar is provided with an adjustment mechanism which is adapted fo regulate theincline of the bar to thereby adjust the distance of the dog from the bicycle. There is alsoprovided a second adjustment mechanism which also serves to adjust the incline of thebar.In accordance with the invention the length of the bars may be adjusted toaccommodate the size of the frame of the bicycle and the resiliency or strength of thespring can be adjusted to accommodate the size of the dog to be exercised. Thus, in apreferred embodiment, the spring may be easily removed and replaced according to theneeds of the user.The fastening device of the invention as previously described may be constructed so asto permit the spring to come out of the grooves when the spring is subjected to anexcessive load.The adjustment mechanisms and may be replaced by a single, adjustable joint (e.g. aball joint) to achieve the same functions as the individual adjustment mechanisms. Thesingle adjustment joint may be affixed to the bar.The bar is rigid and has a U-shape. The resilient means and the bar may be formedintegral with each other. The bar may be provided at one end with a loop. Anattachment device is secured to the loop of the bar and includes a first hook forremovably attaching to the loop and a second hook which is adapted to removablyattach to the collar of the dog. The hooks and are preferably affixed to an elasticmember such as a rubber band or similar member. The hooks are adapted toinstantaneously disengage from the loop and the collar of the dog, respectively whensubjected to a heavy load if the dog or bicycle should hit a stationary object such as atree wherein the dog will be easily disengaged from the device to thereby preventinjury.The bar may be provided with a bore or hole at an end remote from the resilient meansfor the purpose of securing a bracket to the frame of the bicycle. The hole is adapted toreceive the end of a securing means. The securing means is also placed through acorresponding hole in a fastening bolt which is sized to fit with the end of the bar.The bracket is provided with bolt holes which receive fastening bolts or screws. Therespective opposed portions of the bracket are adapted to be secured about the generally cylindrical frame of the bicycle. The bracket may also be provided with a protective lining on the inner surface of the portions to protect the frame of the bicycle. A preferred fastening arrangement for the bar comprises a support prop which may be fastened in one end of the fastening bolt which may have an oblong shape and has in arearward end a W-shaped fastening bracket for securing the device to the back wheel supports of the bicycle. Such a device is suited to prevent the bar from twisting about the frame when subjected to a heavy load.It employs a safety device such as a split ring capable of instantaneously disengaging the dog from the apparatus. Such a device may be placed between the loop and the carbine hook, and/or the carbine hook and the leash of the dog. The split is positioned between the loop and the hook and the split ring is positioned between the hook and theleash. Either or both split rings may be used. The safety device is adapted to free the dog instantly under a load which wouldotherwise injure the dog such as if the leash becomes stuck or entangled in a stationary object such as a tree.

Ans: Title-"Bicycle Dog Exercising Device with Resilient and Safe Leash Attachment"

ABSTRACT:

The present invention provides a device meant for exercising dogs that attaches to a bicycle or similar moving vehicle and enables users to operate the vehicle and exercise the dog in a safe and efficient manner. The device includes a bracket adapted to be attached to the frame of the bicycle, extending outward from the frame, and essentially perpendicular to it. The device also includes a rigid, U-shaped bar attached to a resilient means, such as a spring, and a fastening device that connects the bar to the resilient means. The device has adjustment mechanisms to regulate the incline of the bar to adjust the distance between the dog and the bicycle. The device also includes a safety device, such as a split ring, that frees the dog instantly under a load that would otherwise injure the dog.

CLAIMS:

I claim:

1. A device for exercising dogs that attaches to a bicycle or similar moving vehicle, comprising a bracket, a rigid U-shaped bar attached to a resilient means, and a fastening device that connects the bar to the resilient means.

2. The device of claim 1, further comprising adjustment mechanisms that regulate the incline of the bar to adjust the distance between the dog and the bicycle.

3. The device of claim 1, comprising a safety device, such as a split ring, that frees the dog instantly under a load that would otherwise injure the dog.

4. The device of claim 1, wherein the bracket is adapted to attach to the frame of the bicycle and extend outward and essentially perpendicular from the frame.

5. The device of claim 1, wherein the fastening device connects the bar to the resilient means with a block having grooves on the exterior surface for securely retaining individual turns of the spring.

6. The device of claim 1, wherein the bar is provided with a loop at one end and an attachment device that includes a first hook for removably attaching to the loop and a second hook that is adapted to removably attach to the collar of the dog.

7. The device of claim 1, wherein the adjustment mechanisms may be replaced by a single adjustable joint, such as a ball joint, affixed to the bar to achieve the same functionality.

8. The device of claim 1, wherein the safety device may be placed between the loop and the carbine hook, and/or the carbine hook and the leash of the dog.

9. The device of claim 1, wherein the bracket is provided with bolt holes that receive fastening bolts or screws to secure the device about the generally cylindrical frame of the bicycle.

10. The device of claim 1, comprising a support prop that may be fastened in one end of the fastening bolt and a W-shaped fastening bracket for securing the device to the back wheel supports of the bicycle.

PART B2

Question 1. A client meets you and provides you with the information below. You are required todraft a compiete specification to file a Patent in the Indian Patent Office.The invention relates to Ignition foiling device

which serves to interfere with the efficientoperation of a vehicle ignition system after a brief, predetermined period of time haselapsed subsequent to the unauthorized start-up of the vehicle engine.Invention1.The ignition pulse train which flows to the ignition coil primary is interfered with ina sporadic way, or else stopped altogether after an anomalous period of time, bya fast acting shunting switch such as a thyristor or a transistor.In this invention the ignition foiling means is disabled or shut-off by theauthorized operator of the vehicle through a separate and usually hidden keyswitch, or otherwise obscured secret switch.in the event that an illegal operator tries to obtain engine start-up, the ignitionfoiling means will of course not be defected and thereby the foiling control effectcomes into play.Once the vehicle moves a little distance giving an illusion of engine misfire andlater will have no fuel to run as the fuel pipe is blocked.The actual time which may elapse from the unauthorized start-up of the vehicleand the onset of ignition fouling may be accomplished most preferably throughthe actual pulse counting of the ignition pulses arriving from the ignition coil,which means there will be a variable time elapse with each foiling operation,since the time delay depends on engine speed.The foiling time delay is determined by a clock means which produces arelatively constant initial delay period, usually followed by an irregular series offoiling intervals which become progressively more objectionable. Therefore, theoverall time elapse from startup until the vehicle operation fails will always besomewhat different, giving the illusion of ordinary failure due to faulty vehicleoperation.Aside from the irregular ignition fouling effect, an irregular honking of the vehiclehorn or other such alarm device after the elapse of the initial delay period. This produces an attention getting public outcry where the illegal operator will end up in abandoning the vehicle.

BACKGROUND OF INVENTION: The protection of a motor vehicle against illegal confiscation, viz. theft, has been accomplished before through the installation of a hidden fuel shutoff valve. When such a valve is turned "off", the protected vehicle is allowed to start up in a normal way and operate for a brief period of time during which it consumes the limited amount of fuel contained in the carburetor bowl, etc. This limited operation of the engine encouragesthe thief to drive the vehicle from its obscure location where the thief feels safe, to amore public view where continued theft activity would be discouraged by exposure.Furthermore, the time the vehicle operates before the limited fuel is consumed will varyfrom one vehicle to another due to differences to residual fuel left after the cutoff valve,and the vehicle's consumption rate. The time will also vary in any given vehicledepending on the presumably illicit driver's driving style, e.g. racing the engine willconsume the limited amount of fuel more quickly than a leisurely, idle speed drive away.The inclusion of such cutoff devices has limited popularity because it involves difficult,costly installation which has limited variability in the choice of a good hidden location forthe shutoff device.It therefore appears that a means for producing the same kind of desired irregular timeduration limited drivability effect prior to total vehicle disablement is desirable. if such adevice can be easily installed at low cost and without inter coupling with the vehicle'sfuel system. The limited operation of the vehicle electrical ignition system is selected asthe best embodiment for my invention, in that inter coupling with the ignition system iseasily undertaken, even by the "Saturday afternoon mechanic". Since the operation isentirely electric in nature, the secret switch can be situated in a multitude of locationsunique to each operator's choice. This advantage of course makes the switch discoverymuch more unlikely, even by a skilled potential thief. The likelihood of easy discovery islargely determined by the ingenuity of the individual installer's choice of location options.Additionally, the hidden switch may be key operated.The resulting theft deterring effect which would be desirable would produce anexperience quite similar to that now produced by fuel cutoff, wherein the vehicle startsup, but then soon exhibits erratic running behaviour which shortly becomesprogressively worse, or else the vehicle falters altogether in its operation after a shortperiod of seemingly normal operation. This false start generally serves to enable thethief to have to expose himself in a way that should lead to his abandonment of the theftproject. It also produces the illusion of faulty vehicle operation, which may discouragethe thief. Prior ArtThe earlier shut off devices do not give irregular firing of the engine and cannotdeter the thefts and the location is not fixed and cannot be detected.

IN THE INDIAN PATENT OFFICE

COMPLETE SPECIFICATION

(Section 10; rule 13)

TITLE: Ignition Foiling Device

FIELD OF THE INVENTION:

The present invention relates generally to the field of vehicle anti-theft devices, more particularly to an ignition foiling device that serves to interfere with the efficient operation of a vehicle engine after a brief, predetermined period of time has elapsed subsequent to the unauthorized start-up of the vehicle engine.

BACKGROUND OF THE INVENTION:

The protection of motor vehicles against theft has been accomplished before through the installation of a hidden fuel shutoff valve. However, such devices have limited popularity due to difficult and costly installation. The present invention provides a means for producing the same kind of desired effect by interfering with the ignition pulse train flowing to the ignition coil primary after a predetermined period of time has elapsed, causing erratic engine behavior and discouraging theft.

SUMMARY OF THE INVENTION:

The present invention provides an ignition foiling device comprising a fast-acting shunting switch such as a thyristor or a transistor that interferes with the ignition pulse train flowing to the ignition coil primary in a sporadic way, or stops it altogether after an anomalous period of time. The foiling means is disabled or shut-off by the authorized operator of the vehicle through a separate and usually hidden key switch or an obscured secret switch. In the event that an illegal operator tries to obtain engine start-up, the ignition foiling means is not defected, and the foiling effect comes into play, resulting in erratic engine behavior and, ultimately, engine failure. The foiling time delay is determined by a clock means which produces a relatively constant initial delay period, followed by an irregular series of foiling intervals which become progressively more objectionable. A horn or other alarm device is activated after the elapse of the initial delay period, producing an attention-getting outcry.

DETAILED DESCRIPTION OF THE INVENTION:

The present invention provides an ignition foiling device that serves to interfere with the efficient operation of a vehicle engine after a brief, predetermined period of time has elapsed subsequent to the unauthorized start-up of the vehicle engine.

In one embodiment, the ignition pulse train flowing to the ignition coil primary is interfered with in a sporadic way, or is stopped altogether after an anomalous period of time by a fast-acting shunting switch such as a thyristor or a transistor.

In one embodiment, the ignition foiling means is disabled or shut-off by the authorized operator of the vehicle through a separate and usually hidden key switch or an obscured secret switch, preventing erratic engine behavior and engine failure.

In one embodiment, the foiling time delay is determined by a clock means which produces a relatively constant initial delay period, followed by an irregular series of foiling intervals which become progressively more objectionable.

In one embodiment, a horn or other alarm device is activated after the elapse of the initial delay period, producing an attention-getting outcry where the illegal operator will end up abandoning the vehicle.

The invention may be easily installed at low cost without intercoupling with the vehicle's fuel system, and the secret switch can be situated in a multitude of locations unique to each operator's choice, making switch discovery much more unlikely, even by a skilled potential thief.

EXAMPLES:

Not Applicable.

CLAIMS:

I claim:

1. An ignition foiling device for a vehicle, comprising a fast-acting shunting switch that interferes with the ignition pulse train flowing to the ignition coil primary in a sporadic way, or stops it altogether after an anomalous period of time.

2. The ignition foiling device of claim 1, wherein the foiling means is disabled or shut-off by an authorized operator of the vehicle through a separate and usually hidden key switch or obscured secret switch.

3. The ignition foiling device of claim 1, wherein the foiling time delay is determined by a clock means which produces a relatively constant initial delay period, followed by an irregular series of foiling intervals which become progressively more objectionable.

4. The ignition foiling device of claim 1, further comprising a horn or other alarm device that is activated after the elapse of the initial delay period, producing an attention-getting outcry.

5. The ignition foiling device of claim 1, wherein the fast-acting shunting switch comprises a transistor.

Question 2: A client meets you and provides you with the information below. You are required todraft a complete specification to file a Patent in

the Indian Patent Office.invention in brief:To achieve continuous delivery of the protein or peptide in vivo, a sustained release or sustained delivery formulation is desirable to avoid the need for repeated administrations. Approaches generally followed: microencapsulation to produce micro particles. Encapsulation of a biologically active or pharmaceutically active agent within a biocompatible, biodegradable wall forming material such as a polymer, to provide sustained or delayed release. Generally agent or drug is dissolved, dispersed or emulsified, using stirrers, agitators, orother dynamic mixing techniques, in one or more solvents containing the wall forming material. The solvent is removed. Prior art discloses a set of inert substances such as poly (lactide) (PLA) or poly (lactide-co-glycolide) (PLGA) microspheres or films containing the active agent to be used assustained-release devices. Desirable attributes: sufficiently good control of the release of the encapsulated active agent; No or minimum side effects; integrity of the active agent is maintained during manufacture; e.g. configuration of most protein and peptide drugs are dependent on a three dimensional conformation for their bioactivity and that conformations can easily be compromised. Pharmaceutical compositions : a stable sustained release complex composed of aprotein and/or peptide and a gallic acid ester that allow for sustained delivery of theprotein or peptide in vivo upon administration of the complex. The complex permitscontinuous delivery of a pharmaceutically active peptide to a subject for periods of timeless than about one or two weeks. The complex is formed by combining a protein orpeptide and a gallic acid ester under specific conditions. The complex is poorly solublein water and can be purified from various aqueous solutions. As the complex is in theform of a solid (e.g., a paste, granules, a powder or a lyophilizate), the complex can be 10prepared for administration to a subject as a stable liquid suspension or semi-soliddispersion.The purified complex of a peptide of 20 amino acids or less and a purified gallic acidester, wherein said peptide is a Bl peptide antagonist. The complex is a salt of thepeptide and the gallic acid ester. The gallic acid ester is selected from the groupconsisting of PentaGalloylGlucose (PGG) and epigallocatechin gallate (EGCG). Thepurified gallic acid ester is PentaGalloylGlucose(PGG). The complex is a salt of thepeptide and PGG, and said salt has a release duration in an animal upto two weeks.When the complex is a salt of the peptide and PGG, the salt has a release duration inan animal less than one week. When the complex is a salt of the peptide and PGG, ithas a release duration in an animal of less than 4 days. The purified gallic acid estermay be epigallocatechin gallate (EGCG). The peptide is selected from i) DOm Lys ArgPro Hyp Gly Cpg Ser Dtic Cpg; and ii) Acetyl Lys Lys Arg Pro Hyp Gly Cpg Ser Dtic Cpgwherein DGrn is the D isomer of ornithine, Hyp is Trans-4-hydroxy-proline, Dtic is the Disomer of 12,3 4-tetrahydroisoquinoline-3-carboxylic acid, and Cpg is cyclopentylglycine. The peptide in the complex is in excess of the purified gallic acid ester on aweight/weight basis. The molar ratio of peptide to purified gallic acid ester is 1:1, 1:2, or1.3.The method of making the sustained release composition: combining a solution of apeptide of 20 amino acids or less, and a solution of purified gallic acid ester. Thecomplex is formed at a pH from 6.5 to 8.6. The complex is precipitated out of thesolution to obtain a sustained release composition. The peptide is selected from i) DOmLys Arg Pro Hyp Gly Cpg Ser Dtic Cpg; and ii) Acetyl Lys Lys Arg Pro Hyp Gly Cpg SerDtic Cpg wherein DOrn is the D isomer of ornithine, Hyp is Trans-4-hydroxy-proline, Dticis the D isomer of 12,3 4-tetrahydroisoquinoline-3-carboxylic acid, and Cpg iscyclopentylgiycine.The gallic acid ester is PGG., and the gallic acid ester is EGCG.The purified complex isformed at a pH from 6.0 to 9.0.ExamplesThis provides a description of a preparation of Peptide B-PGG salt (1:1 molar ratio ofPeptide B (POm Lys Arg Pro Hyp Gly Cpg Ser Dtic Cpg)"to PGG). A stock solution ofPGG was made by dissolving 94 mg of PGG in 2 mi of NaOH solution (concentration ofNaOH from 0.10 to 0.20 N) following by filtering it through a 0.2 um filter. To a stocksolution of PGG (1.56 mi) was added sequentially a solution of 109,4 mg of Peptide Bacetate salt in 0.8 ml water with stirring and a precipitate formed. The precipitate wasrecovered by centrifugation. The supernatant was decanted and the precipitate waswashed with 0.5 ml water 3 times. The precipitate was dried in vacuum at approximately30-35°C for approximately 20 hours to yield 125 mg (76%). The Peptide B-PGG saltwas an off-white powder.AaN wo 11Salts of Peptide A-PGG and tannate were made in a similar way to Peptide B-PGG inearlier example.Peptide A was Acetyl Lys Lys Arg Pro Hyp Gly Cpg Ser Dtic Cpg-The study of the effect of salt formation pH (i.e. concentration level of NaOH) on theyield, peptide content and solubility of Peptide B-PGG salt was investigated. FourPeptide B-PGG salts at pH 7.0, 7.2, 7.6 and 8.6 were prepared and isolated. Theirsolubility in water and PBS, and also their peptide content were then determined. Theseresults demonstrate (Table 3) that aqueous solubility, yield of salt formation and peptidecontent increase with increasing pH during salt formation. The sustained release ofPeptide B/PGG and Peptide B/tannate salts in rats is demonstrated here. The ratpharmacokinetics (PK) studies were performed by a single subcutaneous injection (10mg/kg dose) of Peptide B/PGG salts and Peptide B/tannate salt suspended in TRISbuffer, and a PBS solution of Peptide B acetate as a control group. The PK resultsshowed one-week sustained release for Peptide B/ tannate salt and Peptide B-PGG saltthat prepared at pH 7,0. However, Peptide B-PGG salts prepared at pH 7.6 and 8.6showed shorter release duration (around 2-3 days) compared to salt prepared at pH 7.0(up to two weeks).A pure anomer (beta-PGG) and a mixture of anomers (alpha + beta-PGG) of PGG saltsof Peptide B (DOr Lys Arg Pro Hyp Gly Cpg Ser Dtic Cpg) were prepared by a similarmethod to that described in Example 1. There was no significant difference in theaqueous solubility of these salts. Based on aqueous solubility, it is expected that the invivo sustained release duration for these salts would be similar.The following describes the use of EGCG to make a salt with a peptide, which wastested in an animal pharmacokinetic (PK) study for sustained release. A stock solutionof EGCG (Sigma-Aldrich) was made by dissolving 184 mg of EGCG in 2 ml of 0.2 NNaOH followed by filtering it through a 0.2 um filter. To a stock solution of EGCG (1,4ml) was slowly added a solution of 138 mg of acetate salt of Peptide B (DOrn Lys ArgPro Hyp Gly Cpg Ser Dtic Cpg) in 1.2 ml water with stirring. The resulting suspensionwas stirred for approximately 10-15 minutes at room temperature. After centrifugation,the supernatant was decanted and the precipitate was washed with 1 mi water (3 timesby centrifugation and decantation of supernatant). The precipitate was dried undervacuum at approximately 30-35°C for approximately 20 hours to yield 218 mg (88%) ofPeptide B-EGCG salt as an off-white powder.The peptide content of the Peptide BIEGCG salts were 47-50%. The aqueous solubilityfor the salt with 1:3 molar ratio of peptide to EGCG is < 0.5 mg/ml in water and < 0.05mg/ml in PBS, and for 1:2 molar ratio of peptide to EGCG, solubility is approximately 1mg/ml in water and approximately 03 mg/ml in PBS. A rat PK study was performedusing a single sc injection (10 mg/Kg dose) of '593/EGCG salt suspended in TRISbuffer, pH7.0. The PK result showed sustained release of Peptide B for multiple dayswith the blood level > 26 ng/ral at 24 hours, then a decrease to. approximately 5 ng/mlat 96 hours. The Y-capacitors 12, 13 are disposed directly between phase and ground wire housing and contacted tothe ground wire at 18. A very low inductance connection is obtained by these extremely short leads.In FIG. 3, a sectional view as indicated in FIG. 2, the organization of internal components of the filter isillustrated. The short lead connections for the Y-capacitors 12 and 13 are clearly illustrated connectingrespectively between flat plugs 11 and 12 and grounded connector 9.

IN THE INDIAN PATENT OFFICE

COMPLETE SPECIFICATION

(Section 10; rule 13)

Title: Pharmaceutical Composition for Sustained Release of Proteins or Peptides

Abstract: The present invention relates to a pharmaceutical composition for the sustained release of a protein or peptide in vivo. The composition comprises a purified complex of a peptide of 20 amino acids or less and a gallic acid ester, allowing for continuous delivery of the protein or peptide for a period of time up to two weeks. The composition is formed by combining the peptide and gallic acid ester under specific conditions, with the molar ratio of peptide to ester being 1:1, 1:2, or 1.3. The gallic acid ester may be PentaGalloylGlucose (PGG) or epigallocatechin gallate (EGCG). The method of making the composition involves precipitating the complex out of a solution of the peptide and ester, at a pH of 6.5 to 9.0.

FIELD OF THE INVENTION:

The present invention relates generally to the field of pharmaceuticals, more particularly to a pharmaceutical composition for the sustained release of proteins or peptides.

BACKGROUND OF THE INVENTION:

Administration of proteins or peptides to the human body to treat various diseases has become a common practice. However, the in vivo half-life of these proteins or peptides is usually very short, requiring repeated administrations which are both inconvenient and costly. To address this issue, a sustained release or sustained delivery formulation is desirable, which can provide continuous delivery of the protein or peptide in vivo, avoiding the need for repeated administrations.

Several approaches are commonly followed to achieve sustained release of proteins or peptides. One of the most commonly used approaches involves microencapsulation to produce micro-particles. In this approach, a biologically active or pharmaceutically active agent, such as a protein or peptide, is encapsulated within a biocompatible, biodegradable wall-forming material such as a polymer. The encapsulation enables sustained or delayed release of the encapsulated active agent.

Another common approach involves dissolving, dispersing or emulsifying the protein or peptide in one or more solvents containing the wall-forming material while using stirrers, agitators, or other dynamic mixing techniques. The solvent is then removed, leaving behind a solid comprising the protein or peptide encapsulated within the wall-forming material.

Prior art discloses the use of a set of inert substances such as poly(lactide) (PLA) or poly(lactide-co-glycolide) (PLGA) microspheres or films containing the active agent to be used as sustained-release devices. However, these prior art methods may not achieve sufficiently good control of the release of the encapsulated active agent, may cause side effects, and may compromise the integrity of the active agent during manufacture.

SUMMARY OF THE INVENTION:

The present invention provides a stable, sustained release complex composed of a protein and/or peptide and a gallic acid ester that allows for sustained delivery of the protein or peptide in vivo upon administration of the complex. The complex permits continuous delivery of a pharmaceutically active peptide to a subject for periods of time less than about one or two weeks. The complex is formed by combining a protein or peptide and a gallic acid ester under specific conditions. The complex is poorly soluble in water and can be purified from various aqueous solutions.

As the complex is in the form of a solid (e.g., a paste, granules, a powder or a lyophilizate), the complex can be prepared for administration to a subject as a stable liquid suspension or semi-solid dispersion.

DETAILED DESCRIPTION OF THE INVENTION:

The present invention provides a pharmaceutical composition for sustained release of proteins or peptides. The composition comprises a purified complex of a peptide of 20 amino acids or less and a gallic acid ester, allowing for continuous delivery of the protein or peptide in vivo upon administration of the complex.

In one embodiment, the peptide in the complex is a B peptide antagonist. The gallic acid ester may be PentaGalloylGlucose (PGG) or epigallocatechin gallate (EGCG). The mixture of those two gallic acid esters is also included, where the molar ratio of peptide to purified gallic acid ester is 1:1, 1:2, or 1.3.

In one embodiment, the purified complex is formed as a salt of the peptide and the gallic acid ester. The complex is selected from the group consisting of a Peptide A-PGG salt, a Peptide B-PGG salt, a Peptide A-tannate salt, and a Peptide B-tannate salt.

In one embodiment, the peptide is selected from i) DOm Lys Arg Pro Hyp Gly Cpg Ser Dtic Cpg; and ii) Acetyl Lys Lys Arg Pro Hyp Gly Cpg Ser Dtic Cpg, wherein DOrn is the D isomer of ornithine, Hyp is Trans-4-hydroxy-proline, Dtic is the D isomer of 12,3 4-tetrahydroisoquinoline-3-carboxylic acid, and Cpg is cyclopentylglycine. The peptide in the complex is in excess of the purified gallic acid ester on a weight/weight basis.

A method of making the sustained release composition, comprising combining a solution of a peptide of 20 amino acids or less and a solution of purified gallic acid ester, at a pH of 6.5 to 9.0, and precipitating the complex out of the solution to obtain a sustained release composition.

In one embodiment, the method of making the sustained release composition involves the following steps:

- preparing a solution of a peptide of 20 amino acids or less and a purified gallic acid ester;

- combining the solution of the peptide and the gallic acid ester at a pH of 6.5 to 9.0, the complex is formed at a pH from 6.0 to 9.0; and

- precipitating the complex out of the solution to obtain a purified complex.

In one embodiment, the sustained release composition is administered to a subject as a stable liquid suspension or semi-solid dispersion.

The pharmaceutical composition of the present invention may be used to treat various diseases, particularly those requiring the delivery of a protein or peptide for a period of time up to two weeks, such as cancer, chronic pain, inflammation, and cardiovascular diseases.

EXAMPLES:

Example 1:

This example provides a description of a preparation of Peptide B-PGG salt with a molar ratio of 1:1. A stock solution of PGG was made by dissolving 94 mg of PGG in 2 ml of NaOH solution (concentration of NaOH from 0.10 to 0.20 N) following by filtering it through a 0.2 μm filter. To a stock solution of PGG (1.56 ml) was added sequentially a solution of 109.4 mg of Peptide B acetate salt in 0.8 ml water with stirring and a precipitate formed. The precipitate was recovered by centrifugation. The supernatant was decanted and the precipitate was washed with 0.5 ml water 3 times. The precipitate was dried in vacuum at approximately 30-35°C for approximately 20 hours to yield 125 mg (76%). The Peptide B-PGG salt was an off-white powder.

Example 2:

This example provides a description of the sustained release of Peptide B/PGG and Peptide B/tannate salts in rats. A rat pharmacokinetics (PK) study was performed by a single subcutaneous injection (10 mg/kg dose) of Peptide B/PGG salts and Peptide B/tannate salt suspended in TRIS buffer, and a PBS solution of Peptide B acetate as a control group. The PK results showed one-week sustained release for Peptide B/tannate salt and Peptide B-PGG salt that prepared at pH 7.0. However, Peptide B-PGG salts prepared at pH 7.6 and 8.6 showed shorter release duration (around 2-3 days) compared to salt prepared at pH 7.0 (up to two weeks).

Example 3:

In this example, a Peptide B-EGCG salt with a molar ratio of 1:2 was prepared. A stock solution of EGCG (Sigma-Aldrich) was made by dissolving 184 mg of EGCG in 2 ml of 0.2 N NaOH followed by filtering it through a 0.2 µm filter. To a stock solution of EGCG (1.4 ml) was slowly added a solution of 138 mg of acetate salt of Peptide B (DOm Lys Arg Pro Hyp Gly Cpg Ser Dtic Cpg) in 1.2 ml water with stirring. The resulting suspension was stirred for approximately 10-15 minutes at room temperature. After centrifugation, the supernatant was decanted and the precipitate was washed with 1 ml water (3 times by centrifugation and decantation of supernatant). The precipitate was dried under vacuum at approximately 30-35°C for approximately 20 hours to yield 218 mg (88%) of Peptide B-EGCG salt as an off-white powder.

CLAIMS:

I claim:

1. A pharmaceutical composition for the sustained release of a protein or peptide, comprising a purified complex of a peptide of 20 amino acids or less and a gallic acid ester, allowing for the continuous delivery of the protein or peptide in vivo upon administration of the complex.

2. The composition of claim 1, wherein the peptide is a B peptide antagonist.

3. The composition of claim 1, wherein the gallic acid ester is PentaGalloylGlucose (PGG) or epigallocatechin gallate (EGCG).

4. The composition of claim 1, wherein the molar ratio of peptide to purified gallic acid ester is 1:1, 1:2, or 1.3.

5. A method of making the sustained release composition, comprising combining a solution of a peptide of 20 amino acids or less and a solution of

purified gallic acid ester, at a pH of 6.5 to 9.0, and precipitating the complex out of the solution to obtain a sustained release composition.

PATENT AGENT EXAMINATION, 2010

(Under Section 126 of the Patents Act, 1970, as amended)

January 23, 2010

PAPER II

TOTAL MARKS: 100

Time: 3 PM to 6 PM (3 hours)

Total number of pages: 7

Instructions:

This paper consists of 2 parts.

The first part (Part A) of 40 marks requires You to answer four questions of 10 marks each.

The second part (Part B) of 60 marks requires you fo answer two questions of 30 marks each.

You must attempt all questions. Please read the questions very carefully before answering them. Please also divide Your time appropriately so that You are able to complete all answers in time.

PART A (40 MARKS)

Instructions:

Each Question Below Carries 10 (Ten) Marks. Please answer all the questions. Your answer must be brief and to the point. While answering the questions, you are expected to support your answer by giving reasons and citing the relevant sections and rules in the Indian Patents Act.

1. A research team working with company CRO completed a very difficult R&D project. CRO has filed a provisional patent application on October 10, 2009 in its name. Since then, its researchers have worked further on the invention and are now in aposition to file a complete specification. The complete specification is expected tohave 61 pages and 113 claims. There are 3 new inventors, of which 2 are foreignersfrom another institution "CRY" whose names have to be included in the patentapplication. There is an understanding between "CRO" and "CRY that the patent application will be filed Jointly in the names of the two institutions.

Suggest a plan of action for the filing of the relevant patent application including the timelines, the essential forms to be filled, fees to be paid and associated formalities to be completed to ensure that the application is in order.

The following is a plan of action for filing the relevant patent application:

1. Prepare the complete specification: The complete specification should be drafted to include the new inventors' names, and must describe the invention in sufficient detail to enable a person skilled in the art to perform the invention. The specification must also comply with the Indian Patents Act, 1970.

2. File the complete specification: The complete specification must be filed within 12 months of the filing date of the provisional application, as per Section 9(1) of the Indian Patents Act. The application should be filed in Form 2 as per the Indian Patents Rules, 2003. The fee for filing the application varies depending on the type of applicant (individual, small entity, or others) and the number of pages and claims included in the specification.

3. Request examination: Within 48 months of the priority date or the filing date of the complete specification (whichever is earlier), the applicant must file a request for examination of the application in Form 18 with the prescribed fee.

This step is critical to ensure that the patent application is examined by the Indian Patent Office and is processed for grant.

4. Respond to examination report: After examination, the Indian Patent Office issues an examination report containing objections, if any. The applicant must respond to this examination report within 6 months from the date of receipt of the report. The response must be filed in Form 13, along with the prescribed fee. Failure to respond to the examination report may result in abandonment of the application.

5. Grant of patent: If the application satisfies the patentability criteria and the objections raised in the examination report are resolved to the satisfaction of the Indian Patent Office, the patent is granted and published in the Indian Patent Office Journal.

The associated formalities to be completed include filing the necessary forms, paying the fees and ensuring that all the required documents are included in the application. The fees for filing the application and the examination request will depend on the status of the entity (individual, small entity, or others). The fees can be paid online via the Indian Patent Office's e-filing system.

The timeline for filing the complete specification is within 12 months of the provisional application filing, as stated in Section 9(1) of the Indian Patents Act. The timeline for the examination request is within 48 months of the priority date or the filing date of the complete specification (whichever is earlier), as per Section 11(B) of the Indian Patents Act and Rule 24 of Patent Rules. The timeline for responding to the examination report is within 6 months from the date of receipt of the report, as per the Indian Patents Rules, 2003.

2. You receive a letter dated November 25, 2009 from the TATAS asking you to & represent them in respect of "Snano". their invention relating to a

car which * guarantees sound sleep to any person travelling within it, barring the driver. The letter informs you that the client first filed a US application in respect of the "Snano™ on May 1, 2007. They later filed a PCT application on December 1, 2007. Now they wish to file a national phase application in India: i)What information do you require from the client to assess whether the Snano can be protected in India?

ii) You receive the client's letter on November 29, 2009. It will take you at least 5 days to get documents ready and file the papers at the Patent office. What steps would you take to protect your clients interest? Assume in (iii) above that the letter reaches you only on December 5, 2009. What would your advice be?

i) To assess whether the Snano can be protected in India, we would need the following information from the client:

1. Priority application number and date of filing of the US application.

2. Date of filing of the PCT application.

3. Publication date of the PCT application.

4. International search report (ISR) and written opinion (WO) issued by the International Search Authority (ISA) in the PCT application.

5. Details of any amendments made to the claims during the PCT stage.

6. Details of any patents or patent applications filed in other jurisdictions.

ii) If we receive the client's letter on November 29, 2009, we would immediately start preparing the necessary documents to file a national phase application in India. We would request the client to provide us with the required documents and information as soon as possible, to enable us to prepare and file the application within the five-day deadline. We would also advise the client to pay the necessary fees and any other charges required to file the application. The 31st month deadline falls on 1st of December. The client can still seek an extension of time under Rule 138 of the Indian Patents Rules, 2003 before the expiry period. We would advise the client on the procedure for filing an application for extension of time and the likelihood of success in obtaining the extension.

iii) If we receive the client's letter on December 5, 2009, we would advise them that the deadline for filing the national phase application in India has already passed. The deadline for entering the national phase in India is 31 months from the priority date or the international filing date, whichever is earlier, the client can not seek an extension of time under Rule 138 of the Indian Patents Rules, 2003. We would not advise the client on the procedure for filing an application for extension of time.

3. Your client "X" writes to you as follows: "Our Indian patent issued in December 2009 describes and claims a process of reacting A with B under certain specified conditions to obtain product C. It is also essential that catalyst Q be present in order that product C may possess the desirable characteristics outlined in our disclosure, Unfortunately, none of the claims in the patent make any reference to catalyst Q at all, even though catalyst Q and the manner in which it is used in the process is clearly described in our disclosure, We would like to take action in the near future against a competitor of ours who has been using our process since the last one year. Do you think we will have difficulty enforcing our patent and, if so, is there anything you can do to improve our prospects for success against our competitor?"

i) Advise X.

ii) Assume that X's invention above has not yet been patented, but is merely the subject of a patent application before the Indian patent office. Would your advice be different? Consider both situations where the application has been published in the official journal as well as situations where it has not been so published?

iii) Assume now that the letter above is worded differently. It indicates that X's addition of the catalyst is an improvement not included anywhere in the specification. What would your advice be?

Ans. i. In this situation, X may face difficulty in enforcing their patent against the competitor who has been using the process without authorization. This is because the claims in the patent do not mention the essential catalyst Q, which is required for obtaining the desirable characteristics of the product. However, all hope is not lost. X can consider filing an amendment to include a claim that specifically refers to the use of catalyst Q in the process. Section 57 of the Indian Patents Act allows for amendments to the specification, claims, or drawings of a patent to be made by the patentee or their legal representatives, subject to certain conditions.

ii. Subject to the provisions of section 59, the Controller may, upon application made under this section in the prescribed manner by an applicant for a patent or by a patentee, allow the application for the patent or the complete specification [or any document relating thereto] to be amended subject to such conditions, if any, as the Controller thinks fit. Therefore, amendment is available at pre grant as well as post grant stage.

iii.If the letter indicates that the addition of catalyst Q is an improvement not included in the specification, the advice may differ. In this case, the matter would fall under Section 54 of the Indian Patents Act, which deals with the addition of new subject matter to a patent application or patent.

4. Motu wishes to license Chotu's patent relating to a slimming device. Chotu is already selling the product in India, by itself and through various other licensees. Motu hopes to manufacture the same device and sell in remote parts of India. He approaches you to find out if he should go ahead with the licensing deal. What are the aspects you would look into in order to protect your clients interest, including ensuring that Chotu's patent is a good one and that he has complied with all the requirements under the Indian Patents Act? If a license is finally taken, what are the various requirements under the Patents Act that Motu must comply with?

Ans: To protect our client's interest, we would look into the following aspects:

1. **Validity of the patent:** We would conduct a search to verify the validity of Chotu's patent and ensure that it has been granted by the Indian Patent Office. We would also look into whether there are any pending legal challenges against the validity of the patent.

2. **Scope of the patent:** We would look into the scope of the patent to ensure that it covers the slimming device that Motu wishes to manufacture. This includes analyzing the claims of the patent and checking if they are sufficiently broad to cover the device.

3. **Compliance with Indian Patents Act:** We would review Chotu's compliance with the Indian Patents Act, including the requirements for filing a complete specification, paying the prescribed fees, and disclosing the invention in a manner that meets the statutory requirements.

4. **License agreement:** We would review the license agreement between Chotu and Motu to ensure that it contains clear terms regarding the scope of the license, duration, payment of royalties, and other relevant clauses.

If the license deal goes through, the following are the various requirements under the Indian Patents Act that Motu must comply with:

1. **Registration of assignment:** If the license involves an assignment of the patent, then it must be registered with the Indian Patent Office within 6 months under Section 69 of the Indian Patents Act, 1970. The registration must be done in Form-16 as per Rule 90 of the Indian Patent Rules, 2003.

2. **Payment of royalties:** Motu must ensure that it pays the royalty fees to Chotu as per the terms of the license agreement. Failure to pay the royalties may result in termination of the license and legal action against Motu.

Overall, it is important for Motu to carefully consider the terms of the license agreement and ensure that it complies with all relevant requirements under the Indian Patents Act to avoid any legal disputes or infringement claims.

PART B (60 MARKS) This part contains two questions of 30 (Thirty) Marks. Please answer both the questions.

Question 1. After reading the below specification carefully, please

1) Draft at least 5 claims;

ii) Provide an appropriate title to the specification.

iii) Draft a suitable abstract

Field of the Invention The present invention discloses a device capable of harvesting and planting of plantable materials, maintaining their integrity during harvesting and transplantation. Further the device has an optional holder and a protective case also capable of functioning as a handle, Background of the Invention "Root-by Root" follicular hair transplantation is an accepted hair replacement alternative for hair loss. It has also become popular as a cosmetic means. Traditional transplantation of large punches became unacceptable due to its poor cosmetic result. Tt also produced loss of valuable hair grafts during and after transplantation procedure. This lead to the preparation of mini, micro and ultimate follicular hair grafts and transplanting them into desired are. The process of hair transplantation demands meticulous harvesting of the plantable material from the donor site and plantation of several hundreds of grafts in short time without damaging the roots. Several methods and instruments have been developed based on steps that involve damage free harvesting of the plantable material from the donor site, creation of appropriate recipient. site, keeping the site open during the plantation process placing the graft into the site maintaining its integrity and ensuring closure of the site after the plantation process is completed. The plantation process generally involves steps that include creation of an ideal recipient site, keeping the site open and placement of the graft into the site maintaining its integrity. Difficulties encountered in instruments involving plurality of grafts are (1) it is difficult to keep the multiple grafts separate as they have a tendency to stick to each Other planting instruments described in the prior art utilize suction, spring device or electricity. Loading of the planting material is done from the sharp piercing end with possibility of direct damage or degloving type injury if the planting material does not well fit into the cavity of piercing end. In instruments where the planting material is pushed by a rod or cylindrical material blindly inside the cavity, it may damage by crushing, folding, squeezing, distorting, bending or jamming. Some of the

Summary of the invention The main object of the invention is to provide a functionally cost effective manually operated instrument that is capabie of performing harvesting as well as plantation of wide range of plant able materials into diverse substrates at enhanced plantation speeds maintaining follicular integrity resulting in better yield. Another object of the invention is to provide an instrument for silent non-traumatic hair transplantation that ensures feather touch non-traumatic method of picking up the hair follicle only by its extra cuticle part of hair from the cool isotonic solution and inserting them in the loading slot of suitable size in a device avoiding the drawbacks of grabbing, holding, pinching, dragging, pushing and drying. Detailed Description of the invention ¢ The device comprises of a solid or hollow elongated structured transplanter of an appropriate length, width, wall thickness and shape longitudinally developing into a slotted groove of an appropriate length, width and shape having a wider slot as a substrate for harvesting and/or planting to appropriate depth determined. The penetration can be controlled by a "stopper" located at appropriate positions along the surface of the transplanter. This transplanter optionally has openings of appropriate number, size. shape at appropriate positions along the transplanter having optional 4 attachment or provision for the attachment to manuver the transplanter. The transplanted may further an optional holder/hub so structured at its lower end to enable for attachment with the upper end of the transplanter and the upper end of the holder/hub appropriately structured to fit the optional handle/case. Further the device is provided with an optional handle so structured at its lower end to enable housing the holder/hub and/or the transplanter during use while the upper end is so structured to accommodate the holder/hub and/or the transplanter when placed inside the handle to function as a case for storage during non-use. The transplanter may have optional number of openings of various sizes and shapes at appropriate positions along the transplanter to function as release for any "air lock" created during transplantation. The shape of the loading area ensures smooth loading, unloading and movement of the planting material along the transplanter for subsequent operations. It is to be noted that the width of the groove at retaining area is such that it does not allow the planting substance to pop out from the groove at the same time allows easy passage of the sliding device with planting material to and from the loading area to the wedge. Further the edges of the wedge of transplanter are sharp and tapered in a manner to allow easy passage of planter into the substrate with rotation and further during harvesting it enables the creation of circumferential cut around the hair follicle and during plantation it enables the creation of an appropriate site for the transplanting operations by maintaining the opening of the cavity stretched and walls of the cavity dilated/separated to facilitate the easy insertion of the plantable material into the created site with the help of a sliding device. Also the "stopper" arrangement is created as an integral part of the groove or along the common surface of the groove and/or the wedge of the transplanter.

Ans: Title: Device for Harvesting and Transplantation of Plantable Materials

Abstract: The present invention discloses a device for harvesting and planting plantable materials with minimal damage to their follicular structure. The device features a slotted groove for harvesting and/or planting materials, with optional stoppers for controlling penetration, and an optional holder/hub and handle/case for easy use and storage. The shape of the loading area and wedge are designed for easy passage and protection of plantable materials during harvesting and transplantation. This device provides a silent, non-traumatic method of picking up and inserting follicles, resulting in better yield and faster transplant speeds.

CLAIMS:

I claim:

1. A device for harvesting and planting of plantable materials with minimal damage.

2. The device as claimed in claim 1 wherein said device contains a slotted groove for harvesting and/or planting materials to an appropriate depth, with optional stoppers for controlling penetration.

3. The device as claimed in claim 1 wherein said device contains an optional holder/hub and handle/case for easy use and storage.

4. The deviceas claimed in claim 1 wherein said device has optional openings for release of air locks and smooth movement of planting material.

5.The deviceas claimed in claim 1 wherein said device having shape of the loading area and wedge are designed for easy passage and protection of plantable materials during harvesting and transplantation.

Question 2: A client meets you and provides you with information below. Please use the said information to write a complete patent specification ready to be filed before the Indian Patent Office. Hh Ld "The invention relates to an aqueous solution for cleaning contact lenses comprising a water-soluble peroxide, transition metal salts and a surfactant. Below are the details: Invention: 1 $ — 1. The solution is a combination of: Lr == i) a water-soluble peroxide ii) a catalytic amount of a water soluble transition metal catalyst in the form of an inorganic or organic salt 2 iii) a coco-hydrolyzed animal protein anionic surfactant. 3) 2. The invention works best when the above solution is made in the following proportion: 1) 0.1% to 15% by weight/volume (w/v) of peroxide ii) 0.25 micromoles to 0.25 millimoles per deciliter of metal catalyst 111) 0.1% to 20% (w/v) of surfactant and water in a quantity sufficient to make volume. 3. The solution need not be sold as it is. Rather, to ensure that it is stable and lasts longer, it can be divided into two separate portions of specific proportions. These two portions can be sold in one package to the consumer who can combine the separate portions at his end to get the solution. The two portions should be as below: i) a granular or aqueous peroxide ii) an aqueous solution consisting of a catalytic amount of water soluble transition metal catalyst in the form of an inorganic or organic salt AND a coco-hydrolyzed animal protein anionic surfactant. 4. The invention in 3 above works best when: one package contains a granular peroxide or an aqueous peroxide solution having a concentration of 0.2% to 30% (w/v) and the second package contains 0.25 micromoles to 0.50 millimoles per deciliter of said metal; 0.1% to 40% (w/v) of said surfactant; and water in a quantity sufficient to make volume, 5. A process for cleaning contact lenses containing all the steps above. Background to Invention This invention relates to solution for cleaning plastic contact lens materials. Specifically it relates to aqueous solutions comprising a water-soluble peroxide, a catalytic amount of a transition metal salt. a surfactant. These solutions effectively clean hard. flexible and soft hydrogel contact lenses. Because of the environment in which contact lenses are handled and employed, a wide variety of materials may adhere to lenses. During wear, lenses are subjected to proteinaceous materials, particularly mucoproteins; and lipids such as sterols, waxes and glveerides. In addition to these naturally occurring materials, cosmetics, greases from the hands and dusts and other airborne and environmental materials can all act to form a strongly adhering lens coating. Proteinaceous materials constitute the major amount of lens soils. They can also be difficult to remove completely and efficiently from plastic lens materials, particularly mn the instance of hydrophilic hydrogel materials which can readily absorb mucoproteins. If lenses are not properly cleaned these proteinaceous materials and other soils can build up to a point where wearer comfort is affected, lens spectral characteristics are affected or sterilization becomes difficult. Hydrogel polymers and other soft flexible lens materials cannot be mechanically scrubbed because they are easily torn or scratched. Therefore some non-mechanical means must be used to remove soil accretions. Additionally, lenses must be sterilized to prevent transmission of pathogenic agents onto the eye. Certain lens polymers, particularly hydrogels, cannot be chemically sterilized because they absorb antimicrobial drugs which are also eye irritants, so alternative sterilization techniques such as heat in the form of boiling water or steam are often used. High temperatures don't clean lenses and in fact tend to accelerate lens soil buildup by precipitating absorbed proteinaceous materials. Sterile saline solutions have little if any effect on soil removal so some additional cleaning procedure is required. Peroxides alone are adequate disinfectants but do not adequately remove lens soils, particularly non-polar materials. It is therefore desirable to find a simple and efficient one step procedure for cleaning contact lenses which will ensure the removal of all soils, especially proteinaceous material. The procedure should be usable with all contact lenses. The method should be effective over a relatively short period of time, certainly not longer than overnight, and should be safe to the user and provide a clean lens which may be readily rinsed and safe for introduction into the eye thereafter without further treatment. Prior Art Patents X and Y disclose lens-cleansing solutions that consist of different kinds of peroxides."

Ans. Title: Aqueous Solution for Cleaning Contact Lenses

Abstract: The present invention relates to an aqueous solution for cleaning contact lenses, comprising a water-soluble peroxide, a transition metal salt, and a coco-hydrolyzed animal protein anionic surfactant. The solution is effective on hard, flexible, and hydrogel contact lenses, removing soils such as mucoproteins and lipids. The solution is stable and can be divided into separate portions for longer shelf-life. This invention offers a one-step cleaning process for contact lenses that is efficient, safe, and usable for all contact lenses. Prior art solutions are also discussed.

Claims:

1. A contact lens cleaning solution comprising a water-soluble peroxide, a transition metal salt and a coco-hydrolyzed animal protein anionic surfactant.

2. The solution of claim 1, wherein the peroxide is present in a concentration of 0.1% to 15% by weight/volume.

3. The solution of claim 1, wherein the metal catalyst is present in a concentration of 0.25 micromoles to 0.25 millimoles per deciliter.

4. The solution of claim 1, wherein the surfactant is present in a concentration of 0.1% to 20% by weight/volume.

5. A contact lens cleaning process comprising the steps of applying the solution of claim 1 to a contact lens, allowing the solution to react with lens soil, and rinsing the lens with sterile water.

THE PATENTS ACT, 1970

PATENT AGENT EXAMINATION, DECEMBER 2008

Qualifying examination under Section 126 of the Patents Act (as amended and updated)

Paper II

Drafting and Interpretation of Patent specification and other Documents

Time 2 2 Hrs

Total pages —

Instruction:- 1. All questions are compulsory. 2. Marks of each question are indicated at the end of the question. 3. Relevant section and rule shall be quoted.

Q.No.l. Attempt any six questions **(a) You have filed an application with provisional specification on behalf of your client on 15.12.2007, the client is not in a position to provide the total inputs to file a complete specification within the prescribed time but only around 15.2.2009 what action will you take? (10)**

Ans.1(a). Section 9[(3) of Patents Act: Where an application for a patent (not being a convention application or an application filed under the Patent Cooperation Treaty designating India) is accompanied by a specification purporting to be a complete specification, the Controller may, if the applicant so requests at any time within twelve months from the date of filing of the application, direct that such specification shall be treated, for the purposes of this Act, as a provisional specification and proceed with the application accordingly.]

(4) Where a complete specification has been filed in pursuance of an application for a patent accompanied by a provisional specification or by a specification treated by virtue of a direction under sub-section (3) as a provisional specification, the Controller may, if the applicant so requests at any time before

[grant of patent], cancel the provisional specification and post-date the application to the date of filing of the complete specification.

(b) The Director of a Company X had filed an Patent application; after six months of filing Company X was acquired by a Company Y and the Director has approached you to handle the further prosecution of the case. Explain what steps will be taken by you. (10)

Ans.1(b).

Section 20 of Patents Act: Powers of Controller to make orders regarding substitution of applicants etc;

(1) If the Controller is satisfied, on a claim made in the prescribed manner at any time before a patent has been granted, that by virtue of any assignment or agreement in writing made by the applicant or one of the applicants for the patent or by operation of law, the claimant would, if the patent were then granted be entitled thereto or to the interest of the applicant therein, or to an undivided share of the patent or of that interest, the Controller may, subject to the provisions of this section, direct that the application shall proceed in the name of the claimant or in the names of the claimants and the applicant or the other joint applicant or applicants, accordingly as the case may require.

(2) No such direction as aforesaid shall be given by virtue of any assignment or agreement made by one of two or more joint applicants for a patent except with the consent of the other joint applicant or applicants.

(3) No such direction as aforesaid shall be given by virtue of any assignment or agreement for the assignment of the benefit of an invention unless--

(a) the invention is identified therein by reference to the number of the application for the patent; or

(b) there is produced to the Controller an acknowledgment by the person by whom the assignment or agreement was made that the assignment or agreement relates to the invention in respect of which that application is made; or

(c) the rights of the claimant in respect of the invention have been finally established by the decision of a court; or

(d) the Controller gives directions for enabling the application to proceed or for regulating the manner in which it should be proceeded with under sub-section (5).

(4) Where one of two or more joint applicants for a patent dies at any time before the patent has been granted, the Controller may, upon a request in that behalf made by the survivor or survivors, and with the consent of the legal representative of the deceased, direct that the application shall proceed in the name of the survivor or survivors alone.

(5) If any dispute arises between joint applicants for a patent whether or in what manner the application should be proceeded with, the Controller may, upon application made to him in the prescribed manner by any of the parties, and after giving to all parties concerned an opportunity to be heard, give such directions as he thinks fit for enabling the application to proceed in the name of one or more of the parties alone or for regulating the manner in which it should be proceeded with, or for both those purposes, as the case may require.

Rule 35 of Patent Rules, 2003

Manner in which a request may be made under section 20(4)

(1) A request under sub-section (4) of section 20 shall be made in Form 6.

(2) The request shall be accompanied by proof of death of the joint applicant and a certified copy of the probate of the will of the deceased or letters of administration in respect of his estate or any other document to prove that the person who gives the consent is the legal representative of the deceased applicant.

Rule 36. Manner of application under section 20(5).—(1) An application under sub-section (5) of section 20 shall be made in **Form 6** in duplicate and shall be accompanied by a statement setting out fully the facts upon which the applicant relies and the directions which he seeks.

(2) A copy of the application and statement shall be sent by the Controller to every otherjoint applicant.

(c) Your client Company A the owner of several patents inadvertently missed to pay the renewal fee for one year from the date of recordal 2.2.08 for one of the patents leading to its cessation what is the course of action you will suggest to your client? 10)

Ans.1(C)Section 53: As per Section 53 of the Indian Patents Act, if the renewal fee for a patent is not paid before the due date and a six-month grace period, the patent shall cease to have effect from the expiration of the last day on which the fee was payable.

In the given scenario, since the renewal fee was not paid for one year from the date of recordal 2.2.08, the patent has ceased to have effect from the last day on which the fee was payable.

However, as per Section 60 of the Indian Patents Act, if a patentee can satisfy the Controller that the failure to pay the renewal fee was unintentional or due to an error, the Controller may, upon payment of the prescribed fee, extend the time for payment of the renewal fee by such further period, as the Controller thinks fit.

Therefore, the course of action that can be suggested to Company A is to immediately approach the Controller of Patents and provide evidence to show that the non-payment of the renewal fee was unintentional or due to an error. Upon satisfaction of the Controller, the company can pay the renewal fee. However, it is important to note that the grant of an extension of time is solely at the discretion of the Controller, and there is no guarantee that the extension will be granted.

Rule 80 of Patent Rules, 2003: Renewal fees under section 53; —(1) To keep a patent in force, the renewal feesspecified in the First Schedule shall be payable at the expiration of the second year from thedate of the patent or of any succeeding year and the same shall be remitted to the patentoffice before the expiration of the second or the succeeding year.

(1A) The period for payment of renewal fees so specified in sub-rule (1) may be extended to such period not being more than **six months** if the request for such extension of time is made in **Form 4** with the fee specified in the First Schedule.

(2)While paying the renewal fee, the number and date of the patent concerned and the year in respect of which the fee is paid shall be quoted.

(3)The annual renewal fees payable in respect of two or more years may be paid in advance.

(4) The Controller shall, after making such enquiry as he may deem necessary, credit any renewal fee and issue a certificate that the fee has been paid.

(d) What are the implications of filing a Form -8. (10)

Ans.1(d) Section 28 of Patents Act: Mention of inventor as such in patent;

(1) If the Controller is satisfied, upon a request or claim made in accordance with the provisions of this section,--

(a) that the person in respect of or by whom the request or claim is made is the inventor of an invention in respect of which application for a patent has been made, or of a substantial part of that invention; and

(b) that the application for the patent is a direct consequence of his being the inventor, the Controller shall, subject to the provisions of this section, cause him to be mentioned as inventor in any patent granted in pursuance of the application in the complete specification and in the register of Patents:

Provided that the mention of any person as inventor under this section shall not confer or derogate from any rights under the patent.

(2) A request that any person shall be mentioned as aforesaid may be made in the prescribed manner by the applicant for the patent or (where the person alleged to be the inventor is not the applicant or one of the applicants) by the applicant and that person.

(3) If any person [other than a person in respect of whom a request in relation to the application in question has been made under sub-section (2)] desires to be

mentioned as aforesaid, he may make a claim in the prescribed manner in that behalf.

[(4) A request or claim under the foregoing provisions of this section shall be made before the grant of patent.]

* * * * *

(6) [Where] a claim is made under sub-section (3), the Controller shall give notice of the claim to every applicant for the patent (not being the claimant) and to any other person whom the Controller may consider to be interested; and before deciding upon any request or claim made under sub-section (2) or sub-section (3), the Controller shall, if required, hear the person in respect of or by whom the request or claim is made, and, in the case of a claim under sub-section (3), any person to whom notice of the claim has been given as aforesaid.

(7) Where any person has been mentioned as inventor in pursuance of this section anyother person who alleges that he ought not to have been so mentioned may at any time apply to the Controller for a certificate to that effect, and the Controller may, after hearing, if required, any person whom he may consider to be interested, issue such a certificate, and if he does so, he shall rectify the specification and the register accordingly.

3) Your client has made an invention in the area of atomic energy, advise him about getting a patent in India and the procedure to file his patent application in USA. 10

Ans.1(e). Section 39: Residents not to apply for patents outside India without prior permission;

(1) No person resident in India shall, except under the authority of a written permit sought in the manner prescribed and granted by or on behalf of the Controller, make or cause to be made any application outside India for the grant of a patent for an invention unless--

(a) an application for a patent for the same invention has been made in India, not less than six weeks before the application outside India; and

(b) either no direction has been given under sub-section (1) of section 35 in relation to the application in India, or all such directions have been revoked.

(2) The Controller shall dispose of every such application within such period as may be prescribed:

Provided that if the invention is relevant for defence purpose or atomic energy, the Controller shall not grant permit without the prior consent of the Central Government.

(3) This section shall not apply in relation to an invention for which an application for protection has first been filed in a country outside India by a person resident outside India.]

(4) Section 4 of Patents Act: Inventions relating to atomic energy not patentable;

No patent shall be granted in respect of an invention relating to atomic energy falling within sub-section (1) of section 20 of the Atomic Energy Act, 1962 (33 of 1962).

(f) An Indian Company has made an anti-pollution device for flue gases, and wants to file a patent application in India as well as in number of countries abroad. After being convinced by a dependable search, what action can be taken by the company? (10)

After being convinced by a dependable search, the Indian company can proceed with filing a patent application in India as well as in countries abroad where they wish to protect their invention. The company can engage a patent attorney or agent to prepare the patent application and file it with the respective patent offices.

It is important to note that the patent application should be filed within the prescribed time limit, which is usually 12 months from the date of the first filing. The company also needs to pay the required fee for filing and prosecution of the application.

Once the patent is granted, the company can enjoy exclusive rights to make, use, and sell their anti-pollution device for a certain period of time. This can provide a competitive advantage in the market and potentially lead to increased revenue and profits.

Ans.1(f). Filing –Kindly refer to PCT Filing.

(g) A Patent application relating to an anti hypertensive agent has been published in the journal on 12.11.08, your client is already manufacturing the said drug since 15.6.2006, take action to protect the interest of your client. (10)

Ans.1(g) Based on this scenario, the client may consider filing an opposition to the patent application under Section 25 of the Patents Act. This is because the client has been manufacturing the drug since 15.6.2006, which is before the publication of the patent application in the journal on 12.11.08.

An opposition can be filed by any person interested in the patent, including the client, within a specific timeframe after the publication of the application. The opposition can be based on various grounds, such as lack of novelty or inventive step, insufficient disclosure, or unlawful claim.

If the opposition is successful, the patent may be revoked or amended, allowing the client to continue manufacturing the drug without infringing the patent. Alternatively, the client may also consider negotiating a license with the patent holder to avoid any potential infringement.

Section 25 of Patents Act: Opposition to patent;

[25. Opposition to the patent.-- (1) Where an application for a patent has been published but a patent has not been granted, any person may, in writing, represent by way of opposition to the Controller against the grant of patent on the ground--

(a) that the applicant for the patent or the person under or through whom he claims, wrongfully obtained the invention or any part thereof from him or from a person under or through whom he claims;

(b) that the invention so far as claimed in any claim of the complete specification has been published before the priority date of the claim--

(i) in any specification filed in pursuance of an application for a patent made in India on or after the 1st day of January, 1912; or

(ii) in India or elsewhere, in any other document:

Provided that the ground specified in sub-clause (ii) shall not be available where such publication does not constitute an anticipation of the invention by virtue of sub-section (2) or subsection (3) of section 29;

(c) that the invention so far as claimed in any claim of the complete specification is claimed in a claim of a complete specification published on or after the priority date of the applicant's claim and filed in pursuance of an application for a patent in India, being a claim of which the priority date is earlier than that of the applicants claim;

(d) that the invention so far as claimed in any claim of the complete specification was publicly known or publicly used in India before the priority date of that claim.

Explanation.--For the purposes of this clause, an invention relating to a process for which a patent is claimed shall be deemed to have been publicly known or publicly used in India before the priority date of the claim if a product made by that process had already been imported into India before that date except where such importation has been for the purpose of reasonable trial or experiment only;

(e) that the invention so far as claimed in any claim of the complete specification is obvious and clearly does not involve any inventive step, having regard to the matter published as mentioned in clause (b) or having regard to what was used in India before the priority date of the applicant's claim;

(f) that the subject of any claim of the complete specification is not an invention within the meaning of this Act, or is not patentable under this Act;

(g) that the complete specification does not sufficiently and clearly describe the invention or the method by which it is to be performed;

(h) that the applicant has failed to disclose to the Controller the information required by section 8 or has furnished the information which in any material particular was false to his knowledge;

(i) that in the case of a convention application, the application was not made within twelve months from the date of the first application for protection for the invention made in a convention country by the applicant or a person from whom he derives title;

(j) that the complete specification does not disclose or wrongly mentions the source or geographical origin of biological material used for the invention;

(k) that the invention so far as claimed in any claim of the complete specification is anticipated having regard to the knowledge, oral or otherwise, available within any local or indigenous community in India or elsewhere,

but on no other ground and the Controller shall, if requested by such person for being heard, hear him and dispose of such representation in such manner and within such period as may be prescribed.

Q.No.2.

State the forms required for filing a Patent application in India and draft a Complete specification along with abstract on the basis of information given by your client as follows: I am in possession of ap. invention which relates to aspirin — isopropylantipyrine (N-3° a-propylphenazonyl-2-acetoxybenazamide), a novel compound shown by the. formula(I) and a process for producing the same, and its utilization as an analgesic, antipyretic and anti-inflammatory agent. » = Celis ORE | (mm It is already known that: Aspirin (acetylsalicylic acid) is being widely used as a relatively safe antipyretic; analgesic and anti-inflammatory agent. It however has the drawback that it has a gastric ulcerogenic activity, with the consequence that it causes nausea and loss of appetite and even induces such gastric disorders as peptic ulcer, hemorrhage of stomach, etc. at times. Especially in the case where aspirin is administered in large doses say for treatment of rheumatic diseases, care must be exercised to guard against gastric disorders ascribable to the ingestion of aspirin. Furthermore, aspirin is hygroscopic, and hence aspirin not only is decomposed by moisture byt when it is mixed with other drugs, for example, other

antipyretic and analgesic preparations, it becomes moist and discolored at times. : It was found that this novel compound that can be expressed by the foregoing formula (I), while possessing superior analgesic, antipyretic and anti-inflammatory activity, demonstrates marked reduction of such activities as cause gastric disorders that are possessed by aspirin and the side effects of the pyrazolonetype antipyretic and analgletic preparations. Moreover, it is not hygroscopic. It is hence a unique compound possessing good stability. The aspirin-isoproopylantipyrime(AIA) of formula (I) of this invention can be prepared by reacting I-phenyl-2-methyl- -3-aninomethyl-4-isopropylpyrazolone of the formula(T) with either acetylsalicylic acid or a reactive acid derivative thereof as shown in the accompanying example. Further the pharmaceutical composition in a form such as exemplified herein or the formula (I) compound itself can be administered in a dose of about 0.02 to about 0.08 g/kg-body/day. The composition of the invention can be administered through various routes. Thus, it may be in an orally administrable form, an inject able form, or a parenterally administrable form (e.g. suppository). Comparitive tests of gastric Ulcerogenic Activity for Aspirin & AIA were carried out on fasted rats and the test compounds were administered orally,the stomachs were removed 7 hrs later and the lengths of the lesions in the glandular portion were measured. Which are given in Table I TABLE Gastric Ulcerogenic Acitivity {Pylorus-ligarated rats Compound Dose Length of stomach lesion (cm) Mg/kg AlA 100 0.11+0.09 Aspirin 100 413+ 1.24 As apparent little or no injury is caused to the stomach by the compound of this invention. Production of Compound:- Aspirin (14.4 g, 0.08 molar) was dissolved in 400 ml of chloroform, after which the solution was cooled to OC. Dicyclohexylcarbodiimide (18.2 g,0.088 mole) was then added to the solution followed by stirring the mixture for 30 minutes and thereafter adding 19.6 g (0.08 mole) of 2 — methy!-3 aminomethyl-1-phenyl-4-isopropylpyrazolone (II). The mixture was then stirred at room temperature for 24 hours. The precipitate of discylohexylurea formed was filtered off, and the solvent was distilled off under reduced pressure. The residue was dissolved in 150 ml of chloroform, and this solution was added to column packed with 1.8 liters of silica gel and its stage wise elution was performed using chloroform and methanol. The elutes were analyzed by thin-layer chromatography The eluted fractions exhibiting only the spot at Rf= 0.52 were collected and concentrated under educed pressure. The concentrate was purified by crystallizing from ethyl acetate to give 25.4 g (yield 80% of N-3a-propylphenazonyl-2-acetox-ybenzamidéy (I). EXAMPLE 2 Pharmaceutical Compositions Tablets The following ingredients are contained in the amounts indicated in each tablet (500 mg) AIA 250.0 mg Cornstarch IEE 120.0 mg Lactose 122.0 mg Hydroxypropyl cellulose (binder) 5.0 mg Talc 1.5 mg Magnesium stearate 1.0 mg (40)

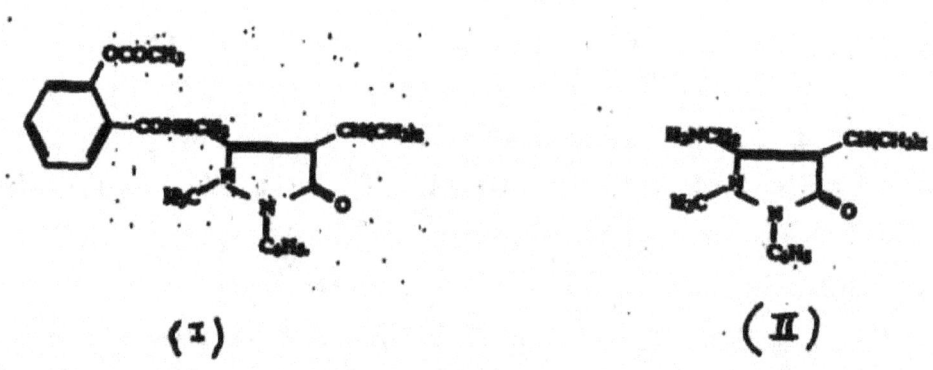

Ans. The following forms are required for filing a patent application in India:

1. Form-1: Application for Grant of Patent

2. Form-2: Complete Specification

3. Form-3: Provisional/Complete Specification for a PCT Application

4. Form-5: Declaration as to Inventorship

5. Form-26: Authorization of Patent Agent/Attorney

6. Form-28: Assignment Deed (if applicable)

In addition to the above forms, the applicant may also need to file other supporting documents such as the proof of right to file the application, priority documents (if the application claims priority from an earlier application) and the fee for filing and prosecuting the patent application.

Title: "A novel compound and its utilization as an analgesic, antipyretic and anti-inflammatory agent"

FIELD OF THE INVENTION

The present invention relates to a novel compound, aspirin-isopropylantipyrine (AIA), its preparation, and its use as an analgesic, antipyretic, and anti-inflammatory agent.

BACKGROUND OF THE INVENTION

Aspirin (acetylsalicylic acid) is widely used as an antipyretic, analgesic, and anti-inflammatory agent. However, it has a drawback of causing gastric ulcerogenic activity, which can lead to nausea, loss of appetite, and gastric disorders, such as peptic ulcer and hemorrhage of the stomach. Aspirin is also hygroscopic and can become discolored when mixed with other drugs.

The present invention provides a novel compound, AIA, which possesses superior analgesic, antipyretic, and anti-inflammatory activity compared to aspirin and with significantly reduced side effects. The AIA compound is also not hygroscopic, making it uniquely stable.

SUMMARY OF THE INVENTION

The present invention provides a novel compound, AIA, expressed by the formula (I), and a process for producing it. AIA is prepared by reacting I-phenyl-2-methyl- -3-aninomethyl-4-isopropylpyrazolone of the formula (T) with either acetylsalicylic acid or a reactive acid derivative thereof.

The present invention also provides a pharmaceutical composition containing AIA as an active ingredient in doses of about 0.02 to about 0.08 g/kg-body/day, which can be administered through various routes, including orally, injectably, and parenterally.

The present invention further provides a comparison of gastric ulcerogenic activity for aspirin and AIA, where AIA caused little to no injury to the stomach.

Additionally, the present invention provides an example of a pharmaceutical composition containing AIA in the form of tablets.

DRAWINGS

None.

DETAILED DESCRIPTION OF THE INVENTION

The present invention provides a novel compound, AIA, which possesses superior analgesic, antipyretic, and anti-inflammatory activity compared to aspirin with significantly reduced side effects. AIA is expressed by the formula (I) and is not hygroscopic.

The AIA compound can be prepared by reacting I-phenyl-2-methyl- -3-aninomethyl-4-isopropylpyrazolone of the formula (T) with either acetylsalicylic acid or a reactive acid derivative thereof.

The pharmaceutical composition of the present invention contains AIA as an active ingredient in doses of about 0.02 to about 0.08 g/kg-body/day, which can be administered through various routes, including orally, injectably, and parenterally.

The present invention further includes a comparison of gastric ulcerogenic activity for aspirin and AIA, where AIA caused little to no injury to the stomach.

An example of a pharmaceutical composition containing AIA in the form of tablets is also provided. The tablets contain AIA, cornstarch, lactose, hydroxypropyl cellulose, talc, and magnesium stearate.

CLAIMS:

I claim:

1. A method for producing AIA comprising the step of reacting I-phenyl-2-methyl- -3-aninomethyl-4-isopropylpyrazolone of the formula (T) with either acetylsalicylic acid or a reactive acid derivative thereof.

2. A pharmaceutical composition containing AIA as an active ingredient in doses of 0.02 to 0.08 g/kg-body/day, for use as an analgesic, antipyretic, and anti-inflammatory agent.

3. The pharmaceutical composition of claim 2, which can be administered through various routes, including orally, injectably, and parenterally.

232

4. A pharmaceutical composition in the form of tablets comprising AIA as an active ingredient, cornstarch, lactose, hydroxypropyl cellulose, talc, and magnesium stearate.

5. The pharmaceutical composition of claim 4, wherein the tablets contain 250.0 mg of AIA, 120.0 mg of cornstarch, 122.0 mg of lactose, 5.0 mg of hydroxypropyl cellulose, 1.5 mg of talc, and 1.0 mg of magnesium stearate.

OR

I have made an improvement in a windmill more particularly to a windmill constructed to generate electricity to make efficient use of wind irrespective of wind direction or wind velocity. Wind has been used since ancient times. These days as the resources such as petroleum and coal are gradually becoming exhausted, interest toward wind as alternative energy source is increasing; a windmill is disclosed in the art, which generates electricity using the wind. Windmills are disclosed in the prior art, however, the conventional windmill is encountered with a problem in'that, only when the wind flows at a velocity greater than a predetermined value and the air has a high density, the propeller-shaped rotor can be rotated to convert the wind into electric power. Therefore, in the case that a gentle wind blow, it is impossible to generate electricity using the conventional windmill. 1 have worked to provide a windmill which has wind guide plates extending in a radial direction and an upper plate for preventing dispersion of the wind, so that the electricity can be generated irrespective of a wind direction or a wind velocity even when a gentle wind blows.

BRIEF DESCRIPTION OF THE DRAWINGS. FIG.1 is a partially enlarged cross-sectional view illustrating the entire windmill with an embodiment of the invention FIG. § & FIG J is a front view illustrating a wind inlet/outlet opening and closing device: of the windmill according to the present invention respectively. As shown in Fig 1 wind blowing in any direction is guided by the wind guide plates: ¥0 to be collected and then introduced into the windmill through the wind inlet 12. Lower ends of the wind guide plates 10 are closed by the charger 23 having substantially a conical sectional shape, and the upper ends of the wind guide plates 10 are 4 closed by the upper plate 1 |. The more the wind flows inward toward the wind inlet 12, the more a sectional area through which the wind passes is reduced. Due to the fact, the wind flows through the wind inlet 12 at an increased velocity. As shown in the partially enlarged upper parts of FIG.I and in FIG.2 the wind inlet 12 comprises the plurality of cells 121 which are defined by plaiting the plurality of wires 120 in the form of a lattice. As can be readily seen from FIG. 2 due to the fact that the wind inlet opening and closing device 13 comprising the plurality of scale shaped pieces is pivotally installed in the air inlet 12, one wind inlet opening and closing device 13 through which the wind is introduced into the windmill is opened by the wind flowing through the wind inlet 12, and another wind inlet opening and closing device 13 which is positioned behind the one wind inlet opening and closing device 13 and through which the wind is discharged out of the windmill is closed by the wind flowing through the wind inlet 12. The wind which is introduced into the windmill through the wind inlet opening and closing device 13 as described above flows through the power generating tunnel 20 and rotates the rotors 21 which are arranged in the power generating tunnel 20. By this fact the generator 22 generates electricity, and the electricity by the generator 22 is charged into the charger 23. The wind rotating the rotors 21 flows downward through the generating tunnel 20 and then is discharged through the wind outlet 30 which is defined below the wind inlet 12. As shown in the partially enlarged lower parts of FIG,.1 and in FIG.3 the wind outlet 30 comprises the plurality of cells, 301 which are defined by plating the plurality of wires 300 in the form of a lattice. Also, as can be readily seen from F1G.3 due to the fact that the wind outlet opening and closing device 31 comprising the plurality of scale-shaped pieces is pivotally installed in the air outlet 30, one wind outlet opening and closing device 31 through which the wind is introduced in to the windmill is closed by the wind flowing through the wind outlet 30, and another wind outlet opening and closing device 31 which is positioned behind the one wind outlet opening and closing device 31 and through which the wind is discharged out of the windmill is opened by the wind flowing through the wind outlet 30

Ans.

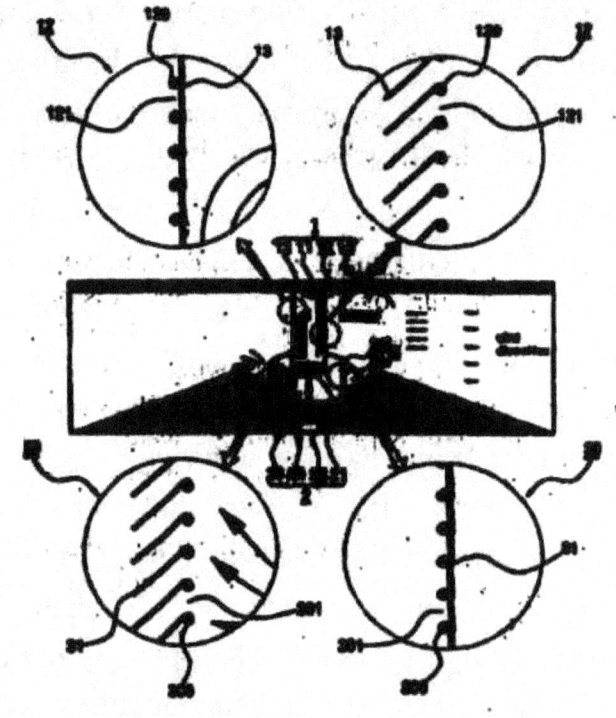

FIG.1

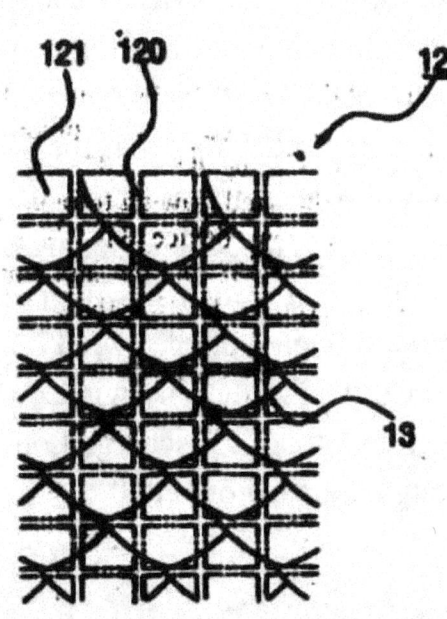

FIG.2

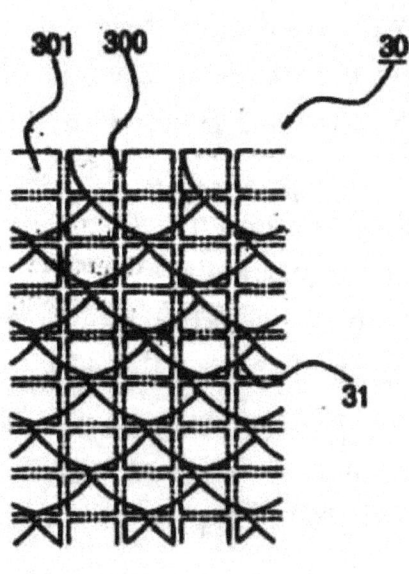

FIG.3

FIELD OF THE INVENTION

The present invention relates to a windmill for generating electricity. Specifically, the invention relates to a windmill designed to efficiently use wind irrespective of wind direction or velocity.

BACKGROUND OF THE INVENTION

Wind has been used as a source of energy since ancient times. As traditional resources such as petroleum and coal are gradually becoming exhausted, interest in wind as an alternative energy source is increasing. Windmills have been developed to generate electricity using wind. However, conventional windmills can only generate electricity when the wind velocity is greater than a predetermined value and the air has a high density. Thus, it is impossible to generate electricity using conventional windmills when the wind blows gently.

SUMMARY OF THE INVENTION

The present invention provides a windmill that can efficiently generate electricity irrespective of wind direction or velocity, even when the wind blows gently. The windmill includes wind guide plates that extend radially and an upper plate for preventing wind dispersion.

The wind guide plates collect wind blowing in any direction and introduce it through the wind inlet. The lower ends of the wind guide plates are closed by a charger having substantially a conical sectional shape, and the upper ends of the wind guide plates are closed by the upper plate. As the wind passes through the wind inlet, the sectional area through which the wind passes is reduced, resulting in an increased wind velocity.

The wind inlet comprises a plurality of cells that are defined by plaiting a plurality of wires in the form of a lattice. The wind inlet opening and closing device, comprising a plurality of scale-shaped pieces, is pivotally installed in the air inlet. As the wind flows through the wind inlet, one wind inlet opening and closing device through which the wind is introduced into the windmill is opened, and another wind inlet opening and closing device through which the wind is discharged out of the windmill is closed.

The wind introduced into the windmill flows through the power generating tunnel and rotates the rotors, which are arranged in the power generating tunnel. The generator generates electricity, which is charged into the charger. The wind rotating the rotors flows downward through the generating tunnel and is discharged through the wind outlet.

The wind outlet comprises a plurality of cells that are defined by plating a plurality of wires in the form of a lattice. The wind outlet opening and closing device, comprising a plurality of scale-shaped pieces, is pivotally installed in the air outlet. As the wind flows through the wind outlet, one wind outlet opening and closing device through which the wind is introduced into the windmill is closed, and another wind outlet opening and closing device through which the wind is discharged out of the windmill is opened.

The present invention provides a windmill that can generate electricity irrespective of wind direction or velocity, including when the wind blows gently.

DRAWINGS

FIG.1 is a partially enlarged cross-sectional view illustrating the entire windmill with an embodiment of the invention. FIG.2 and FIG.3 are front views illustrating a wind inlet/outlet opening and closing device of the windmill according to the present invention, respectively.

DETAILED DESCRIPTION OF THE INVENTION

The present invention provides a windmill that can efficiently generate electricity irrespective of wind direction or velocity, including when the wind blows gently.

The windmill includes wind guide plates that extend radially and an upper plate for preventing wind dispersion. The wind guide plates collect wind blowing in any direction and introduce it through the wind inlet. The lower ends of the wind guide plates are closed by a charger having substantially a conical sectional shape, and the upper ends of the wind guide plates are closed by the upper plate.

The wind inlet comprises a plurality of cells that are defined by plaiting a plurality of wires in the form of a lattice. The wind inlet opening and closing device, comprising a plurality of scale-shaped pieces, is pivotally installed in the air inlet to regulate the amount of wind flowing into the windmill.

The wind introduced into the windmill flows through the power generating tunnel and rotates the rotors, which are arranged in the power generating tunnel. The generator generates electricity, which is charged into the charger. The wind rotating the rotors flows downward through the generating tunnel and is discharged through the wind outlet.

The wind outlet comprises a plurality of cells that are defined by plating a plurality of wires in the form of a lattice. The wind outlet opening and closing device, comprising a plurality of scale-shaped pieces, is pivotally installed in the air outlet to regulate the amount of wind flowing out of the windmill.

The present invention provides a windmill that can generate electricity irrespective of wind direction or velocity. The invention is particularly useful for generating electricity from gentle winds, which are typically not harnessed by conventional windmills.

CLAIMS:

I claim:

1. A windmill for generating electricity comprising wind guide plates that extend radially, an upper plate for preventing wind dispersion, a charger having substantially a conical sectional shape, rotors arranged in a power generating tunnel, and a generator for generating electricity, wherein the wind guide plates collect wind blowing in any direction, the wind flows through the power generating tunnel and rotates the rotors to generate electricity, and the wind is discharged through the wind outlet, wherein the wind inlet comprises a plurality of cells that are defined by plaiting a plurality of wires in the form of a lattice, and the wind inlet opening and closing device comprising a plurality of scale-shaped pieces is pivotally installed in the air inlet, whereby one wind inlet opening and closing device through which the wind is introduced into the windmill is opened by the wind flowing through the wind inlet, and another wind inlet opening and closing device through which the wind is discharged out of the windmill is closed by the wind flowing through the wind inlet, and wherein the wind outlet comprises a plurality of cells that are defined by plating a plurality of wires in the form of a lattice, and the wind outlet opening and closing device comprising a plurality of scale-shaped pieces is pivotally installed

in the air outlet, whereby one wind outlet opening and closing device through which the wind is introduced into the windmill is closed by the wind flowing through the wind outlet, and another wind outlet opening and closing device through which the wind is discharged out of the windmill is opened by the wind flowing through the wind outlet.

2. The windmill of claim 1, wherein the wind guide plates extend radially from the wind inlet.

3. The windmill of claim 1, wherein the wind inlet and wind outlet are positioned at the top and bottom of the windmill, respectively.

4. The windmill of claim 1, wherein the wind inlet opening and closing device comprises a plurality of scale-shaped pieces that pivotally open and close within the wind inlet.

5. The windmill of claim 1, wherein the wind outlet opening and closing device comprises a plurality of scale-shaped pieces that pivotally open and close within the wind outlet.

6. The windmill of claim 1, wherein the wind inlet and wind outlet are defined by a plurality of cells that are plaited by a plurality of wires in the form of a lattice.

7. The windmill of claim 1, wherein the rotors are arranged in a power generating tunnel.

The Patents Act, 1970

Qualifying Examination under section 126 of the Patents Act

(As amended & updated)

PAPER-II

Drafting and Interpretation of Patent specification and other Documents

November, 2007

Time :- 2 Hrs., Total Marks —-100

Total Pages - 7

Instructions : 1. All questions are compulsory.

2. Marks of each question are indicated at the end of the question

3. Answers should be precise and to the point supported by relevant provisions of the Act and Rules.

Q.No.1. a) Your client ABC Pharma, Chennai approaches you with a known molecule having slight modification therein by adding a methyl group in the benzene ring. They wish to obtain a Patent for this invention. Advise appropriately to your client about the available provisions in the Indian Patent Act.

Ans. **Ans.1(a)Section 3 (e) of the Patents Act**: a substance obtained by a mere admixture resulting only in the aggregation of the properties of the components thereof or a process for producing such substance;

Section 3 (d) of the Patents Act: the mere discovery of a new form of a known substance which does not result in the enhancement of the known efficacy of that substance or the mere discovery of any new property or new use for a known substance or of the mere use of a known process, machine or apparatus unless such known process results in a new product or employs at least one new reactant.

Section 3 (f) of the Patents Act: the mere arrangement or re-arrangement or duplication of known devices each functioning independently of one another in a known way;

b) Your client has filed an application for patent. They received first examination report from the Controller of Patents with the objection that "your said application contains the claims from 8 to 15 distinct from rest of the claims not falling under the single inventive concept". Advise your client suitably about the provisions in the Patent Act in this regard.

Ans.1(b) Section 16 of the Patents Act: Power of Controller to make orders respecting division of application;

(1) A person who has made an application for a patent under this Act may, at any time [before the grant of the patent], if he so desires, or with a view to remedy the objection raised by the Controller on the ground that the claims of the complete specification relate to more than one invention, file a further application in respect of an invention disclosed in the provisional or complete specification already filed in respect of the first mentioned application.

(2) The further application under sub-section (1) shall be accompanied by a complete specification, but such complete specification shall not include any matter not in substance disclosed in the complete specification filed in pursuance of the first mentioned application.

(3) The Controller may require such amendment of the complete specification filed in pursuance of either the original or the further application as may be necessary to ensure that neither of the said complete specifications includes a claim for any matter claimed in the other.

[Explanation.-- For the purposes of this Act, the further application and the complete specification accompanying it shall be deemed to have been filed on the date on which the first mentioned application had been filed, and the further application shall be proceeded with as a substantive application and be examined when the request for examination is filed within the prescribed period.]

c) Your client Nokia Corporation, USA wishes to file an application for Patent in India based on the application filed in USA dated 01.01.2007. The invention of US application has been published in a journal on 01.10.2007 in India and US. Explain to your client the relevant provisions to protect the invention in India appropriately.

Ans.1(c): Convention Application

a) Where a person has made an application for a patent in respect of an invention in a Convention country (basic application), and that person or the legal representative or assignee of that person makes an application under this Act for a patent within twelve months after the date on which the basic application was made, the priority date of a claim of the complete specification, being a claim based on matter disclosed in the basic application, is the date of making of the basic application.

b) Where applications have been made for similar protection in respect of an invention in two or more convention countries, the period of twelve months referred to in this sub-section shall be reckoned from the date on which the earlier or earliest of the said applications was made.

c) Where applications for protection have been made in one or more convention countries in respect of two or more inventions which are cognate or of which one is a modification of another, a single convention application may be made in respect of those inventions at any time within twelve months from the date of the earliest of the said applications for protection. However, the fee payable in respect of such application shall be the same as if separate applications have been made in respect of each of the said inventions.

Documents to be submitted

1) Every convention application shall:

i. be accompanied by a complete specification;

ii. specify the date on which the first of such applications was made and the convention country in which such application for protection is sought and

iii. state that no application for protection in respect of the invention had been made in a convention country before that date by the applicant or by any person from whom he derives title.

2) a complete specification filed with a convention application may include claims in respect of developments of, or additions to, the invention in respect of which the application for protection was made in a convention country, being developments or additions in respect of which the applicant would be entitled under the provisions of section 6 to make a separate application for a patent.

3) be accompanied by an abstract

4) a certified copy of the priority document, if the Controller requires the same, may be filed within 3 months from the date of communication by the Controller of such requirement.

5) accompanied by a verified English translation of such document, if the priority document is in a language other than English.

PCT International application by Indian applicant

An Indian applicant can file a PCT International application in the following manner:

i. If the international application is filed before 6 weeks from the date of the priority in India, the foreign filling permission under section 39 has to be obtained from the appropriate patent office.

ii. If the international application is filed directly at RO/IB or RO/IN (i.e. without a priority claim), foreign filling permission under section 39 has to be obtained from the appropriate patent office.

If the applicant fails to obtain the foreign filling permission under section 39, the application will not be considered as international application by RO/IN.

If any person fails to comply with any direction given under section 35 or makes or causes to be made an application for the grant of a patent in contravention of section 39, he shall be punishable with imprisonment for a term which may extend to two years, or with fine, or with both.

An International patent application can be filed in Indian Patent Office as a Receiving Office, in request form (PCT/RO/101),offline or online.

Functions of Indian Patent Office as Receiving Office:

Receiving Office (RO)receives International Application (IA) and does the following verifications:
Nationality/residence Check
☐ At least one of the applicants must have the right to file with the RO
☐ The application must be in a language accepted by the RO (English/Hindi)
☐ If formality criteria are not satisfied, then IA may be referred to IB for further processing.

☐ Accords or refuses the international filing date (Article 11(1))

The application must contain:

☐ A request which has the effect of making all possible designations (Article 4 and Rules 3 and 4.9)

The name of applicant

A description

A claim

☐ Decides on requests for incorporation by reference of missing elements or parts (Rules 20.5 to 20.7)

☐ Checks whether translation of international application is required (Rules 12.3 and 12.4)

☐ Checks if the required fees (RO/IB /ISA) are timely paid (Rule14,15, 16bis)

☐ Checks priority claim(s) (Rules 4.10 and 26bis)

☐ Decides on requests for restoration of the priority right (Rule 26bis.3)

☐ Specifies the *International Searching Authority*

☐ Specifies *the International Preliminary Examining Authority*

☐ Checks for national security clearance/FFL (as per section 39 of Patent Act 1970)

☐ Forwards the record copy to IB and the search copy to ISA, including any required translation (Article 12, Rules 22.1 and 23.1)

☐ Forwards and receives correspondence from applicants and the international authorities

☐ Prepares the priority documents of PCT applications filed with it.

d) Your client isolated a new DNA sequence from the cells of a plant of Apple. The said DNA sequence on modification ir vivo developed resistance to a disease. The client wishes to protect following : (1) A modified DNA sequence of the plant (11) A method for isolation of DNA sequence (111) ~~ A DNA sequence in the cells of the plant (iv) A method of modifying DNA sequence in vivo (v) A method of treatment of plant by modification of the DNA sequence in vivo as claimed in claim 1. Advise appropriately to your client about the relevant provisions for the protection of above kind of invention.

Ans.1(d)(i) Section 3 (j) of the Patents Act: plants and animals in whole or any part thereof other than micro-organisms but including seeds, varieties and species and essentially biological processes for production or propagation of plants and animals;

(ii)method patentable
(iii) Not patentable
(iv) patentable
(v) patentable

e) Your client LG Chemicals Pvt. Ltd., Korea wishes to enter into the National Phase of India for obtaining Patent as early as possible based on his international application (without claiming any priority of earlier filing) filed in Korea. With this intention he approached you at 12th month from the date of international application filing with the prior art search report and preliminary examination report from the International Search Authority. Advise your client the available provisions in the Indian Patents Act and rules to proceed with such National Phase application in the circumstances as mentioned above.

Ans.1(e)

Section 135 of Patents Act: Convention applications;

(1) Without prejudice to the provisions contained in section 6, where a person has made an application for a patent in respect of an invention in a convention country (hereinafter referred to as the "basic application"), and that person or the legal representative or assignee of that person makes an application under this Act for a patent within twelve months after the date on which the basic application was made, the priority date of a claim of the complete specification, being a claim based on matter disclosed in the basic application, is the date of making of the basic application.
Explanation.--Where applications have been made for similar protection in respect of an invention in two or more convention countries, the period of twelve months referred to in this sub-section shall be reckoned from the date on which the earlier or earliest of the said applications was made.
(2) Where applications for protection have been made in one or more convention countries in respect of two or more inventions which are cognate or of which one is a modification of another, a single convention application may, subject to the provisions contained in section 10, be made in respect of those inventions at any time within twelve months from the date of the earliest of the said applications for protection:
Provided that the fee payable on the making of any such application shall be the same as if separate applications have been made in respect of each of the said

inventions, and the requirements of clause (b) of sub-section (1) of section 136 shall, in the case of any such application, apply separately to the applications for protection in respect of each of the said inventions.

[(3) In case of an application filed under the Patent Cooperation Treaty designating India and claiming priority from a previously filed application in India, the provisions of sub-sections (1) and (2) shall apply as if the previously filed application were the basic application:

Provided that a request for examination under section 11B shall be made only for one of the applications filed in India.]

f) The Pfizer Pharma l.td, USA obtained a patent on a pharmaceutical product from the Indian Patent office. Your client Zindal Pharma Pvt. Ltd., came to know about the said patent on receipt of a notice of infringement from the Pfizer Pharma Ltd., USA. The Zindal Pharma Pvt. Ltd. approached you for remedial action. They informed you that they are already manufacturing the same product and are exporting to Zambia. They have taken appropriate license to export the Drug from the authorities. Advise your client the course of action which may be adopted to benefit your client. (10 x 5 =50)

Ans. **Ans.1(f)**

Section 107A of Patents Act: Certain acts not to be considered as infringement;

[**107A. Certain acts not to be considered as infringement.**--For the purposes of this Act,--

(a) any act of making, constructing, [using, selling or importing] a patented invention solely for uses reasonably related to the development and submission of information required under any law for the time being in force, in India, or in a country other than India, that regulates the manufacture, construction, [use, sale or import] of any product;

(b) importation of patented products by any person from a person [who is duly authorised under the law to produce and sell or distribute the product], shall not be considered as an infringement of patent rights.]

Ans.2. Rule 138 of the Patent Rules, 2003: Power to extend time prescribed;

(1) Except for the time prescribed in clause (i) of sub-rule (4) of rule 20, sub-rule (6) of rule 20, rule 21, sub-rules (1), (5) and (6) of rule 24B, sub-rules (10) and (11) of rule 24C, sub-rule (4) of rule 55, sub-rule (1A) of rule 80 and sub-rules (1) and (2) of rule 130, the time prescribed by these rules for doing of any act or the taking of any proceeding thereunder may be extended by the Controller for a period of one month, if he thinks it fit to do so and upon such terms as he may direct.

(2) Any request for extension of time prescribed by these rules for the doing of any act or the taking of any proceeding thereunder shall be made before the expiry of such time prescribed in these rules.

Q.No.2. Your client Maruti Pvt. Ltd., Gurgaon sent a request for examination through speed post in respect of an application filed by them. The said document was delivered in Patent office by Post office two days after the last date for the filing of the request for the examination. Patent office sent a communication to Maruti Pvt. Ltd., Gurgaon stating that the request for examination has been filed after the due date and therefore cannot be taken on record. Your client approaches you to take remedial action. Draft appropriate documents to justify the stand in favour of your client.

Ans.2. Rule 138 of the Patent Rules, 2003: Power to extend time prescribed;

(1) Except for the time prescribed in clause (i) of sub-rule (4) of rule 20, sub-rule (6) of rule 20, rule 21, sub-rules (1), (5) and (6) of rule 24B, sub-rules (10) and (11) of rule 24C, sub-rule (4) of rule 55, sub-rule (1A) of rule 80 and sub-rules (1) and (2) of rule 130, the time prescribed by these rules for doing of any act or the taking of any proceeding thereunder may be extended by the Controller for a period of one month, if he thinks it fit to do so and upon such terms as he may direct.

(2) Any request for extension of time prescribed by these rules for the doing of any act or the taking of any proceeding thereunder shall be made before the expiry of such time prescribed in these rules.

or

Draft an application in favour of your client XYZ Pharmaceutical Ltd., 23, Industrial Estate, Hyderabad 500049 for obtaining compulsory license for export of patented anticancer pharmaceutical product "sunitinib" u/s 92(A) of the Patent Act, 1970 to "Angola". The facts of the Patent is as under : Patentee Royal Pharma, Roland Industrial Zone, UK Patent No. 205774 Documents and evidence (1)Drug license issued by Angola Govt. in favour of in support of obtaining | XYZ Pharmaceutical Ltd., Hyderabad for supply of compulsory license u/s 92 (A) | 20000 tablet per month (11) Letter from Angola Govt. authorizing XYZ Pharmaceutical Ltd., Hyderabad for export of its Drug to Angola for the purpose of export to Angola Terms and conditions | The Royalty of the three percents (3%) on net ex- acceptable to XYZ | factory price is payable to the Patentee Pharmaceutical Ltd., Hyderabad with regard to Royalty on issuance of the Compulsory License under section 92(A) for export (20 x 1=20)

Q.No.3 Draft Complete specification including claims for filing patent application on the basis of the information given by the applicant : Applicant's Name: Sanjeevani Herbals Pvt. Ltd, Industrial Estate, Okhla, New Delhi Disclosure of the Invention: We have developed a herbal formulation for treating AIDS and also have developed a process for preparing the same. The herbal formulation consists of Tulasi seeds, Momordica charantia seeds, Silaja, Silajit, Karanajaka, Chanaka , Kaphyog, Cinnamomum zeylanicum bark, Curcuma zedoaria root, Allilum sativum bulb and Betula alba bark . The herbs are used in amounts effective to produce a physiological benefit in combination with an amount of sodium chloride, more preferably sea salt, which is effective to promote the digestibility (palatability) and storage stability of the therapeutic composition.   Presently there is no specific and proven herbal medicine available for the treatment of AIDS. Currently the patients with AIDS are being treated using synthetic drugs, which are not only expensive but also have negative side effects like nausea, weight loss, cardiac irregularities and other related secondary effects. 2   This herbal formulation is based on plants, which are easily available in India, and so the treatment is cheaper. The composition of herbs described herein functions to augment the immune system through the synergistic interaction of the herbal components. The herbs are used in amounts effective to produce a physiological benefit in combination with an amount of sodium chloride, more preferably sea salt, which is effective to promote the digestibility (palatability) and storage stability of the therapeutic composition. the formulation is therapeutically effective and shows good clinical efficacy and at the same time shows a drastic reduction of side effects. The formulation can be formulated in tablets, tonic and has good taste. The term "sea salt" is used to describe preferred salt which is used in the present invention to promote the digestibility and storage stability of compositions according to the present invention. Although any source of sodium chloride may be used in the present invention, provided that the amount of sodium chloride represents approximately 1% to about 20% by weight, more preferably about 3% to about 5% by weight of the final composition. The above herbs are typically dried and ground to a fine powder. All ingredients are washed. Ripened seeds of Tulasi and Momordica charantia are selected. All ingredients are pulverized to fine powder and then mixed with sodium chloride. The antioxidant such as Vitamin C& Vitamin E is used as gum and stabilizers and other known ingredients such as flavors may be used upto 2%. All weights are expressed in milligrams and all percentages are by weight of the essential elements in the composition. The composition is typically an intimate mixture of powders. However, extracted herbs may also be used. The composition is then combined with effective amounts of sodium chloride, more preferably sea salt, in amounts effective to substantially enhance the digestibility and the storage stability of the composition. This amount generally ranges from about 1% to about 20% by weight of the composition, more preferably about 3% to about 5% by weight of the composition. 3% by weight of salt is most preferably included in the present compositions. The herbal mixture comprises from about 1.5% to about 75% Tulasi seeds, from about 1.5% to about 75% Momordica charantia seeds; from about 0.7% to about 35% Silaja bark; from about 0.6% to about 30% Silajit root; from about 0.6% to about 30% Karanajaka fruit; from about 0.6% to about 30% Chanaka, from about 1.5% to about 75% Kaphyog root, from about 1.5% to about 35% Cinnamomum zeylanicum bark,; from about 0.4% to about 25% Curcuma zedoaria root bark from about 0.4% to about 25% Allilum sativum bulb; and from about 0.4% to about 25% Betula alba bark. The antioxidant such as Vitamin C& Vitamin E is used as gum and stabilizers and other known ingredients such as flavors may be used upto 2%.

Ans.

TITLE-Herbal composition and method of treating HIV infection

FIELD OF INVENTION

The present invention relates to a herbal formulation for treating AIDS and a process for preparing the same. Particularly, the invention relates to the use of specific herbs and sodium chloride or sea salt in a synergistic combination for the treatment of AIDS.

BACKGROUND OF THE INVENTION

AIDS is a severe immunodeficiency disease that is caused by the human immunodeficiency virus (HIV). It causes a significant global health burden, with millions of people infected and affected worldwide. Presently, there is no specific and proven herbal medicine available for the treatment of AIDS. Currently, the patients with AIDS are being treated using synthetic drugs, which are not only expensive but also have negative side effects like nausea, weight loss, cardiac irregularities and other related secondary effects.

SUMMARY OF THE INVENTION

The present invention provides a herbal formulation for treating AIDS that is based on a synergistic combination of specific herbs and sodium chloride or sea salt. The herbal formulation comprises Tulasi seeds, Momordica charantia seeds, Silaja, Silajit, Karanajaka, Chanaka, Kaphyog, Cinnamomum zeylanicum bark, Curcuma zedoaria root, Allilum sativum bulb, and Betula alba bark in amounts effective to produce a physiological benefit. An amount of sodium chloride or sea salt is also added, which is effective to promote the digestibility and storage stability of the therapeutic composition.

The present invention also provides a process for preparing the herbal formulation. Ripened seeds of Tulasi and Momordica charantia are selected. All ingredients are washed, dried, and pulverized to a fine powder. The ingredients are then mixed with sodium chloride or sea salt and vitamin C & vitamin E as gum and stabilizers to form the therapeutic composition.

DETAILED DESCRIPTION OF THE INVENTION

The present invention provides a herbal formulation for treating AIDS comprising specific herbs and sodium chloride or sea salt in a synergistic combination. The herbs used in the formulation are commonly found in India and have been traditionally used for their medicinal properties.

The composition of herbs described herein functions to augment the immune system through the synergistic interaction of the herbal components. The herbs are used in amounts effective to produce a physiological benefit in combination with an amount of sodium chloride or sea salt, which is effective to promote the digestibility (palatability) and storage stability of the therapeutic composition.

The term "sea salt" is used to describe the preferred salt which is used to promote the digestibility and storage stability of compositions according to the present invention. Although any source of sodium chloride may be used in the present invention, provided that the amount of sodium chloride represents approximately 1% to about 20% by weight, more preferably about 3% to about 5% by weight of the final composition. The herbal mixture comprises from about 1.5% to about 75% Tulasi seeds, from about 1.5% to about 75% Momordica charantia seeds; from about 0.7% to about 35% Silaja bark; from about 0.6% to about 30% Silajit root; from about 0.6% to about 30% Karanajaka fruit; from about 0.6% to about 30% Chanaka, from about 1.5% to about 75% Kaphyog root, from about 1.5% to about 35% Cinnamomum zeylanicum bark,;

252

from about 0.4% to about 25% Curcuma zedoaria root bark from about 0.4% to about 25% Allilum sativum bulb; and from about 0.4% to about 25% Betula alba bark.

The present invention also provides a process for preparing the herbal formulation for treating AIDS. The process comprises a series of steps that include selecting ripened seeds of Tulasi and Momordica charantia, washing all ingredients, drying the ingredients, and pulverizing the ingredients to a fine powder. The herbal mixture is then combined with effective amounts of sodium chloride or sea salt, which is effective to substantially enhance the digestibility and the storage stability of the composition. Vitamin C & vitamin E are added as gum and stabilizers, and other known ingredients such as flavors may be used up to 2% of total composition.

The herbal formulation according to the invention is the result of extensive research and development. It has been found to be therapeutically effective and shows good clinical efficacy while at the same time shows a drastic reduction of side effects. The formulation can be formulated in tablets, tonic and has a good taste.

Accordingly, the present invention provides a herbal formulation for treating AIDS comprising specific herbs and sodium chloride or sea salt in a synergistic combination, as well as a process for preparing the same.

CLAIMS:

I claim:

1. A herbal formulation for treating AIDS comprising Tulasi seeds, Momordica charantia seeds, Silaja, Silajit, Karanajaka, Chanaka, Kaphyog, Cinnamomum zeylanicum bark, Curcuma zedoaria root, Allilum sativum bulb, and Betula alba bark in amounts effective to produce a physiological benefit, and an amount of sodium chloride or sea salt effective to promote the digestibility and storage stability of the therapeutic composition.

2. The herbal formulation according to claim 1, wherein the sodium chloride or sea salt represents 1% to about 20% by weight of the final composition.

3. The herbal formulation according to claim 1, wherein all ingredients are pulverized to a fine powder and then mixed with sodium chloride or sea salt.

4. The herbal formulation according to claim 1, comprising from about 1.5% to about 75% Tulasi seeds, from about 1.5% to about 75% Momordica charantia seeds, from 0.7% to about 35% Silaja bark, from 0.6% to about 30% Silajit root, from 0.6% to 30% Karanajaka fruit, from 0.6% to 30% Chanaka, from 1.5% to 75% Kaphyog root, from 1.5% to 35% Cinnamomum zeylanicum bark, from 0.4% to 25% Curcuma zedoaria root bark, from 0.4% to 25% Allilum sativum bulb, and from 0.4% to 25% Betula alba bark.

5. A process for preparing a herbal formulation for treating AIDS comprising the steps of: selecting ripened seeds of Tulasi and Momordica charantia; washing all ingredients and drying them; pulverizing the ingredients to a fine powder and then mixing with an amount of sodium chloride or sea salt effective to promote the digestibility and storage stability of the composition; and adding vitamin C & vitamin E as gum and stabilizers to the composition.

Q. Draft a complete specification for the protection of process and product in a single application. or Applicant's Name: M/S Thomson and Thomson Co. Pvt .Ltd, 198, E Block, Sector-23, Gurgaon, Haryana, India Disclosure of the Invention: This invention aims to provide a toothbrush which can effectively remove by brushing plaque on surfaces such as between teeth or between teeth and gums where plaque is easy to accumulate and at the same time massage gums. Toothbrushing has become an established custom for public people in everyday lives in recent years. The toothbrushing aims to prevent dental caries, periodontitis and foul breath and to massage gums, and which is widely done using toothbrush. The toothbrushes are used to remove plaque adhered to teeth as well as food residue between teeth and to massage gums as well. For conventional toothbrush filament, mainly monofilament made of uniform resin with round sectional shape has been used. Concerning tip shape of such monofilaments, hemispherical or tapering shape is known. Further toothbrushes are known which uses filaments with only one 3 tip shape or two or more tip shapes for individual tuft and they are embedded in tuft holes on the block head. As public interest in oral care grows strong in recent years, to remove effectively plaque which will cause carious teeth or periodontitis, a number of toothbrushes have been developed as shown above. However in the case of toothbrushes whose bristles have all needlelike tapering tips to remove plaque adhered to the surface between teeth and gums, because the bristles near tips becomes too thin and too flexible, the bristle tips lose their stiffness necessary to remove plaque sufficiently, and the purpose of toothbrushes to prevent periodontitis cannot be attained after all. On the other hand, toothbrushes whose bristle ends being round or hemispherical are suitable to clean flat surfaces of teeth or to massage gums, however it is difficult for such toothbrushes to remove plaque between teeth or in boundary spaces between teeth and gums because the bristle tips are too thick to enter such boundary spaces to remove plaque therein. That is, it is difficult for conventional toothbrushes having bristles with same tip shape or those with different tip shapes being uniformly mixed to clean up in every nook and corner in the mouth. The preferred embodiment of the present invention essentially comprises a toothbrush effective regardless of toothbrushing method or technique to prevent carious teeth or periodontitis which can more easily and effectively clean up in every nook and corner in the mouth than conventional ones, that is, the toothbrush can remove plaque and food residue adhered to surfaces between teeth, between teeth and gums and occlusal surface and give a proper stimulus to gums by massaging to quicken the circulation of the blood. The toothbrush head comprises tufts 4, 5 of bristles of polygonal cross-section, and tufts 6 of bristles of sheath-core construction which shows in cross-section as concentric circles. The polygonal bristles enable the cleaning of flat tooth surfaces and gum massage. The sheath-core bristles have a hard core for penetration between teeth and a softer sheath reducing bending. The cross-sections, lengths, profiles, tip shapes and materials of the bristles are extensively described. In the drawings, FIGURE 1 (a) illustrates a plan view of a block head of a toothbrush in accordance with the present invention and FIGURE 1(b) a side view thereof. FIGURE 2 illustrates a front view of on rush portion and a block head of a toothbrush in accordance with the present invention. Figure 3(a) illustrates a plan view of a toothbrush in accordance with the present invention, and Figure 3(b) a side view thereof. Figure 4(a) to (d), each illustrates a portion of sectional view showing condition polygonal filaments being densely embedded, that is, Figure 4(a) shows a triagonal filament, (b) a tetragonal filament, (¢) a hexagonal filament and (d) a octagonal filament, and Figure 4(e) illustrates the condition of conventional filaments having round cross section. In the Figures, the following reference symbols are used: 1- block head, 2-handle, 3- block head surface, 4 and 5 tufts of polygonal filaments, 6-tuft composed of sheath- core structural filament, 7- brush end, o- an angle of the first cut surface to the block head surface, 3- angle of the third cut surface to the block head surface. Draft a complete specification from your client including statement of claims. (30 x 1 = 30)

Figure 1

(a)

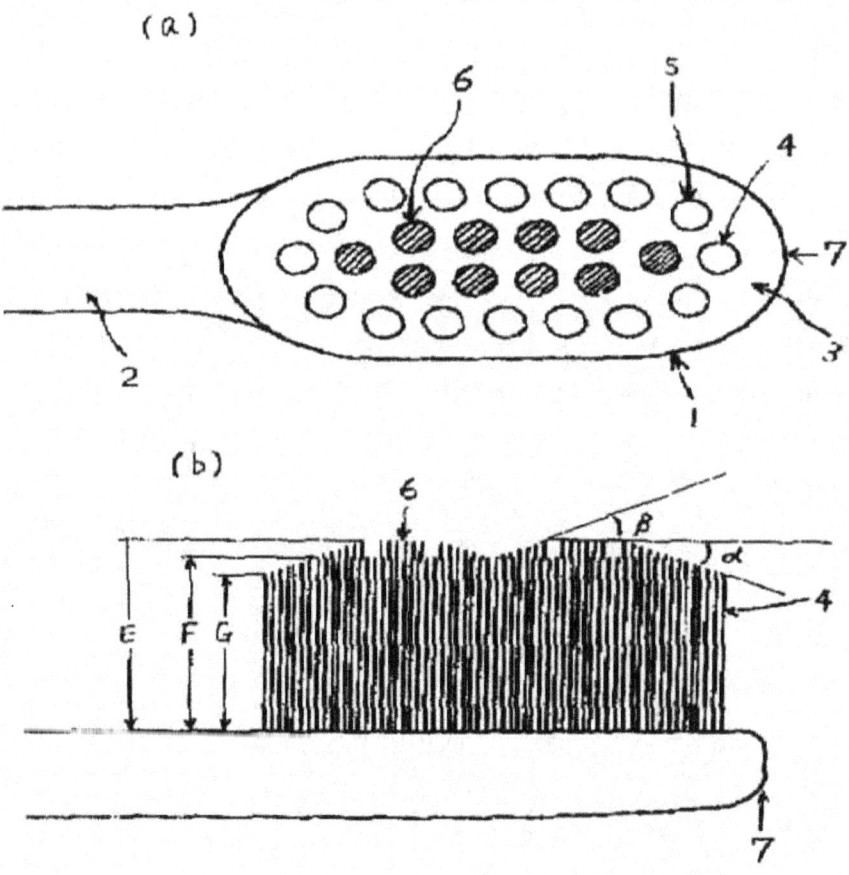

(b)

Figure 2

Figure 3

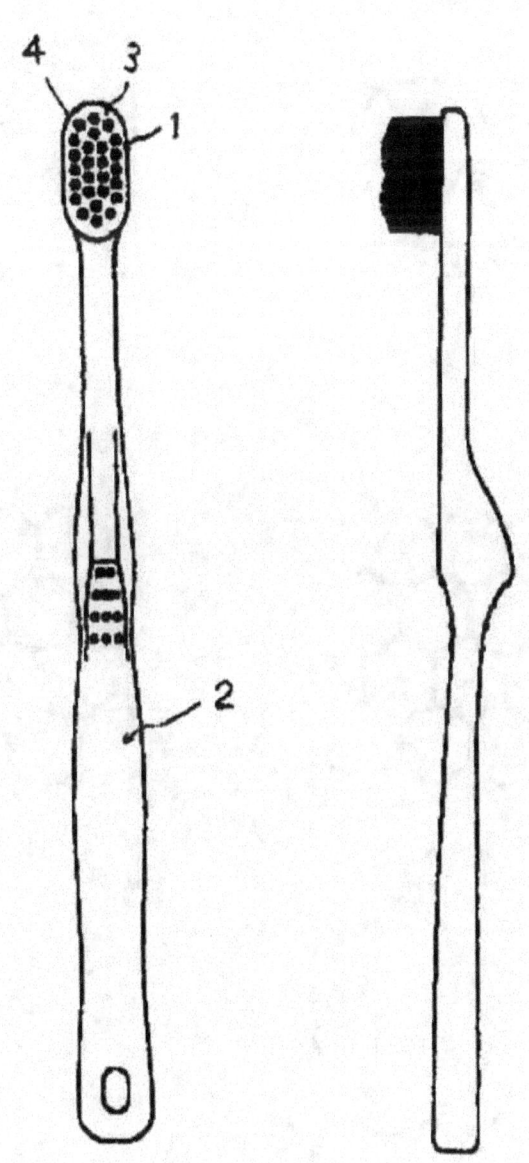

Figure 4

(a)

(b)

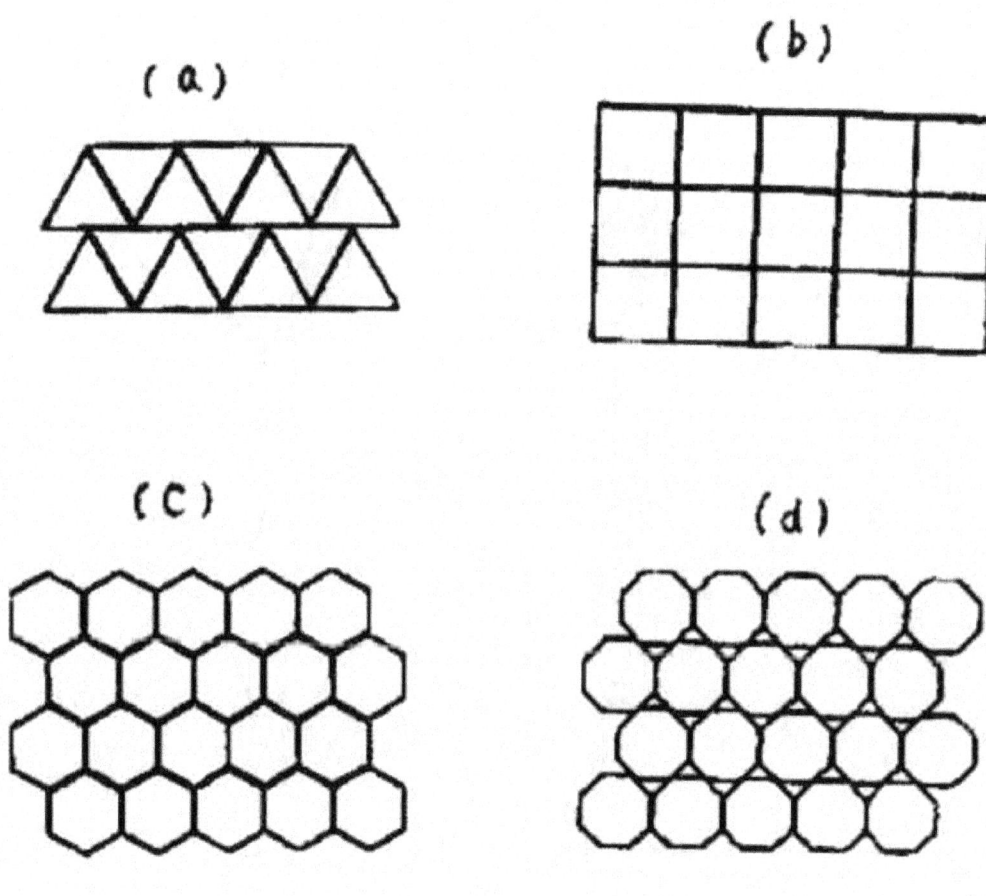

(C)

(d)

(e)

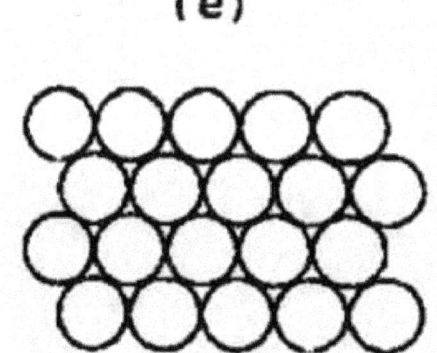

Ans. Kindly refer to US5991957A

TITLE-Toothbrush

FIELD OF THE INVENTION

The present invention relates to a toothbrush that effectively removes plaque and massages gums. More specifically, the invention relates to a toothbrush with a unique bristle configuration that enables it to effectively clean every nook and corner in the mouth.

BACKGROUND OF THE INVENTION

Toothbrushing has become a popular custom for maintaining good oral health. The goal of toothbrushing is to prevent dental caries, periodontitis, foul breath, and to massage gums. To achieve this goal, toothbrushes with different bristle configurations have been developed. However, conventional toothbrushes with monofilament bristles and tapering or hemispherical tip shapes have limitations in effectively removing plaque from between teeth and in boundary spaces between teeth and gums.

SUMMARY OF THE INVENTION

The present invention provides a toothbrush that effectively removes plaque and massages gums. The toothbrush head comprises tufts of bristles of polygonal cross-section for cleaning flat tooth surfaces and massaging gums. Additionally, the toothbrush includes tufts of bristles of sheath-core construction, which penetrate between teeth and reduce bending.

The present invention provides a unique bristle configuration that enables the toothbrush to effectively clean every nook and corner in the mouth. The toothbrush enables the removal of plaque and food residue adhered to surfaces between teeth, between teeth and gums, and occlusal surfaces.

DRAWINGS

In the drawings, FIGURE 1(a) illustrates a plan view of a block head of a toothbrush in accordance with the present invention and FIGURE 1(b) a side view thereof. FIGURE 2 illustrates a front view of the brush portion and a block head of a toothbrush in accordance with the present invention. Figure 3(a) illustrates a plan view of a toothbrush in accordance with the present invention, and Figure 3(b) a side view thereof. Figure 4(a) to (d) illustrates a portion of a sectional view showing the condition of polygonal filaments being densely embedded, and Figure 4(e) illustrates the condition of conventional filaments having a round cross-section.

DETAILED DESCRIPTION OF THE INVENTION

The present invention provides a toothbrush with a unique bristle configuration that enables it to effectively clean every nook and corner in the mouth.

The toothbrush head comprises tufts of bristles of polygonal cross-section and tufts of bristles of sheath-core construction. The polygonal bristles enable the cleaning of flat tooth surfaces and gum massage. The sheath-core bristles have a hard core for penetration between teeth and a softer sheath reducing bending. The cross-sections, lengths, profiles, tip shapes, and materials of the bristles are extensively described.

The toothbrush handle may be made of various materials including plastic or wood. The bristles are embedded in a block head made of plastic or other suitable material.

In a preferred embodiment, the polygonal bristles are densely embedded in tufts of approximately 9-13 mm in length. The bristles have a cross-section of a polygonal shape, such as a triangle, tetragon, hexagon, or octagon. The sheath-core bristles are also densely embedded in tufts of approximately 9-13 mm in length. The bristles have a cross-sectional shape of concentric circles, where the core is harder than the sheath to penetrate between teeth.

In one embodiment, the pyramid or conical tip shapes are preferred for polygonal bristles as shown in FIGURE 4. In another embodiment, the bristle length may be varied, such as a flat-ended tip for gum massage, or a pointed tip for interdental cleaning.

In another embodiment, the toothbrush head is angled with respect to the handle. The toothbrush head may be angled at a first angle relative to the block head surface and a second angle relative to the handle. The overall angle between the head and handle may be from about 85° to about 125°.

Accordingly, the present invention provides a toothbrush effective in preventing carious teeth and periodontitis, more easily cleaning up every nook and corner in the mouth than conventional toothbrushes, and provides effective removal of plaque and food residue adhered to surfaces between teeth, between teeth and gums, and occlusal surfaces.

CLAIMS:

I claim:

1. A toothbrush for effectively removing plaque and massaging gums, comprising a block head and a handle, wherein the block head has tufts of bristles of polygonal cross-section for cleaning flat tooth surfaces and gum massage, and tufts of bristles of sheath-core construction for penetrating between teeth and reducing bending.

2. The toothbrush of claim 1, wherein the polygonal bristles are densely embedded in tufts of 9-13 mm in length.

3. The toothbrush of claim 1, wherein the sheath-core bristles are densely embedded in tufts of 9-13 mm in length.

4. The toothbrush of claim 1, wherein the cross-sections of the polygonal bristles are a polygonal shape, such as a triangle, tetragon, hexagon, or octagon.

5. The toothbrush of claim 1, wherein the cross-sections of the sheath-core bristles are concentric circles.

6. The toothbrush of claim 1, wherein the bristle tip shapes are pyramid or conical.

7. The toothbrush of claim 1, further comprising an angled block head relative to the handle, wherein the block head is angled at a first angle relative to the block head surface and a second angle relative to the handle.

Reproductions or any process for their production. Under this Section (j) any invention related to the atomic energy is not granted patent according to the Atomic Energy Act, 1962.

Under Section 3(k), the following inventions are not patentable:

- A mathematical method or
- A business method or
- A computer program per se or
- Algorithms

The client 3D GRAPHICS has invented:
1. A new software code
2. An engine for the code

The software code per se is not patentable as per Section 3(k). However, if the software code has a technical effect and works in combination with the engine (hardware), it may be patentable.

The engine which is a hardware invention can be patented as it is a machine/apparatus.

To obtain patent in the minimum possible time, the client should:

1. File a provisional or complete specification along with Form 1 and Form 2.
2. File a request for early publication under Section 11A read with Rule 24A in Form 9, so that the application is published before the expiry of 18 months.
3. File a request for examination under Section 11B read with Rule 24B in Form 18. An express request for examination can be filed for early examination.
4. Respond to the First Examination Report (FER) within the prescribed time.

By filing a request for early publication and request for examination at the earliest, the patent can be obtained in the minimum possible time.

(k) a mathematical or business method or a computer programme per se or algorithms;

Patent filing procedure:

To obtain a patent for your client's software code and engine in India, they need to follow these steps:

1. Conduct a prior art search: It is important to conduct a patentability search to determine if the invention is novel and non-obvious before filing a patent application.

2. Write the patent specification: The patent specification should include a detailed description of the invention, patent claims outlining the scope of the invention, and any necessary drawings or diagrams.

3. File a provisional patent application: A provisional patent application can be filed to establish a priority date while providing additional time to refine the invention and prepare a final patent application.

4. File a complete patent application: The complete patent application must be filed within 12 months of the provisional application filing date.

4A. File request for early publication: Form 9

5. Examination: After filing the complete patent application, they can request for expedited examination under the procedure by paying the required fees.

6. Respond to objections and attend hearings (if necessary): The patent examiner may issue objections to the application during the examination process, and your client must respond within the deadlines provided. In case a hearing is required, they may attend the hearing and present their arguments to the patent office.

7. Grant of patent: If the patent office is satisfied with the invention, they will grant a patent that provides exclusive rights to the invention for up to 20 years.

b) Your client Mr. WISE has got a patent in India for a method of manufacturing a product X. The patent is in force from 10-01-2004. Your client has improved upon the patented method and seeks your advice for protecting the improvement. Suggest him the best and economic way for its

protection. Also inform him the necessary fees to be paid for the grant of patent and the maintenance fees for the entire term of patent.

Ans.1.(b) Mr. Wise, can protect the improvement to the patented method by filing a patent application for the improvement under Section 54 of the Indian Patent Act, which allows for the filing of a patent application for an improvement over an existing patent.

c) An Indian Research student invents a new form of drug for small pox. He claims that this drug is 30% more efficient than all other available drugs. He wishes to get it patented only in the USA, Advise him the necessary procedures to be carried out with Indian Patent Office.

Ans.1.(c)

The Indian Research student must follow certain procedures with the Indian Patent Office as per Section 39 of the Indian Patent Act.

As per Section 39, the inventor of a patent application filed in India is required to seek permission from the Indian Patent Office before filing a corresponding application outside India.

Therefore, the Indian Research student should file a patent application in India for the new form of drug for small pox.

After filing the application in India, the student must file a request for permission to file a corresponding application outside India.

The request for permission must be in writing and should include the details of the country where the student wishes to file the patent application, along with the reasons for seeking a corresponding application outside India.

The Indian Patent Office will examine the request for permission and may grant or refuse permission based on the following grounds:

1. National Security or defense

2. Public Safety or Health

3. The invention relates to atomic energy

d) A Patent is granted to M/s. Greedi Ltd. for manufacture of a product X in the year 2003. The patentee in order to extract maximum benefit inflates the price and supplies the product in the market in a limited quantity. Being disturbed by this unjust exploitation of the patent, your client M/s. Right Ltd. who is interested to make and market that product approaches you. What provisions of the Patents Act would you suggest to them under which they can get a licence ? Advise your client the necessary procedures to be carried out with the Patent Office.

Ans.1.(d) Under Section 84, any person interested may apply for a compulsory license for a patent if the reasonable requirements of the public with respect to the patented invention have not been satisfied, or if the patented invention is not available to the public at a reasonably affordable price, or if the patented invention is not worked in the territory of India.

The application for compulsory licensing under Section 84 must be made in the prescribed form (Form 17) along with the prescribed fees. The application must contain a statement that sets out the nature of the applicant's interest and the facts upon which the application is based.

The Controller of Patents will consider the application and take into account the nature of the invention, the measures already taken by the patentee to make full use of the invention, the ability of the applicant to work the invention to the public advantage, and the capacity of the applicant to undertake the risk in providing capital and working the invention.

If the Controller is satisfied that the reasonable requirements of the public have not been satisfied, or the patented invention is not available to the public at a reasonably affordable price, or the patented invention is not worked in the territory of India, he may grant a compulsory license upon such terms as he may deem fit.

Section 84 of Patents Act: Compulsory licences;

(1) At any time after the expiration of three years from the date of the [grant] of patent, any person interested may make an application to the Controller for grant of compulsory licence on patent on any of the following grounds, namely:--

(a) that the reasonable requirements of the public with respect to the patented invention have not been satisfied, or

(b) that the patented invention is not available to the public at a reasonably affordable price, or

(c) that the patented invention is not worked in the territory of India.

(2) An application under this section may be made by any person notwithstanding that he is already the holder of a licence under the patent and no person shall be estopped from alleging that the reasonable requirements of the public with respect to the patented invention are not satisfied or that the patented invention is not worked in the territory of India or that the patented invention is not available to the public at a reasonably affordable price by reason of any admission made by him, whether in such a licence or otherwise or by reason of his having accepted such a licence.

(3) Every application under sub-section (1) shall contain a statement setting out the nature of the applicants interest together with such particulars as may be prescribed and the facts upon which the application is based.

(4) The Controller, if satisfied that the reasonable requirements of the public with respect to the patented invention have not been satisfied or that the patented invention is not worked in the territory of India or that the patented invention is not available to the public at a reasonably affordable price, may grant a licence upon such terms as he may deem fit.

(5) Where the Controller directs the patentee to grant a licence he may, as incidental thereto, exercise the powers set out in section 88.

(6) In considering the application filed under this section, the Controller shall take into account,--

(i) the nature of the invention, the time which has elapsed since the sealing of the patent and the measures already taken by the patentee or any licensee to make full use of the invention;

(ii) the ability of the applicant to work the invention to the public advantage;

(iii) the capacity of the applicant to undertake the risk in providing capital and working the invention, if the application were granted;

(iv) as to whether the applicant has made efforts to obtain a licence from the patentee on reasonable terms and conditions and such efforts have not been successful within a reasonable period as the Controller may deem fit:

Provided that this clause shall not be applicable in case of national emergency or other circumstances of extreme urgency or in case of public non-commercial use or on establishment of a ground of anti-competitive practices adopted by the patentee,

but shall not be required to take into account matters subsequent to the making of the application.

[Explanation.--For the purposes of clause (iv), "reasonable period" shall be construed as a period not ordinarily exceeding a period of six months.]

(7) For the purposes of this Chapter, the reasonable requirements of the public shall be deemed not to have been satisfied--

(a) if, by reason of the refusal of the patentee to grant a licence or licences on reasonable terms,--

(i) an existing trade or industry or the development thereof or the establishment of any new trade or industry in India or the trade or industry of any person or class of persons trading or manufacturing in India is prejudiced; or

(ii) the demand for the patented article has not been met to an adequate extent or on reasonable terms; or

(iii) a market for export of the patented article manufactured in India is not being supplied or developed; or

(iv) the establishment or development of commercial activities in India is prejudiced; or

(b) if, by reason of conditions imposed by the patentee upon the grant of licences under the patent or upon the purchase, hire or use of the patented article or process, the manufacture, use or sale of materials not protected by the patent, or the establishment or development of any trade or industry in India, is prejudiced; or

(c) if the patentee imposes a condition upon the grant of licences under the patent to provide exclusive grant back, prevention to challenges to the validity of patent or coercive package licensing, or

(d) if the patented invention is not being worked in the territory of India on a commercial scale to an adequate extent or is not being so worked to the fullest extent that is reasonably practicable, or

(e) if the working of the patented invention in the territory of India on a commercial scale is being prevented or hindered by the importation from abroad of the patented article by--

(i) the patentee or persons claiming under him; or

(ii) persons directly or indirectly purchasing from him; or

(iii) other persons against whom the patentee is not taking or has not taken proceedings for infringement.

e) An Indian automobile firm is doing research on a novel brake system, which could be completed in another ten months. They approach you to get a patent in India, Europe and China. Explain him the possible ways of getting a patent, the necessary documents needed, various fees involved, time period required and various other requirements.

To obtain a license to manufacture and market the product X which is patented by M/s. Greedi Ltd, your client M/s. Right Ltd may apply for a compulsory license under Section 84 of the Indian Patents Act, 1970.

Ans.1(e) Filing procedure; convention application;advantages

f) Three students approach you for getting a patent on their novel machine and all three are the applicants and inventors of the machine. Explain to them the rights of the co-owners on the patent. (5x 10 = 50)

Ans. 1(f) Section 50 of Patents Act: Rights of co-owners of patents;

(1) Where a patent is granted to two or more persons, each of those persons shall, unless an agreement to the contrary is in force, be entitled to an equal undivided share in the patent.

(2) Subject to the provisions contained in this section and in section 51, where two or more persons are registered as grantee or proprietor of a patent, then, unless an agreement to the contrary is in force, each of those persons shall be entitled, by himself or his agents, to [the rights conferred by section 48] for his own benefit without accounting to the other person or persons.

(3) Subject to the provisions contained in this section and in section 51 and to any agreement for the time being in force, where two or more persons are registered as grantee or proprietor of a patent, then, a licence under the patent shall not be granted and a share in the patent shall not be assigned by one of such persons except with the consent of the other person or persons.

(4) Where a patented article is sold by one of two or more persons registered as grantee or proprietor of a patent, the purchaser and any person claiming through him shall be entitled to deal with the article in the same manner as if the article had been sold by a sole patentee.

(5) Subject to the provisions contained in this section, the rules of law applicable to the ownership and devolution of movable property generally shall apply in relation to patents; and nothing contained in sub-section (1) or sub-section (2) shall affect the mutual rights or obligations of trustees or of the legal representatives of a deceased person or their rights or obligations as such.

(6) Nothing in this section shall affect the rights of the assignees of a partial interest in a patent created before the commencement of this Act.

Q.No.2.

Your client Biopharma, Mysore, India, patentee of patent No0.202625 dated 10-10- 2005 wishes to change their name to Biosafe Pharmaceuticals, Further, they want to grant a licence to another company Altius Pharmaceuticals Ltd. on non-exclusive basis with a royalty of 3% on the net ex-factory price. Draft the necessary letters and agreements for your client.

Ans.2. Letter to Controller of Patents:

To,

The Controller of Patents,

Intellectual Property Office Building,

Plot No. 32, Sector 14, Dwarka,

New Delhi- 110078.

Dear Sir/Madam,

We, Biopharma, Mysore, India, hereby request you to change our name to Biosafe Pharmaceuticals in the records of the Patent Register associated with our patent No. 0.202625 dated 10-10-2005. We are enclosing the necessary documents for the same and request you to kindly make the necessary changes.

We thank you for your prompt attention and cooperation.

Yours faithfully,

Biosafe Pharmaceuticals

License Agreement:

This is a License Agreement between Biosafe Pharmaceuticals (herein referred to as the "Licensor"), with its registered office at _____ and Altius Pharmaceuticals Ltd. (herein referred to as the "Licensee"), with its registered office at _____

1. Purpose of the Agreement:

The Licensor is the owner of the Patent No. 0.202625 dated 10-10-2005 (herein referred to as the "Patent"). The Licensor wishes to grant a non-exclusive license to the Licensee to make, use and sell the products covered under the Patent in the territory mentioned in this agreement.

2. License Grant:

The Licensor hereby grants to the Licensee, a non-exclusive, non-transferable, worldwide license to use the Patent solely for such purposes and under such terms and conditions stated under this Agreement.

3. Royalty:

As consideration for this License grant, the Licensee shall pay the royalties equal to 3% of the net ex-factory price of the products covered under the Patent to the Licensor.

4. Duration:

This Agreement shall remain in effect for a period of _____ from the Effective Date.

5. Termination:

Either party may terminate this Agreement immediately upon giving written notice to the other party in the event of a material breach of this Agreement by the other party.

6. Governing Law and Jurisdiction:

This Agreement shall be governed by and construed in accordance with the laws of India and any disputes arising out of this Agreement shall be subject to the jurisdiction of the courts in Mysore.

7. Representations and Warranties:

The Licensor represents and warrants that it is authorized to grant the license and that it has not granted any rights conflicting with the rights granted under this Agreement.

The Licensee represents and warrants that it shall comply with all applicable laws and regulations and it shall not make, use or sell the products covered under the Patent, which are infringing upon the rights of any third party.

IN WITNESS WHEREOF, the Parties have executed this Agreement on the date set forth below.

For Biosafe Pharmaceuticals: _____

Authorized Signatory

For Altius Pharmaceuticals Ltd.: _____

Authorized Signatory

Date: _____

Section 57: Amendment of application and specification before Controller;

(1)Subject to the provisions of section 59, the Controller may, upon application made under this section in the prescribed manner by an applicant for a patent or by a patentee, allow the application for the patent or the complete specification [or any document relating thereto] to be amended subject to such conditions, if any, as the Controller thinks fit:

Provided that the Controller shall not pass any order allowing or refusing an application to amend an application for a patent or a specification [or any document relating thereto] under this section while any suit before a court for the infringement of the patent or any proceeding before the High Court for the revocation of the patent is pending, whether the suit or proceeding commenced before or after the filing of the application to amend.

(2) Every application for leave to amend an application for a patent 2[or a complete specification or any document relating thereto] under this section shall state the nature of the proposed amendment, and shall give full particulars of the reasons for which the application is made.

[(3) Any application for leave to amend an application for a patent or a complete specification or a document related thereto under this section made after the grant of patent and the nature of the proposed amendment may be published.]

(4) Where an application is [published] under sub-section (3), any person interested may, within the prescribed period after the [publication] thereof, give notice to the Controller of opposition thereto; and where such a notice is given within the period aforesaid, the Controller shall notify the person by whom the application under this section is made and shall give to that person and to the opponent an opportunity to be heard before he decides the case.

(5) An amendment under this section of a complete specification may be, or include, an amendment of the priority date of a claim.

[(6) The provisions of this section shall be without prejudice to the right of an applicant for a patent to amend his specification or any other document related thereto to comply with the directions of the Controller issued before the grant of a patent.]

OR .

M/s. Alpha Pharma received patent rights in India for a novel compound B claiming priority from 1% January 2002. Patent Grant notification was made in the Official Journal on 1st July 2006. M/s. Beta Pharma, your client, on seeing the notification, is of the opinion that the compound B was imported to India on July 2001 and being commercially sold at all places from August 2001. M/s. Beta Pharma approaches you on 1st March, 2007 for necessary advice and suitable actions to be taken. Help them suitably. (1x 20 = 20)

Post grant opposition or Revocation as a remedy

Section 25 of Patents Act: Opposition to patent;

(2) At any time after the grant of patent but before the expiry of a period of one year from the date of publication of grant of a patent, any person interested may give notice of opposition to the Controller in the prescribed manner on any of the following grounds, namely:--

(a) that the patentee or the person under or through whom he claims, wrongfully obtained the invention or any part thereof from him or from a person under or through whom he claims;

(b) that the invention so far as claimed in any claim of the complete specification has been published before the priority date of the claim--

(i) in any specification filed in pursuance of an application for a patent made in India on or after the 1st day of January, 1912; or

(ii) in India or elsewhere, in any other document:

Provided that the ground specified in sub-clause (ii) shall not be available where such publication does not constitute an anticipation of the invention by virtue of sub-section (2) or subsection (3) of section 29;

(c) that the invention so far as claimed in any claim of the complete specification is claimed in a claim of a complete specification published on or after the priority date of the claim of the patentee and filed in pursuance of an application for a patent in India, being a claim of which the priority date is earlier than that of the claim of the patentee;

(d) that the invention so far as claimed in any claim of the complete specification was publicly known or publicly used in India before the priority date of that claim.

Explanation.--For the purposes of this clause, an invention relating to a process for which a patent is granted shall be deemed to have been publicly known or publicly used in India before the priority date of the claim if a product made by that process had already been imported into India before that date except where such importation has been for the purpose of reasonable trial or experiment only;

Section 64 of Patents Act: Revocation of granted patents;

(1) Subject to the provisions contained in this Act, a patent whether granted before or after the commencement of this Act, may, [be revoked on a petition of any person interested or of the Central Government by *** on a counter-claim in a suit for infringement of the patent by the High Court] on any of the following grounds, that is to say--

(a) that the invention, so far as claimed in any claim of the complete specification, was claimed in a valid claim of earlier priority date contained in the complete specification of another patent granted in India;

(b) that the patent was granted on the application of a person not entitled under the provisions of this Act to apply therefor:

3* * * * *

(c) that the patent was obtained wrongfully in contravention of the rights of the petitioner or any person under or through whom he claims;

277

(d) that the subject of any claim of the complete specification is not an invention within the meaning of this Act;

(e) that the invention so far as claimed in any claim of the complete specification is not new, having regard to what was publicly known or publicly used in India before the priority date of the claim or to what was published in India or elsewhere in any of the documents referred to in section 13:

* * * * *

(f) that the invention so far as claimed in any claim of the complete specification is obvious or does not involve any inventive step, having regard to what was publicly known or publicly used in India or what was published in India or elsewhere before the priority date of the claim:

3* * * * *

(g) that the invention, so far as claimed in any claim of the complete specification, is not useful;

(h) that the complete specification does not sufficiently and fairly describe the invention and the method by which it is to be performed, that is to say, that the description of the method or the instructions for the working of the invention as contained in the complete specification are not by themselves sufficient to enable a person in India possessing average skill in, and average knowledge of, the art to which the invention relates, to work the invention, or that it does not disclose the best method of performing it which was known to the applicant for the patent and for which he was entitled to claim, protection;

(i) that the scope of any claim of the complete specification is not sufficiently and clearly defined or that any claim of the complete specification is not fairly based on the matter disclosed in the specification;

(j) that the patent was obtained on a false suggestion or representation;

(k) that the subject of any claim of the complete specification is not patentable under this Act;

(l) that the invention so far as claimed in any claim of the complete specification was secretly used in India, otherwise than as mentioned in sub-section (3), before the priority date of the claim;

(m) that the applicant for the patent has failed to disclose to the Controller the information required by section 8 or has furnished information which in any material particular was false to his knowledge;

(n) that the applicant contravened any direction for secrecy passed under section 35 [or made or caused to be made an application for the grant of a patent outside India in contravention of section 39];

(o) that leave to amend the complete specification under section 57 or section 58 was obtained by fraud;

[(p) that the complete specification does not disclose or wrongly mentions the source or geographical origin of biological material used for the invention;

(q) that the invention so far as claimed in any claim of the complete specification was anticipated having regard to the knowledge, oral or otherwise, available within any local or indigenous community in India or elsewhere.]

(2) For the purposes of clauses (e) and (f) of sub-section (1),--

(a) no account shall be taken of [personal document or secret trial or secret use]; and

(b) where the patent is for a process or for a product as made by a process described or claimed the importation into India of the product made abroad by that process shall constitute knowledge or use in India of the invention on the date of the importation, except where such importation has been for the purpose of reasonable trial or experiment only.

(3) For the purpose of clause (l) of sub-section (1), no account shall be taken of any use of the invention--

(a) for the purpose of reasonable trial or experiment only; or

(b) by the Government or by any person authorised by the Government or by a Government undertaking, in consequence of the applicant for the patent or any person from whom he derives title having communicated or disclosed the invention directly or indirectly to the Government or person authorised as aforesaid or to the Government undertaking; or

(c) by any other person, in consequence of the applicant for the patent or any person from whom he derives title having communicated or disclosed the invention, and without the consent or acquiescence of the applicant or of any person from whom he derives title.

(4) Without prejudice to the provisions contained in sub-section (1), a patent may be revoked by the High Court on the petition of the Central Government, if the High Court is satisfied that the patentee has without reasonable cause failed to comply with the request of the Central Government to make, use or exercise the patented invention for the purposes of Government within the meaning of section 99 upon reasonable terms.

(5) A notice of any petition for revocation of a patent under this section shall be served on all persons appearing from the register to be proprietors of that patent or to have shares or interests therein and it shall not be necessary to serve a notice on any other person.

(e) that the invention so far as claimed in any claim of the complete specification is obvious and clearly does not involve any inventive step, having regard to the matter published as mentioned in clause (b) or having regard to what was used in India before the priority date of the claim;

(f) that the subject of any claim of the complete specification is not an invention within the meaning of this Act, or is not patentable under this Act;

(g) that the complete specification does not sufficiently and clearly describe the invention or the method by which it is to be performed;

(h) that the patentee has failed to disclose to the Controller the information required by section 8 or has furnished the information which in any material particular was false to his knowledge;

(i) that in the case of a patent granted on convention application, the application for patent was not made within twelve months from the date of the first application for protection for the invention made in a convention country or in India by the patentee or a person from whom he derives title;

(j) that the complete specification does not disclose or wrongly mentions the source and geographical origin of biological material used for the invention;

(k) that the invention so far as claimed in any claim of the complete specification was anticipated having regard to the knowledge, oral or otherwise, available within any local or indigenous community in India or elsewhere,

but on no other ground.

(3) (a) Where any such notice of opposition is duly given under sub-section (2), the Controller shall notify the patentee.

(b) On receipt of such notice of opposition, the Controller shall, by order in writing, constitute a Board to be known as the Opposition Board consisting of such officers as he may determine and refer such notice of opposition along with the documents to that Board for examination and submission of its recommendations to the Controller.

(c) Every Opposition Board constituted under clause (b) shall conduct the examination in accordance with such procedure as may be prescribed.

(4) On receipt of the recommendation of the Opposition Board and after giving the patentee and the opponent an opportunity of being heard, the Controller shall order either to maintain or to amend or to revoke the patent.

(5) While passing an order under sub-section (4) in respect of the ground mentioned in clause (d) or clause (e) of sub-section (2), the Controller shall not take into account any personal document or secret trial or secret use.

(6) In case the Controller issues an order under sub-section (4) that the patent shall be maintained subject to amendment of the specification or any other document, the patent shall stand amended accordingly.]

Q.No.3. Draft Complete Specification including claims for filing patent application on the basis of the information given by your client: Your client M/s. Apco Construction, Salem, India furnishes the following information: : We have invented wall ties having an elongate shank fabricated from hard drawn stainless steel for tying together the two leaves of a cavity wall, for example two brick leaves. + Conventional wall tie is formed from wire and has a simple shank with one or two'shallow U-shaped bends known as lips which help in collecting condensed water and promoting formation of drops which when of sufficient size, fall down to the bottom of the cavity. Such lips create a complication in to brick laying as it is essential that they be incorporated in the correct orientation, that is bend downwards, if they are to function properly with respect to drip formation, Preferred embodiment of the invention is described with illustration as follows: - Fig.1 isa plan of a wall tie according to the invention. Fig. 2 is a side elevation of tie of Fig, 1. Fig.3 isan end elevation of the tie of Figs.1 & 2. 10 - wall tie 12 - elongate shank 14,16 - triangular heads 18,20 - crimped portion of heads. 22 - double lips 24,26 - adjacent bends 28 - straight portion making an angle of 40° to axis of shank. According to the preferred embodiment of the present invention there is provided a wall tie (10) having an elongate shank (12). At each end triangular heads (14, 16) are provided for embedding in a mortar course. The shank (12) is also provided with one or more pairs of adjacent bends (24, 26) extending in opposite directions in a plane normal to that of said head. Such a He is reversible and will promote drip- formation equally well in either orientation. The adjacent bends (24, 26) thus have a generally S-shaped configuration, the intermediate portion between the two U-bends constituting the S preferably being straight and forming an angle of less than 45° to the axis of the shank (12). Preferably the wall tie is made from a single length of hard drawn stainless steel wire with at least one triangular head (14,16). To enhance the anchorage of the head when embedded in mortar, the wire forming the head or heads may be crimped at one or more places. Drawings enclosed.

Title: Wall ties for cavity walls

Field of Invention: This invention relates to wall ties for use in cavity walls, and particularly to wall ties that simplify bricklaying and promote drip formation without the need for complicated orientation.

Background of the Invention: Traditional wall ties are formed from wire and have a simple shank with one or two U-shaped bends known as lips which promote drip formation by collecting condensed water. However, these lips can create a complication in bricklaying as they must be incorporated in the correct orientation to function properly. This invention provides a wall tie that is reversible and promotes drip formation equally well in either orientation.

Summary of the Invention: The invention is a wall tie for cavity walls consisting of an elongate shank with triangular heads at either end for embedding in mortar, and one or more pairs of adjacent bends extending in opposite directions in a plane normal to the heads. The intermediate portion between the two U-bends constitutes an S-shape, and the straight portion forms an angle of less than 45 degrees to the axis of the shank. The wall tie is preferably made from a single length of hard drawn stainless steel wire with at least one crimped head for enhanced anchorage.

Brief Description of the Drawings: Figure 1 is a plan of the wall tie, Figure 2 is a side elevation, and Figure 3 is an end elevation.

Detailed Description of the Invention: The wall tie of the present invention provides a simple and effective solution to the complications of traditional wall ties. The elongate shank is formed from hard drawn stainless steel wire, which is more durable and resistant to corrosion than traditional wire.

At either end of the shank are triangular heads for embedding in mortar. The heads may be crimped at one or more places to enhance anchorage. The wall tie also includes one or more pairs of adjacent bends extending in opposite directions in a plane normal to the heads. The intermediate portion between the two U-bends constitutes an S-shape, with the straight portion forming an angle of less than 45 degrees to the axis of the shank.

The adjacent bends promote drip formation by collecting condensed water, and the S-shape allows the wall tie to be reversible, promoting drip formation equally well in either orientation. This simplifies bricklaying and eliminates the need for complicated orientation of the wall tie.

In end, the wall tie of the present invention provides a simple and effective solution for promoting drip formation in cavity walls without the complications of traditional wall ties. The use of hard drawn stainless steel wire and crimped heads enhances the durability and anchorage of the tie, and the S-shaped configuration allows for reversible orientation.

CLAIMS:

I claim:

1. A wall tie for tying together two leaves of a cavity wall comprising an elongate shank fabricated from hard drawn stainless steel, provided with one or more pairs of adjacent bends extending in opposite directions in a plane normal to that of the head, wherein the adjacent bends have a generally S-shaped configuration, the intermediate portion between the two U-bends forming the S being straight and forming an angle of less than 45° to the axis of the shank.

2. The wall tie according to claim 1, wherein the adjacent bends are located at a distance from the triangular head of the tie.

3. The wall tie according to claim 1, further comprising at least one triangular head provided at each end of the shank for embedding in a mortar course.

4. The wall tie according to claim 1, wherein the shank is made from a single length of hard drawn stainless steel wire.

5. The wall tie according to claim 1, wherein the wire forming the triangular head or heads is crimped at one or more places to enhance anchorage of the head when embedded in mortar.

OR

Your client M/s. Ranepal Ltd, Hyderabad, India furnishes the following information to you:- We have invented superabsorbent polymers which absorb water, aqueous liquids and blood wherein the polymers of our invention have improved properties. These properties include an improved relationship between gel bed permeability and fluid retention including achieving higher gel bed permeability without the disadvantages of low retention that are characteristics of higher gel strengths. The super absorbent polymers that are currently available are cross linked poly acrylic acids or cross linked starch-acrylic acid graft polymers, in which some of the carboxyl groups are neutralized with sodium hydroxide solution or potassium hydroxide solution. - In particular, gel blocking is a well-known problem that may be associated with the use of superabsorbent polymers in absorbent articles such as diapers. To overcome the above mentioned problem we have invented an absorbing polymer composition that exhibits excellent properties such as capabilities of maintaining high liquid permeability and liquid retention even when the super absorbent polymer is increased in percent by weight based on the absorbent structure. According to our invention, the superabsorbent polymer composition comprises from about 55 to about 99.9 wt. % of polymerizable unsaturated acid group containing monomers; from about 0.001 to about 5.0 wt. % of internal crosslinking agent; from about 0.001 to about 5.0 wt. % of surface crosslinking agent applied to the particle surface; from 0 to about 5 wt. % of a penetration modifier immediately before, during or immediately after the surface crosslinking step; from 0 to about 5 wt. % of a multivalent - metal salt on the surface; from about 0 to 2 wt % surfactant on the surface; and optionally from about 0.01 to about 5 wt% of an insoluble, inorganic powder and from . about 0.01 to about 5 wt% of a thermoplastic polymer is applied on the particle surface coincident with or followed by a temperature at least the thermoplastic melt temperature or greater. The improved properties of superabsorbent polymer are as follows: - Centrifuge retention capacity of about 25 g/g or more; and a gel bed permeability II of about $300 \times 10^{-9} cm^2$ or more, or in the alternative, a gel bed permeability T of about $500 \times 10^{-9} cm^2$ or more and a shear modulus of less than about 9500 dynes/cm^2. Further monomers, used for the preparation of the absorbent polymers according to the invention, are 0 40 wt% of ethylenically unsaturated monomers which can be copolymerised with a), such as eg acrylamide, methacrylamide, hydroxyethyl acrylate, dimethylaminoalkyl (meth)-acrylate, ethoxylated (meth)- acrylates, dimethylaminopropylacrylamide or acrlamidopropyltrimethylammonium chloride. More than 40 wt.% of these monomers impair the swellability of the polymers. The internal crosslinking agent has at least two ethylenically unsaturated double bonds or one ehylenically unsaturated double bond and one functional group which is reactive towards acid groups of the polymerizable unsaturated acid group containing - monomers or several functional groups which are reactive towards acid groups can be used as the internal crosslinking component and which is present during the polymerization of the polymerizable unsaturated acid group containing monomers. The absorbent polymers according to the invention can also include from about 0.01 to about 5 wt% of water-insoluble, inorganic powder. Examples of insoluble, inorganic powders include silicon dioxide, silicic acid, silicates, titanium dioxide, aluminum oxide, magnesium oxide, zinc oxide, talc, calcium phosphate, clays, diatomataceous earth, zeolites, bentonite, kaolin, hydrotalcite, activated clays. It is also desirable to employ surface additives that perform several roles during surface modifications. For example, a single additive may be a surfactant, viscosity modifier and react to crosslink polymer chains. The superabsorbent polymers may also include from 0 to about 2.0 wt% of dedusting agents, such as hydrophilic and hydrophobic dedusting agents. Further, additives of the superabsorbent polymers according to the invention may optionally be employed, such as odor-binding substances, such as cyclodextrins, zeolites, inorganic or organic salts and similar materials; anti-caking additives, flow modification agents and the like. (1 x 30 = 30) FIG3

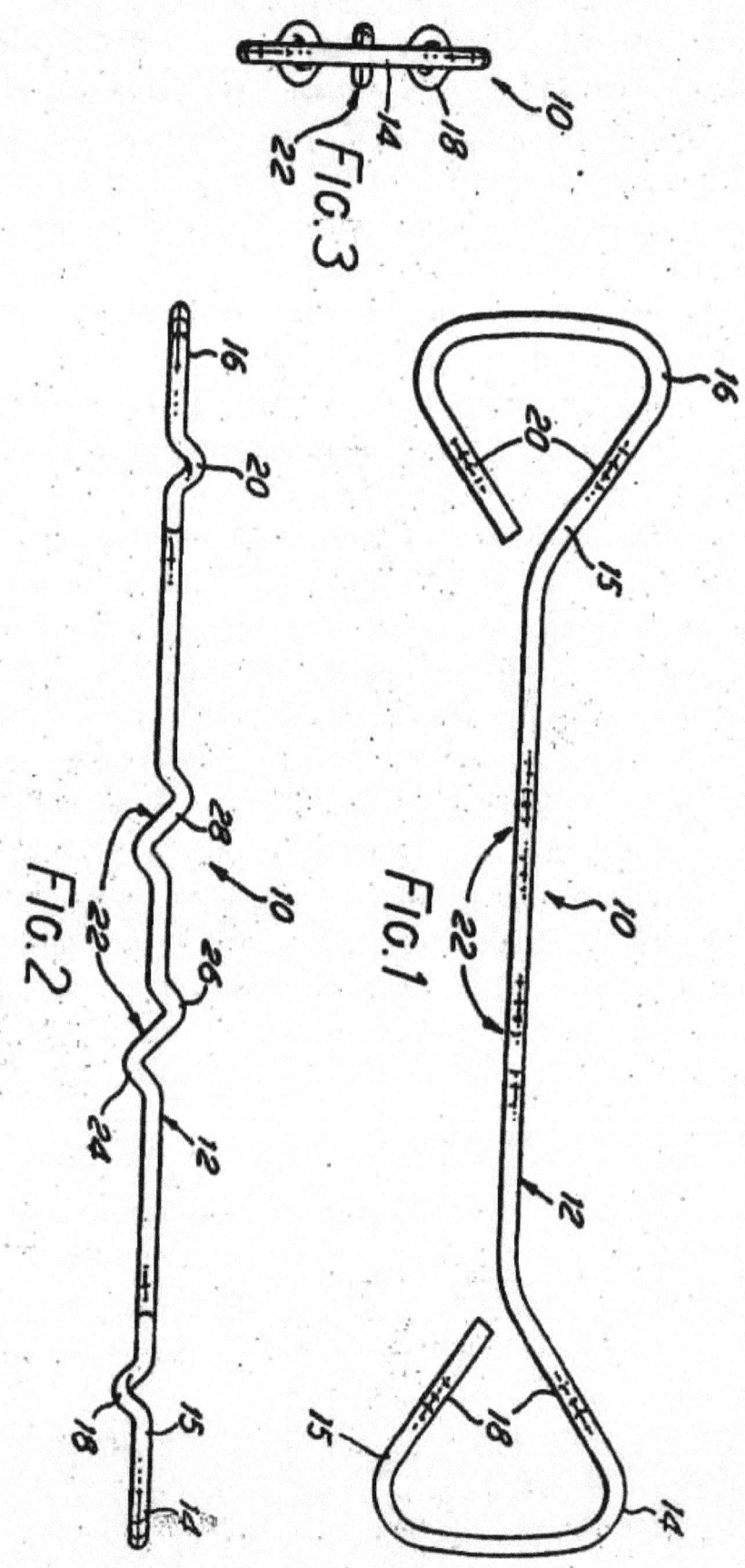

FIG.3

FIG.2

FIG.1

Title: Superabsorbent Polymers with Improved Properties

Field of Invention: This invention relates to superabsorbent polymers that absorb water, aqueous liquids, and blood, and specifically to polymers that have improved properties, including a higher gel bed permeability without the disadvantages of low retention.

Background of the Invention: Superabsorbent polymers are widely used as absorbing materials in a variety of applications such as diapers, feminine care products, and medical dressings. However, traditional superabsorbent polymers have limitations such as gel blocking, which can impede liquid permeability and retention. This invention provides a solution to the problem of gel blocking by creating a superabsorbent polymer composition that exhibits excellent properties.

Summary of the Invention: The invention is a superabsorbent polymer composition that comprises polymerizable unsaturated acid group containing monomers, an internal crosslinking agent, a surface crosslinking agent applied to the particle surface, a penetration modifier immediately before, during, or after the surface crosslinking step, multivalent metal salt on the surface, a surfactant on the surface, and optionally, an insoluble, inorganic powder and a thermoplastic polymer applied on the particle surface. The specific weight percentages of these ingredients are defined in the specification.

The superabsorbent polymer composition of the invention has improved properties, including centrifuge retention capacity of about 25 g/g or more, a gel bed permeability II of about $300.times.10.sup.-9cm.sup.2$ or more, a gel bed permeability T of about $500.times.10.sup.-9 cm.sup.2$ or more, and a shear modulus of less than about 9500 dynes/cm.sup.2.

The composition also includes ethylenically unsaturated monomers which can be copolymerized with the polymerizable unsaturated acid group containing monomers. The internal crosslinking agent has at least two ethylenically unsaturated double bonds or one ethylenically unsaturated double bond and one functional group that reacts towards acid groups of the polymerizable unsaturated acid group containing monomers.

The use of the insoluble, inorganic powder enhances the properties of the superabsorbent polymer composition, and surface additives may perform several roles during surface modifications, such as acting as a surfactant, viscosity modifier, and crosslinking polymer chains. Additionally, odor-binding substances, anti-caking additives, flow modification agents, and other additives may be employed in the composition.

Brief Description of the Drawings:

Detailed Description of the Invention: The superabsorbent polymer composition of the present invention provides a solution to the gel blocking problem that is typically associated with superabsorbent polymers. The composition includes specific weight percentages of several ingredients, and the use of an insoluble, inorganic powder, surface additives, and other additives enhances the properties of the composition.

The internal crosslinking agent has at least two ethylenically unsaturated double bonds or one ethylenically unsaturated double bond and one functional group that reacts towards the acid groups of the polymerizable unsaturated acid group containing monomers. The use of such an internal crosslinking agent allows for improved properties compared to traditional crosslinked polymers.

The use of a surface crosslinking agent applied to the particle surface also contributes to improved properties by enhancing the gel bed permeability and liquid retention of the superabsorbent polymer composition. A penetration modifier may be used immediately before, during, or after the surface crosslinking step, and a multivalent metal salt on the surface, surfactant on the surface, and optional additives may also be employed.

In end, the superabsorbent polymer composition of the present invention provides excellent properties, which greatly enhance the absorbent capabilities of the polymer. The specific ingredients and their weight percentages are defined in the specification, and the use of inorganic powders, surface additives, and other additives enhance the properties of the composition.

CLAIMS:

I claim:

1. A superabsorbent polymer composition comprising from 55 to 99.9 wt. % of polymerizable unsaturated acid group containing monomers, from 0.001 to 5.0 wt. % of internal crosslinking agent, from 0.001 to 5.0 wt. % of surface crosslinking agent applied to the particle surface, from 0 to 5 wt. % of a penetration modifier, from 0 to 5 wt. % of a multivalent metal salt on the surface, from 0 to 2 wt. % surfactant on the surface, and optionally, from 0.01 to about 5 wt% of an insoluble, inorganic powder and from 0.01 to 5 wt% of a thermoplastic polymer applied on the particle surface.

2. The superabsorbent polymer composition according to claim 1, wherein the polymerizable unsaturated acid group containing monomers are selected from acrylic acid, methacrylic acid, or maleic acid.

3. The superabsorbent polymer composition according to claim 1, wherein the internal crosslinking agent comprises at least two ethylenically unsaturated double bonds or one ethylenically unsaturated double bond and one functional group that is reactive towards acid groups of the polymerizable unsaturated acid group containing monomers.

4. The superabsorbent polymer composition according to claim 1, wherein the surface crosslinking agent comprises a di- or polyfunctional compound having at

least two reactive groups capable of being crosslinked with the internal crosslinking agent.

5. The superabsorbent polymer composition according to claim 1, further comprising from about 0.01 wt% to 5 wt% of an insoluble, inorganic powder selected from the group consisting of silicon dioxide, silicic acid, silicates, titanium dioxide, aluminum oxide, magnesium oxide, zinc oxide, talc, calcium phosphate, clays, diatomataceous earth, zeolites, bentonite, kaolin, and hydrotalcite

PATENT AGENT EXAMINATION

SEPTEMBER, 2005

PAPER -II

Time :-2 Hrs

Total pages —4+1 Total Marks — 100

Instructions: 1. All questions are compulsory.

2 .Marks of each question are indicated at the end of the question.

3.Answers should be precise and to the point supported by relevant provisions of the Act and Rules.

0.1. Answer any 5 of the following. (2) Your client PASCO LTD, which is a detergent manufacturing Company and having tough competition from rival company SAUSCO LTD, interested to get a Patent on its latest invention relating to detergent composition as soon as possible preferably within one year from the date of filing the application in India. Advise your client the possible procedure to obtain the Patent right within the expected minimum time lo grab the monopoly in the field .

Ans:To obtain a patent right as soon as possible, preferably within one year from the date of filing the application in India, the following procedures can be followed:

1. File the Patent Application with Complete Specification: PASCO LTD can file the patent application in Form 1 along with a complete specification in Form 2 as per Section 7 and 10 of the Patents Act, 1970.

2. File Declaration as to Inventorship: PASCO LTD also needs to file a declaration as to inventorship in Form 5 as per Section 10(6) and Rule 13(6) of the Patents Rules, 2003.

3. Request for Early Publication: Section 11A(2) of the Patents Act, 1970 allows the applicant to request early publication of the application. PASCO LTD can

file Form 9 for early publication along with the prescribed fee if it wants to get its invention published as soon as possible.

4. Request for Examination: Section 11B of the Patents Act, 1970 allows the applicant to request an early examination of the application. To obtain a patent right within the expected minimum time, PASCO LTD can file Form 18 to request early examination of the patent application along with the prescribed fee.

The procedure involved to obtain a patent in the minimum possible time:

Patent Application filed in Form 1 along with Complete Specification in Form 2, Section 7,10

Form 5: Declaration as to inventorship r/w Section 10(6), Rule13(6)

Form 9-Early Publication r/w Section 11A(2), Rule-24

Request for Examination-Form 18, Section 11B,Rule 24B

(bh) Your client Mr. AMRIT LAL invented a novel molecule for treatment of diabetes two years ago while doing his Ph.D and published the same in journal of medicinal chemistry. Now as a result of further extensive research work the molecule has been found to have potential therapeutic values for the treatment of Cancer. He now wants to have patent protect for the same molecule with anticancer properties in India and USA. Advise your client the provisions available in Indian Patents Act for protection of invention as mentioned by the client. What are his chances in USA?

Ans: In India, Mr. AMRIT LAL can file a patent application under the Patent Act, 1970 for his discovery of the novel molecule with anticancer properties. As per the Indian Patents Act, the invention should be new, non-obvious, and should have industrial applicability to qualify for a patent.

Section 3(d) of the Indian Patents Act states that incremental inventions that do not result in improved efficacy of a substance or composition may not be granted a patent. Therefore, if Mr. AMRIT LAL claims that the molecule has enhanced efficacy against cancer, then he has more chances of getting a patent for the same.

As for the USA, Mr. AMRIT LAL can file a utility patent application with the United States Patent and Trademark Office (USPTO) to protect his invention. The criteria for patentability in the USA are similar to India, i.e., the invention should be novel, non-obvious, and have industrial applicability.

(¢c) **Your client JOSOMAHA CORPORATION based in Tokyo, Japan filed a PCT international application in Japanese language in receiving office, Japanese Patent Office. on 1.1.2004 without claiming any priority. After receiving good search report from the International searching Authority on 30.10.2004 it is interested to enter the national phase in India to obtain a patent as early as possible. Advise your client the relevant provisions available in Indian patent law to file a national phase application in abovementioned circumstances. Also advise client about the provisions in the Indian Patents Act for getting early examination of the national phase Application.**

Ans: In order to enter the national phase in India, the client JOSOMAHA CORPORATION needs to file a Form 1 application along with the required documents and fees within 31 months from the priority date. Since the client did not claim any priority, the 31-month deadline would begin from the PCT filing date, i.e., 1.1.2004.

The client must also provide a translation of the international application in English within 31 months from the priority date, as per Rule 20(5) of the Indian Patents Rules. This English translation would be used for the examination of the national phase application.

If the client wishes to obtain an early examination of the national phase application, they can file a request for the same under Rule 20(4) of the Indian Patents Rules. This request must be made along with the Form 18 and the prescribed fees. Upon receiving the request for early examination, the Indian Patent Office will examine the application out of turn and expeditiously.

In summary, the relevant provisions for filing a national phase application in India are as follows:

1. File a Form 1 application within 31 months of the priority date

2. Provide an English translation of the international application

3. Request for early examination under Rule 20(4) for expedited processing of the application.

(d) Due to malnutrition, lots of people in LOBANG, a least developing country, are suffering from tuberculosis. LOBANG has no manufacturing capacity for the manufacturing of SIMTADIN. a PHARMACEUTICAL COMPOUND, very effective and cheap for the treatment of tuberculosis. However. it authorises by notification M/S CIPLA LTD in India to manufacture and export the said pharmaceutical compound to LOBANG. M/S CIPLA LTD informs that the pharmaceutical compound is patent protected in India by LIZA INC USA and therefore unable to manufacture and export due to fear of possible infringement. Advise vour client M/S CIPLA LTD about various relevant provisions available under the Patents Act 1970 as amended in order to enable the said company to manufacture and export the said product to LOBANG without any infringement.

Ans:In order for M/S CIPLA LTD to manufacture and export the pharmaceutical compound SIMTADIN to LOBANG without infringing upon LIZA INC USA's patent, they can explore the following provisions available under the Indian Patents Act, 1970:

1. Section 92A - This provision allows certain acts related to inventions, including the manufacture and export of patented products, to be carried out without the permission of the patent holder in certain circumstances. The provision allows for the grant of compulsory licenses to manufacture and export a patented product to countries that are declared as "eligible importing

countries." LOBANG, being a least developing country, may be eligible to receive such a license, which would allow M/S CIPLA LTD to manufacture and export the patented product without infringing upon LIZA INC USA's patent.

2. Section 84 - This provision allows for the grant of compulsory licenses to manufacture a patented product in the domestic market under certain circumstances such as national emergency, extreme urgency or public non-commercial use. In case the government of LOBANG allows the use of this provision for its citizens, then M/S CIPLA LTD can apply for a compulsory license in India to manufacture and supply SIMTADIN.

M/S CIPLA LTD can consider making an application under Section 92A of the Indian Patents Act to obtain a compulsory license to manufacture and export the SIMTADIN to LOBANG. The company can also explore the option of applying for a voluntary license with LIZA INC USA for the manufacture and export of SIMTADIN to LOBANG.

(e) You have filed a patent application for your client ABC INC, USA on 12.06.2005 in Indian Patent office. Your client could not provide a proof of the assignment of the invention in the name ABC INC. US from the inventor at the time of filing the application. Advise your client about the provisions regarding filing a proof of right to make an application as per Indian Patents Act & Rules. Quote relevant rules and sections.

Ans:

As per Indian Patents Act and Rules, it is important to provide proof of right to make an application when filing a patent application. In the given scenario, as the client ABC INC, USA could not provide a proof of assignment of invention from the inventor at the time of filing the application, the client can follow the provisions under Section 7(2) and Rule 10 of the Indian Patents Act and Rules respectively.

According to Section 7(2) of the Indian Patents Act, if an application for a patent does not include a declaration of the inventorship or the right to make an application, the Patent Office can request the applicant, at any time during the proceedings, to file such a declaration.

Rule 10 of the Indian Patents Rules specifies that the proof of right to make an application should be filed within six months from the date of the first request made by the Indian Patent Office, or within the period prescribed. Failure to do so can result in the application being deemed abandoned.

Therefore, in this case, the client ABC INC, USA can file a proof of right to make an application within six months from the date of the request made by the Indian Patent Office. The proof of right could be in the form of a signed assignment agreement between the inventor and ABC INC, USA or any other relevant documentation proving the assignment of the invention to the company. If the proof of right is not provided within the prescribed period, the application may be deemed abandoned by the Indian Patent Office.

(f) Your client ITC Company, Kolkata has filed an application through you on 1.05.2005. On 16.06.2005 the ITC Company assigns the rights of invention to another company CBZ Pvt. Ltd. Mumbai. CBZ Pvt. Lid also wants to pursue' the patent application through you. What will be the formalities to be dene by you to record the abovementioned change in the Patent Office? Also draft a power of authority on behalf of CBZ Pvt.Ltd, Mumbai in your favour. (5x10=50)

Ans: In order to record the change in ownership of the invention from ITC Company to CBZ Pvt. Ltd., the following formalities need to be undertaken by us:

1. Preparation of Assignment Deed: A valid assignment deed must be executed between ITC Company and CBZ Pvt. Ltd. This document must be signed by authorized representatives of both the companies and must clearly mention the date of the assignment, the title of the invention, and the considerations for the assignment.

2. Filing the Request for Recording of Change in Ownership: We need to file a request for recording the change in ownership with the Indian Patent Office by

filing Form 16. This form should be accompanied by a certified copy of the Assignment deed and proof of payment of the prescribed fee. Rule 90 of the Indian Patents Rules, 2003 governs the procedure for recordal of change in ownership.

3. Publication in Patent Journal: Once the change in ownership has been recorded with the Patent Office, the same will be published in the Patent Journal.

4. Draft Power of Authority: In order to authorize our firm to represent CBZ Pvt. Ltd. Mumbai before the Indian Patent Office, the following Power of Authority can be drafted:

POWER OF AUTHORITY

To,

The Patent Agent,

[Address]

I, [Name], [Designation], of [Company Name], do hereby authorize [Name of the Attorney/ Patent Agent], of [Address], to act on behalf of the company CBZ Pvt. Ltd, Mumbai in all matters relating to the patent application bearing No. [Application No.] filed by ITC Company, Kolkata, including but not limited to, filing a request to record the change in ownership, maintain the records, ability to sign and execute documents, and other actions required as per the Indian Patents Act and Rules.

This Power of Authority is valid until further notice from CBZ Pvt. Ltd, Mumbai.

Signed on behalf of CBZ Pvt. Ltd., Mumbai:

[Signature of Authorized Signatory]

[Name]

[Designation]

Date: [Date]

After drafting the Power of Authority, we need to obtain the signatures of an authorized signatory of CBZ Pvt. Ltd and send a copy of the same to them for their reference.

Q.2. **Your Client M/S Aditya Pharmaceuticals, Bangalore, India; the patentee for the Indian Patent No.184203 dated 12.01.1999 wants to grant a license to M/S More Pan Labs. Pvt. Lid., Kalka, India on the following terms & conditions: a) Patentee:- Aditya Pharmaceuticals, Bangalore, India b) Licensee: M/S More Pan Labs. Pvt. Lid.. Kalka. India ¢) Title: A novel process for preparation of anti malarial medicament "composition d) Nature of License: Non Exclusive License e) Royalty to be paid by licensee. 3% on the net Ex-Factory Price f) Maintaining & Information of Accounts: Licensee shall maintain monthly account of the production and sale made by them and fumish quarterly statement of the account to the Patentee. ¢) Conditions for settlement of disputes as you deem fit**

Draft a License agreement with all other conditions to protect the interest of the patentee.

Ans: License Agreement between Aditya Pharmaceuticals (Patentee), Bangalore, India and M/S More Pan Labs. Pvt. Ltd. (Licensee), Kalka, India

1. Title: This Agreement shall be known as the License Agreement for A Novel Process for Preparation of Anti-Malarial Medicament Composition.

2. Grant of License: The Patentee grants a non-exclusive license to the Licensee for the use of the patented process for the preparation of anti-malarial medicament composition.

3. Royalty: The Licensee shall pay a royalty of 3% on net Ex-Factory Price to the Patentee for the use of the patented process.

4. Maintenance and Information of Accounts: The Licensee shall maintain monthly accounts of the production and sale of the anti-malarial medicament composition and furnish a quarterly statement of the account to the Patentee.

5. Term: This Agreement shall remain in effect for a period of ____ from the Effective Date.

6. Dispute Resolution: Any dispute arising out of this Agreement shall be settled through mutual discussion between both the parties. If they fail to reach a settlement, then the matter shall be referred to a sole arbitrator appointed by the Patentee. The arbitration shall be held in Bangalore, India, and the decision of the arbitrator shall be final and binding on both parties.

7. Termination: This Agreement shall be terminated by either party upon giving written notice with a notice period of 30 days in case of a material breach of any of the terms and conditions of this Agreement. Upon termination, the Licensee shall cease to use the patented process for the preparation of anti-malarial medicament composition.

8. Governing Law: This Agreement shall be governed by and construed in accordance with the laws of India.

9. Confidentiality: The Licensee shall maintain confidentiality with respect to the patented process and shall not disclose any information regarding the process to any third party without the prior written consent of the Patentee.

10. Intellectual Property Rights: The Licensee acknowledges the Patentee's ownership of the patented process, and nothing in this Agreement shall be construed as granting the Licensee any rights, title, or interest in the Patentee's intellectual property rights.

11. Representations and Warranties: The Patentee represents and warrants that it is the rightful owner of the patented process and has the authority to grant the license. The Licensee represents and warrants that it shall comply with all applicable laws and regulations.

IN WITNESS WHEREOF, the Parties have executed this Agreement on the date set forth below.

For Aditya Pharmaceuticals: _____

Authorized Signatory

For M/S More Pan Labs. Pvt. Ltd.: _____

Authorized Signatory

Date: _____

Or

Draft petitions under rule 137 and rule 138 of the Patent Rules 2005 requesting condonation of the delay in filing and extension of time to submit the information regarding foreign applications made for the same or substantially same inventions L/S stating the full particulars of the circumstances which resulted in the delay & which to your best knowledge were beyond your client's control.

To,

The Controller of Patents,

The Patent Office,

[Address]

Dear Sir/Madam,

We hereby submit this petition under Rule 137 and Rule 138 of the Patent Rules 2005 for condonation of delay in filing the information regarding foreign applications made for the same or substantially same invention (L/S).

We understand that under Rule 12 of the Patent Rules 2005, we were required to furnish the information regarding foreign applications made for the same or substantially same invention (L/S) within 6 months from the date of filing. However, due to an inadvertent error on our part, we failed to comply with the requirement within the prescribed time limit.

The circumstances which resulted in the delay were beyond our control and were due to reasons such as [explain the reasons for the delay in detail]. We have stated the full particulars of the circumstances in the annexure attached herewith.

We request you to kindly condone the delay and allow us to submit the required information as soon as possible.

Thanking you.

Yours faithfully,

[Applicant/Agent]

Annexure: Full particulars of the circumstances which resulted in the delay.

(20) Your Client Riwaj Ayurvedic medicines Pvt. Lid. Nagpur, furnishes the following information for preparing a complete specification for filing a Patent application in India: We have developed an ayurvedic medicinal formulation for treatment of Parkinson disease along with process of preparing the same. The ayurvedic formulation consists of Unpowdered Mucuana seeds, Stabilizers, antioxidants and optionally other ingredients. At present there is no specific and proven Ayurvedic medicine available for the treatment of Parkinson's disease. Currently, the Parkinson's diseases being treated with synthetic drugs which are effective but are very expensive and have inherent side effects. such as gastro intestinal irregularities along with nausea, anorexia, cardiac irregularities. orthostatic hypo tension, weight gain & psychiatric symptoms such as agitations, hallucinations, nightmares. Bul our plant based Ayurvedic formulation for the treatment of Parkinson's discase is cheaper and therapeutically active and cl inically efficacious and at the same time drastically reducing the side effects .It is a geriatric tonic also, This Ayurvedic formulation is readily soluble in water

and is delicious and flovourous . We followed the following steps for preparing: Selected ripened seeds of Mucuna pruriens bak (Atmagupta)plant were Pulverized to fine powder and then mixing 80% to 90% of pulverized seed by weight of the total Ayurvedic formulation with 5% to 15% by weight of the total formulation the antioxidant and 5 to 10 % stabilizer. The main skill involved in formulation of medicine is the selection of particular kind of ripened seeds of mucuna pruriens plants having at least three percent of alkaloid and the percentage of the ingredients mixed. The antioxidant such as Vitamin C & Vitamin E is used & gum as Stabilizers are used and other known ingredients such as flavors and taste enhancer may also be used upto 3%. Draft a complete specification for the protection of Process and the Product in a single application. Or four client M/s Banerjee Furnitures, 155, d block, Sector 53 ,Gurgacn, Haryana, India furnishes the following informations; We have invented a folding chair that has an improved folding manner for easy transport and with less space of storage in the folded position. Chairs are widely used in daily activities. A conventional type of chair will not able to provide comfort for user and often not stored after used. It is therefore the foldable chairs have the advantage of being folded and for easy transport and storage. The use of folding vhairs is known in the prior art. Folding chairs are devised and utilized for the purpose of providing a seat that folds up for easy storage and transport. It is basically consisting of lamiliar, expected and obvious structural configurations. There are varieties of folded chairs have been made it the market. These folding chairs normally require big volume of space during transportation and storage. This leads to the increase in the storage space as well as the transportation fee and space. the present invention provides compact folding chair to tacilitate transport and storage of the folding chair. It further provides locking element where the chair will lock automatically once the chair is in an unfolded or opened out position. The opened out position is extremely stable and eliminates the possibility of collapsing when the chair is being placed into such position of use. The preferred embodiment of present invention essentially comprises of a sitting base being pivotally connected to the backrest by a plurality of connecting means and supported by a plurality of legs. The said legs consist of a pair of rear legs and a set of front legs, whereby the upper end of the front legs are connected to the said sitting base by connecting means. A pivoting bar is provided to connect the said backrest and said rear legs by a plurality of connecting means in order to the said backrest to be rested on the said tear legs. The opening and closing of the chair is governed by a tie bar which link the lower part of the said backrest and said front legs, wherein to prevent the said backrest from expanding to further unstable position. A set of blocks is placed between the said pivoting bar and the said tie bar in order to parallel the connecting of the said backrest to the said front legs. The said two pair of legs. sitting hase, backrest, tie bars, pivoting bars and blocks can be brought together thereby producing an extremely compact folded position to the chair for less space during transport and storage. The said chair is locked automatically when in opened position by a locking mechanism comprises of a locking bar which is mounted on the underside of the said sitting base.. FIG. | is a side view of the folding chair according to the preferred embodiment of the present invention in its open condition. FIG. 2 is a front view of the sitting base. FIG. 3 illustrates the locking mechanism with the locking bar in its locking position. FIG. 4 illustrates the locking mechanism with the locking bar in its release position. Following are the elements:- I backrest, 2- sitting base , 3-rear legs , 4- front legs , 5- A set of level blocks . 6- first connecting means, 7- A set of pivoting bars, 8- a second connecting means, 9- A set of tie bars , 1{1- connecting means which could be nuts and bolts assemblies, fastners.screws.snaps,clamps,clips.ete, | 1-pivotal means , |2-pivotal connected means, 13- arrow, 14- locking bar, 15-the recesses. 25- A notch formed on the top end of the inclined front leg (4). In the locked condition, the said locking bar (14) is is caught into the notch (25) Draft a complete specification for your client including statement of claims. Drawing enclosed. [End of the document]

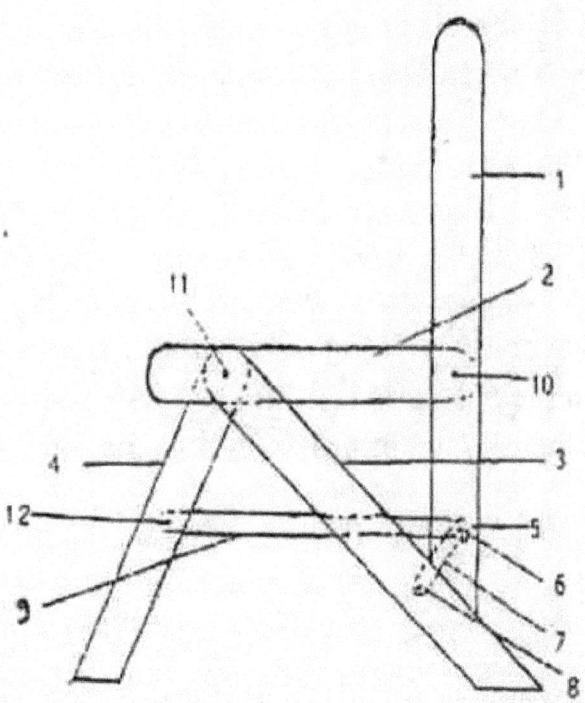

Figure 1

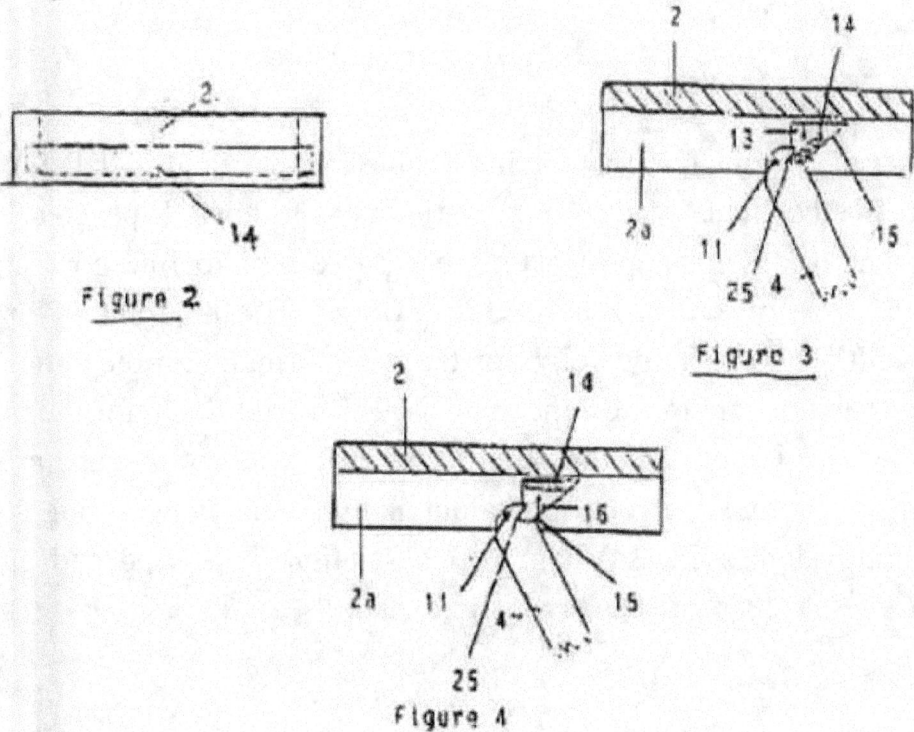

Figure 2

Figure 3

Figure 4

Complete Specification

Title: Ayurvedic Medicinal composition for Treatment of Parkinson's Disease

FIELD OF INVENTION: The present invention relates to an ayurvedic medicinal formulation for treatment of Parkinson's disease and a process for preparing the same.

PRIOR ART: At present, there is no specific and proven Ayurvedic medicine available for the treatment of Parkinson's disease. Currently, the Parkinson's diseases being treated with synthetic drugs which are effective but are very expensive and have inherent side effects such as gastro intestinal irregularities along with nausea, anorexia, cardiac irregularities, orthostatic hypo tension, weight gain, and psychiatric symptoms such as agitations, hallucinations, and nightmares.

DESCRIPTION: The present invention relates to an ayurvedic medicinal formulation for the treatment of Parkinson's disease. The said ayurvedic formulation consists of Unpowdered Mucuana seeds, Stabilizers, antioxidants, and optionally other ingredients. The said formulation is found to be cheaper and therapeutically active and clinically efficacious and drastically reduces the side effects.

The said Ayurvedic formulation is readily soluble in water and is delicious and flavoursome. The technique used for preparation is as follows. Ripened seeds of Mucuna pruriens bak (Atmagupta) plant were pulverized to fine powder, and then, 80% to 90% of pulverized seed by weight of the total Ayurvedic formulation with 5% to 15% by weight of the total formulation the antioxidant and 5 to 10 % stabilizer are mixed. The main skill involved in the formulation of medicine is the selection of particular kinds of ripened seeds of mucuna pruriens plants having at least three percent of alkaloid and the percentage of ingredients mixed. The antioxidant such as Vitamin C & Vitamin E is used and gum as

Stabilizers are used and other known ingredients such as flavours and taste enhancers may also be used up to 3%.

CLAIMS:

I claim:

1. An ayurvedic medicinal formulation for the treatment of Parkinson's disease, comprising Unpowdered Mucuana seeds, Stabilizers, antioxidants, and optionally other ingredients.

2. The ayurvedic medicinal formulation of claim 1, wherein stabilizers are gum arabic or gum acacia.

3. The ayurvedic medicinal formulation of claim 1, wherein additional ingredients comprise flavor and taste enhancers.

4. The ayurvedic medicinal formulation of claim 1, wherein the percentage of ingredients mixed is obtained by selecting ripened seeds of mucuna pruriens plants having at least three percent of alkaloid.

5. The ayurvedic medicinal formulation of claim 1, wherein the antioxidant is vitamin C & vitamin E.

OR

Complete Specification

Title- Folding Chair

FIELD OF INVENTION: The present invention relates to a folding chair that has an improved folding mechanism that enables the chair to occupy less storage space and ensure safe transport.

PRIOR ART: The use of folding chairs is known in the prior art. Folding chairs are devised and utilized for the purpose of providing a seat that folds up for easy storage and transport. It is basically consisting of lamiliar, expected and obvious structural configurations. There are varieties of folded chairs have been made it the market. These folding chairs normally require a big volume of space during transportation and storage. This leads to the increase in the storage space as well as the transportation fee and space.

DESCRIPTION: The present invention provides a folding chair that has an improved folding mechanism that makes transportation and storage of the chair easy. The folding chairs currently available in the market often require a lot of space during storage and transport. The present invention is a unique, compact folding chair that enables easy storage and transportation. The folding chair has a locking element where the chair will lock automatically once the chair is in an unfolded or opened out position, ensuring safety during use. The opened out position is extremely stable and eliminates the possibility of collapsing when the chair is being placed into such position of use.

The preferred embodiment of the present invention essentially comprises of a sitting base being pivotally connected to the backrest by a plurality of connecting means and supported by a plurality of legs. The legs consist of a pair of rear legs and a set of front legs whereby the upper end of the front legs are connected to the said sitting base by connecting means. A pivoting bar is provided to connect the backrest and the rear legs by a plurality of connecting means in order for the backrest to be rested on the rear legs. The opening and closing of the chair is governed by a tie bar that links the lower part of the backrest and the front legs, wherein to prevent the backrest from expanding to further unstable position. A set of blocks is placed between the pivoting bar and the tie bar to parallel the connecting of the backrest to the front legs.

The two pair of legs, sitting base, backrest, tie bars, pivoting bars, and blocks can be brought together, thereby producing an extremely compact folded position to the chair for less space during transport and storage. The chair is locked automatically when in opened position by a locking mechanism comprising a locking bar that is mounted on the underside of the sitting base. The invention includes the steps of manufacturing the folding chair with an improved folding mechanism.

DRAWINGS:

The drawings accompanying the present specification are:

1. FIG. 1 is a side view of the folding chair according to the preferred embodiment of the present invention in its open condition.

2. FIG. 2 is a front view of the sitting base.

3. FIG. 3 illustrates the locking mechanism with the locking bar in its locking position.

4. FIG. 4 illustrates the locking mechanism with the locking bar in its release position.

CLAIMS:

I claim:

1. A folding chair with an improved folding mechanism, comprising a pair of rear legs and a set of front legs with a sitting base pivotally connected to the backrest.

2. The folding chair of claim 1, wherein the connecting means join the sitting base to the front legs.

3. The folding chair of claim 1, wherein the backrest is rested on the rear legs.

4. The folding chair of claim 1, wherein the tying mechanism links the lower part of the backrest to the front legs.

5. The folding chair of claim 1, wherein the locking mechanism comprises a locking bar mounted on the underside of the sitting base.

6. The folding chair of claim 1, wherein the folding and unfolding is governed by a tie bar that links the lower part of the backrest and the front legs.

7. The folding chair of claim 6, wherein blocks placed between the pivoting bar and the tie bar parallel the connecting of the backrest to the front legs.

8. The folding chair of claim 1, wherein a notch is formed on the top of the front legs for locking the chair in the unfolded position.